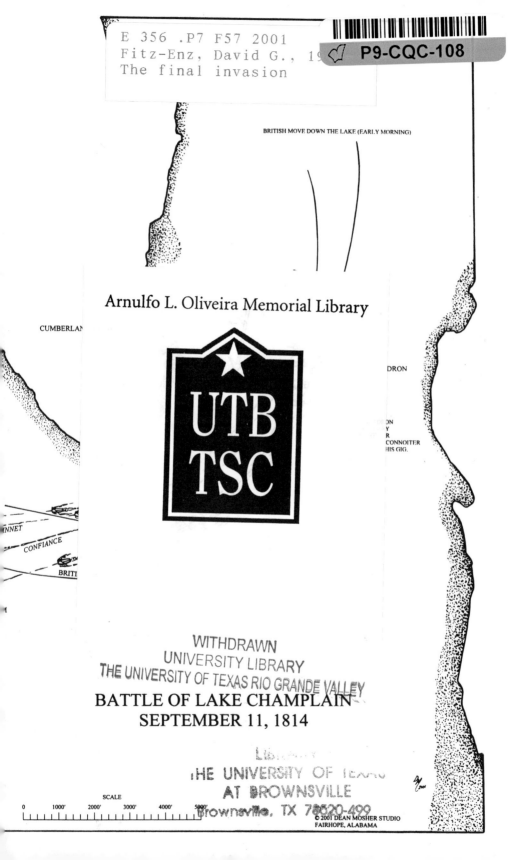

BRITISH MOVE DOWN THE LAKE (EARLY MORNING)

CUMBERLA

DRON

CONNOITER
HIS GIG.

NNET

CONFIANCE

BRITI

BATTLE OF LAKE CHAMPLAIN
SEPTEMBER 11, 1814

SCALE

0   1000'   2000'   3000'   4000'   5000'

© 2001 DEAN MOSHER STUDIO
FAIRHOPE, ALABAMA

THE FINAL INVASION

THE FINAL INVASION

Plattsburgh, the War of 1812's Most Decisive Battle

COLONEL DAVID G. FITZ-ENZ

Edited by Colonel John R. Elting

Foreword by Sir Christopher Prevost, Baronet

Introduction by Colonel David Jablonski

 Cooper Square Press

First Cooper Square Press edition 2001

This Cooper Square Press hardcover edition of *The Final Invasion* is an original publication. It is published by arrangement with the author.

Published by Cooper Square Press
An Imprint of the Rowman & Littlefield Publishing Group
150 Fifth Avenue, Suite 814
New York, New York 10011

Distributed by National Book Network

Library of Congress Cataloging-in-Publication Data

Fitz-Enz, David G., 1940–
    The final invasion : Plattsburgh, the War of 1812's most decisive battle / David G. Fitz-Enz.
    p. cm.
    ISBN 0-8154-1139-1 (alk. paper)
    1. Plattsburgh (N.Y.), Battle of 1814. I. Title.

E356.P7 F58 2001
973.5'256—dc21

                                2001028417

Printed in the United States of America

♾™ The paper used in this publication meets the minimum requirements of American National Standard for Information Sciences—Permanence of Paper for Printed Library Materials, ANSI/NISO Z.39.48-1992.

To my Childhood Sweetheart,
my Wife Carol

CONTENTS

ACKNOWLEDGMENTS

This book is a companion volume to the Cannonade Filmworks documentary of the same name, which I coproduced and cowrote with Bruce Carlin, and which has appeared on PBS television. When I began research on the War of 1812, the obscurity of the subject presented two challenges: first, to unearth the facts and, second, to furnish enough images for a television production. I thought that one would lead to the other. But since the facts were contained in letters, documents, scraps of newspaper, and personal anecdotes, concealed in the yellowed pages of long unopened books, my premise proved wrong. This pivotal incident in American history occurred well before the innovation of photography and since it did not interest the British or the young American republic, few images exist in contemporary collections. Bruce Carlin, creator of the documentary film, gave me the easy job: to "do the research and write a draft script." He took on the task of filming the images.

Since winners usually record our mainstream views of history, I thought it important to understand what the losers had to say before their actions were maligned in American writings. In London, my research partner—my wife Carol—and I presented letters of introduction that had been procured before leaving home. At the British Army Museum, the Royal Navy Museum, and the Royal Artillery Institute, our reception was warm. However, each time we were confronted with the curators' sad news that "we have looked into the matter and have nothing of interest in our collection." Brigadier K. A. Timbers, secretary of the Artillery Institute, had assembled a panel of experts to back him up. Intrigued by my cause, they went to work anew and Captain Adrian Caruana came through, breaking open the naval gun strategy that changed the whole complexion of the battle. Curator Stan Walter and staffers Ed Cullen and Marc Sherrif located the Congreve rocket launcher and furnished me with Wellington's pistol to demonstrate how to fire a cannon with no fuse. The Woolwich Artillery Rotunda is an amazing place, cared for by a most accommodating staff of experts. It is well worth the forty-five-minute train ride from London. The bonus was lunch in the Royal Artillery officers' mess with Brigadier Timbers and his wife Bridget.

The Royal Navy Collection yielded facts, but more important, paintings and prints I had not seen before. The busy staff at the Army Museum in Chelsea located magazines of the time and firsthand accounts. At the Chelsea Royal Hospital Museum, just next door, curator Major R. A. G. Courage and Sergeant Major M. A. Ford presented the painting of Queenstown and the backdrop for the interview with Sir Christopher Prevost. Not only did they allow us to film in the great Wren dining hall, they also uncovered precise color drawings of the flags captured by the British. At Kneller Hall, Twickenham, near London, Majors Roger Swift and Gordon Turner led me through the Royal Military School of Music Museum's collection and pointed out that "the soldiers marched off for Plattsburgh to the strains of 'The Girl I Left Behind Me.'" Lunch in the officers' mess with the commandant, Colonel Hoggarth, was a treat.

Lionel Leventhal, publisher of Greenhill Press, whose books on the Napoleonic Wars I have pored over for years, provided the link to Paddy Griffith, formerly of the Royal Military College at Sandhurst, who opened his home to us. In his comfortable study, he provided me with insight into the character of the British soldier of 1814, bringing that figure to life again. A phone call to Sir Christopher and Lady Prevost in Portugal resulted in a January trip to the coast at Albufeira and a stay in their villa. Here was a find of a lifetime. They opened to us the family papers, which included not only the diary of Sir George Prevost's teenage daughter from the days of the battle, but also the long-lost secret order that sent the invasion force into northern New York. Wanting very much to have his ancestor's story told, he sent us to the Royal Green Jackets Museum in Winchester. There, Major R. D. Cassidy and his welcoming staff encouraged the film crew to probe the corners and to shoot what they needed. Of all the museums we visited, the Peninsula Barracks proved to be a small jewel and a must-see for anyone interested in military history. Inniskilling fusiliers at Enniskillen, Northern Ireland, and the Dorchester regiment in southern England provided similar assistance. At Canterbury, housed in the town library, is the East Kent Regimental Museum. Although the museum is tiny, the old records are well cared for by B. W. Crocker. Here C. R. B. Knight's history of the regiment provided many firsthand accounts not mentioned in any history before. All of this led us to the Public Records Office at Kew Gardens, London. "Vast" does not begin to describe the collection. "It is all there if you can find it," I was told time and again. We learned the system from one of the extremely helpful directors and filled out many a reference sheet. Many turned up nothing, but now and then we found a gem. The "Conduct of Court Martial of Captain Daniel Pring, RN, Aug 1815," was priceless. I cannot describe the feeling of opening a shoe box filled with original documents tied with faded ribbons, and unfolding the stiff brown pages covered with faded ink. The smell of old vellum is memorable. The London Library at St. James is invaluable but requires time and patience, which the helpful staff makes up for. When all is said and done, the Naval and Military Club is a resting place that coddles the weary researcher.

In Canada, there are two views to be considered. Donald Graves, of Ensign Heritage Group, strides the pages of the Englishman's history with a master's insight. Rene Chartrand wants you to look more carefully at the complex picture, which is dominated by the courage of his French Canadians, who go back to the colony's beginning and remain a strong presence today. Ottawa's national collection, close to the ground that was the host for this conflict, contained both insular history and image. It reminded us that the distrust between the English and French cultures was put aside during the War of 1812, as Canadians, for the first time in their history, banded together as a nation.

The United States has lost touch with the War of 1812, even though it was a defining event for the new nation. It was its first war since the Revolution and the last time England and Canada would be less than allies. Helen Allen, at the Clinton County Historical Association in Plattsburgh, has nearly on her own maintained the notes and preserved the artifacts. Orville Paye did some great digging for facts, ignoring rumors and old wives tales. Bob Mulligan Jr., New York military historian Major Bill Glidden, and Dr. Joe Meany upheld the militia's end of the story. At Annapolis, curator Jim Cheevers showed the Naval Academy's Congreve cannon, archives, and the flags of the captured English ships. Bob Summerall, curator of model ships, provided the naval architectural drawings of the American ships on Lake Champlain, which allowed us to build the virtual models on the screen. Hard days under their tutelage provided great rewards to the book and film. They sent us on to the Navy Museum in Washington, D.C., which is unique. At Fort Myer, Virginia, Colonel Bryan Shelburne, commander of the United States Army Band, offered the help of his music library and staff Sergeant Paul Murtha. At Fort McNair, Tom Groppel, and Mark Murray of the Military District of Washington took time from their demanding schedules to ensure that I obtained the proper legal releases that are so troublesome these days.

The definitive work on the War of 1812 is Colonel John Elting's 1995 book, *Amateurs, to Arms!: A Military History of the War of 1812*. A World War II veteran, former assistant professor at West Point, and one of America's most revered military historian's, Elting had the most amazing memory. His encouragement to dig deeper and his assistance as an editor made this book possible. He consented to edit the text, requiring proof of every item and eliminating any wild imaginings. He provided carte blanche access to his formidable library and, more importantly, to the volumes of color military prints that he had commissioned over the past fifty years. The well-known prints from the Company of Military Historians come with a written history that is irrefutable.

The U.S. Naval War College suggested that Dr. Donald Hickey, a visiting professor and author of *The War of 1812: A Forgotten Conflict,* would be of help. He gave me the world history perspective needed to truly understand this pivotal northern battle. Colonel David Jablonski, professor of national security affairs, U.S. Army War College, impressed upon me that events do not occur in a vacuum. Michael McGaulley, an experienced and noted editor, perused carefully the first draft of the manuscript and turned it into a book. Scott Schuler, a fine artist, computer creator, and leader in his field, listened patiently as I described the computer-generated graphics required for the documentary.

Carol, my wife of thirty-nine years, dug through the archives of four countries, sifted though mountains of mildew-stained documents, and found previously unknown historical gems. She found things that I had lost for the fifth time, corrected my spelling of "antiquarian" for the tenth time, and somehow seemed to enjoy it all. She has put up with it all, now that I have retired from the regular army and have become "unemployed."

FOREWORD

Sir Christopher Prevost, Baronet

A letter was forwarded to me in Portugal in October 1995 from a gentleman requesting information on one of my ancestors. I little realized to what extent that letter was to change my concept of my family's history. I thought I could just respond, as I had done in the past, and that would be the end of the matter.

How wrong I was! My reply was followed up immediately with a second letter, asking if it was possible for the writer to examine the papers in my possession. This is how I came to meet Colonel David Fitz-Enz and his wife Carol.

On a sunny day in Portugal, Colonel Fitz-Enz delved into the documentation and books in my possession with such energy, enthusiasm, and knowledge of his subject that I too started to read more carefully what had been handed down through generations of my family. David triggered an enthusiasm in me to assemble the large amount of family papers and official documents that had been stored for many years. With the help of computers, the collection is now far more accessible, and many more historical facts about my family have come to light in America.

It is a privilege to be asked to write this foreword to a book on a subject that caused considerable grief to my ancestor, Sir George Prevost, the commander of the British land forces at Plattsburgh, and to his immediate family. David's descriptions of the naval battle vividly evoke the horrors that the sailors had to endure. Victory or defeat was hanging in the balance for both sides. David also brings to light the "secret orders" that Sir George possessed. Previous military researchers writing about these events make no mention of orders.

The secret orders do much to defend the conduct in battle of Sir George, who had the support of his government, the commander-in-chief of the army, and his king, who granted his widow the title "'Supporters' to the Coat of Arms." This exceptional honor was in lieu of a peerage, which she declined to accept.

SIR CHRISTOPHER PREVOST, BARONET
Albufeira, Portugal
July 2001

INTRODUCTION

Colonel David Jablonski

The War of 1812 is perhaps the most obscure major conflict in American history, primarily remembered for the British burning of the White House and for the American victory at New Orleans, which occurred after the peace treaty between the United States and Great Britain had been negotiated, but before news of it reached the United States. It should not be surprising, therefore, that the decisive encounter of that war—the Battle of Plattsburgh on Lake Champlain—has long been lost to history. This unique book by Colonel David Fitz-Enz expands on his highly praised film documentary concerning the battle. It is a fast-moving, literate remedy to the neglect of those events that unfolded in northern New York in September 1814.

At the time of the war, America was not yet forty years old and consisted of fifteen states that more closely resembled the loose confederation of the ancient Greek city-states than a united republic. Citizens generally looked to their states, not to the national government, for rules and regulations. As a consequence, the federal government had great difficulty collecting the amount in taxes necessary to equip, train, and commit an army and navy to anything other than loose and limited defenses. Nevertheless, this did not diminish the bravado with which American congressmen took the irrevocable step of declaring war on Great Britain, the greatest global power of the day.

The immediate results were predictable enough. Colonel Fitz-Enz succinctly brings the reader through the first two turbulent years of the conflict, a period marked by American defeats and casualties caused by politically appointed commanders leading untrained and ill-prepared troops. All this contributed to the general decline of a patriotic fervor far removed from that of the Revolutionary generation. The unpopularity of the war with the merchants and farmers—long used to a lucrative trade with the nations of Europe—compounded this crisis. In many cases, these professions turned to smuggling. On the northern border, New Yorkers and Vermonters supplied 80 percent of the food and ship-building materials to the British throughout the war. The selling of intelligence to the enemy was not uncommon. By contrast, the British were committed to the war. Some of their greatest officers would fight on American soil—men who had earned their reputations throughout the British Empire and who were anxious to maintain those reputations in the War of 1812. Many were sons of British officers who had fought in the American Revolution; some had been born in the colonies during the conflict. At the highest level, British leaders believed strongly that a significant victory on land would awaken loyalist sentiment for the throne in the former colonies. Reinforcing this notion, British spies in New England assured the London government that a portion of the northern states would negotiate, once occupied by British troops. Finally, there was the enthusiastic support of King George III, who had presided over the loss of the American colonies earlier in his reign.

All this, of course, begs the question of why Britain did not devote all of its resources to the speedy and victorious termination of its war with the former colonies. The answer, as Colonel Fitz-Enz convincingly demonstrates, lies in the realm of grand strategy. Britain was a global power, engaged at the time (as it had been throughout much of the eighteenth century) in a worldwide conflict with France. The war with Napoleon was reaching its denouement on the European continent with the catastrophic French invasion of Russia, in the year that Britain's war with America began. In exploring this larger picture, Colonel Fitz-Enz has forged from his exhaustive and extensive research in primary sources a compelling picture of the grand strategic linkage between the two wars.

As coalition forces moved toward the initial victory over Napoleon in 1814, it was natural that British leaders in Whitehall would refocus their grand strategy to resolve the conflict in North America. The Duke of Wellington was offered command of the expedition, but declined; it was left to Lieutenant General Sir George Prevost to lead the British invasion. The plan for the expedition has remained one of the best-kept secrets in military and diplomatic history. A document outlining this plan was discovered in London in 1922, but disappeared a few years later. Fortunately, Colonel Fitz-Enz located a rare copy in Portugal at the villa of Sir Christopher Prevost, a descendant of the British invasion commander. It is an astounding document, revealing in great detail the strategic and operational concepts designed to conquer much of what constitutes the present-day United States.

Against the backdrop of this plan, Colonel Fitz-Enz weaves the fascinating and hitherto untold story of Sir George Prevost's efforts as expedition commander. As that story unfolds, the reader develops a grand strategic appreciation of those efforts. It was no coincidence, for example, that the battle of Plattsburgh occurred nearly simultaneously with the British assault on Baltimore, forever immortalized by Francis Scott Key. All in all, it was an extraordinarily close call for the young republic. In evaluating the leadership of Sir George and the performance of his British force, we can look to Winston Churchill's judgment of a

different age: "The terrible 'Ifs' accumulate," the British statesman wrote as he reflected on the long hot summer of 1914 that
resulted in World War I. So did they also a century earlier at
Plattsburgh, in one of the few decisive battles in history.

COLONEL DAVID JABLONSKI, PH.D.
Professor, National Security Affairs
U.S. Army War College
Carlisle, Pennsylvania
July 2001

CHAPTER 1

The defeat at Plattsburgh crippled the British advance and was the most decisive engagement of the war.
—Sir Winston Churchill, *History of the English Speaking People*

In June 1814, the British government, riding high after defeating Napoleon's troops in Spain, sent word of a secret plan to its military commander in Canada. If the plan, which ultimately failed, had worked, the fledgling American democracy—barely forty years old—would have been destroyed, and what we know as the United States would have reverted to their former status as British colonies. That this secret plan did not work was due to the outcome of an almost unheralded battle, the battle of Plattsburgh on Lake Champlain, feverishly fought by now forgotten American soldiers and sailors.

Why is this battle so obscure? One reason is that occurring on nearly the same day was the battle of Baltimore, witnessed by Francis Scott Key as he wrote the words to what became the U.S. national anthem. With its stirring descriptions of "the rockets red glare," the poem was published widely and captured the imagination of the emerging country, setting Key's words on the path to the stars and eclipsing the strategic victory over the invasion force from the north at Plattsburgh, New York. But there is a second reason for Plattsburgh's obscurity: because its secret plan failed, the British government kept it confidential

1

for over a century. Only now are we beginning to realize just how audacious the plan was, and hence how crucial the American victory at Plattsburgh on Lake Champlain.

The War of 1812 took place after the end of a century that witnessed the American Revolution, or as British schoolchildren were taught to call it, "the skirmish." The impact of the Revolution was profound. At that time, most states around the world were ruled from hereditary thrones. It is therefore not surprising that many Americans believed that this was the only way to be governed. George Washington was offered the American throne, but turned it down. Martha, his wife, was referred to as Lady Washington.[1] In the minds of some former colonists, it was quite logical to think that a new dynasty in the Americas should be spawned, if with certain safeguards. Many believed that the power of a throne could be curbed with the introduction of a system similar to the figurehead system in Great Britain today. And it might have worked in that age, because the states were quite autonomous, which would have fit with a central authority with little power.

But in the 1780s, wiser heads prevailed and the new central government was set up in New York City, along republican lines. The new United States feared even the thought of European-style potentates, whom many of its citizens had fled. Now separated by the Atlantic Ocean from their motherlands, Americans couldn't contain their desire for freedom. In 1775 the fiery words of Thomas Paine's "Common Sense" columns were reprinted time and again in Europe, and American revolutionary ideas were exported to the continent. In France in 1789, these ideas led to the revolt against the Bourbon king, Louis XVI. The revolution that began in America was now more than mere rhetoric in Europe. The ten-year-old experiment in the United States of America offered a break from oppression and proved it was possible for a large nation to be ruled by republican principles, free from the excesses of kings, without fear of disintegration. Authority, held firmly in the hands of the hereditary rulers throughout Europe, watched anxiously. The terror which followed the French Revolution alarmed them. France struggled with the new birth, as the heads of French aristocrats fell. The internal chaos in France convinced the British to take steps to reverse its course before it was launched across the English Channel. By the early 1790s Britain was spending money at a rapid rate to contain the revolution within French borders. Britain funded armies in Austria, Prussia, and Russia. Its own army was very small, for it was the Royal Navy which garnered most of the military budget. Britain believed it could support France's bordering states in their efforts to destroy the revolutionary process in France. The king's ministers believed that with the internal political disarray in France, the new republic could not defend its borders. Encouraging this notion was the French republic's destruction of the old royal French army and navy, which had been respected institutions throughout Europe. The naval officer corps, in particular, was decimated. The successive outrageous regimes in Paris between 1789 and 1794 replaced the old army leadership with a new army officer corps which rose from among the people. With British naval power at France's waterline and European armies at her throat, the idea of republic could be strangled. It was a good plan and should have worked, leaving the thrones of Britain and its allies intact.

But intrigue and interference had the opposite effect. France was forced to turn away from internal political hubbub to defend itself. Following the American example, she created a citizen army built on conscripts who believed in the revolution. With characteristic French resistance to being dictated to by outsiders, France and its new kind of force fought fiercely for "liberty, equality, and fraternity." Successful on the field of battle by 1795, France demonstrated that self-motivated soldiers could beat the archaic armies of Old World monarchs. Young republican leaders, elected from within the ranks, defeated old, privileged leaders appointed by the throne. Ever so slowly, the citizen army solidified the traditional borders and began to spread the revolution into neighboring principalities. Before the turn of the century France was occupying new lands and had invaded and taken Egypt, disrupting the British eastern trade route. The French government, once in turmoil, became more stable, and every citizen saw himself an ambassador of liberation. Now the French army campaigned not as a conquering army but as the neighbor who brought a new order. Spreading the revolution was on the minds of every soldier. Conquering new territory was on the minds of French politicians. The French army gained confidence with each campaign, as her soldiers were often welcomed by the populace and condemned by fleeing dethroned ruling families.

In the fall of 1793 a new, most extraordinary leader emerged to rule France. Napoleon Bonaparte, who came of age on the battlefield at Toulon against a British force, provided the genius to conquer. Britain and her allies became decisively engaged: they could not pull back. If France succeeded in dominating Europe, Britain and its form of government could become a thing of the past.

Britain, which had already lost much of North America after 1776, adopted a global strategy to contain Napoleon. Britain ruled the oceans of the world and therefore the trade. A very important aspect of the plan was to deny expanding France materials from outside. America was trading heavily with the warring parties of Europe. Britain introduced wide restrictions to keep American goods out of the hands of the French revolutionaries. The United States would only be allowed to trade within British interests. American merchant ships were kept out of Europe by the Royal Navy's men-of-war, which presented floating blockades outside French ports. In fact, many of the British blockaders sat offshore within sight of American harbors and made a show of attacking merchantmen at will.

The Royal Navy, the agent of the political power, had a tradition that chafed all who knew it. For more than three hundred years, it had been crewed by impressed sailors. And it did not discriminate. In towns along the English coast, "press gangs" seized drunks on their way home from the pubs. Royal Navy ships would lay offshore of home ports, within sight of British soil, and stop its own merchant ships as they arrived, selecting the most fit sailors. Captives were forcibly enlisted in the Royal Navy for a period of a dozen years. Never allowed ashore for fear of desertion, the unwilling sailors were transferred at sea, from one Royal Navy ship to another. In 1798, the *Morning Chronicle* of London referred to Jonathan Swift, who, appalled by the practice, wrote about it in *Gulliver's Travels:* "Though he drew occasionally upon his imagination to heighten or multiply follies, he could not stretch so far as this." With the impressment of his own subjects so widespread, it was of no concern to King George that Americans should contribute to the manning of his ships of the line. In 1807 the frigate *Leopard* fired on the American frigate *Chesapeake* within sight of the U.S. coast. Earlier, at the port of Norfolk, Virginia, the British captain had claimed four men from the American man-of-war but the American skipper questioned the men and determined that only one, perhaps, could have been a British citizen. The attack killed four American sailors and did significant damage to the *Chesapeake.* After interrogating the ship's company, the British took several more American sailors because they appeared to be British citizens, according to the victorious English captain. At that time an English accent could be sufficient to risk kidnapping.

In all, six thousand Americans would be impressed over the length of the conflict. Outraged, President Thomas Jefferson, whose hatred of the English was well known, imposed an embargo on all British goods. It made little impression on the British government at first, but began to hurt as time passed. The main impact was to the merchants of major American cities along the Atlantic coast. And it was soon largely ineffective because of the new industry it fostered: smuggling.

SMUGGLING

Not looked upon as a crime, but a necessity, smuggling became a way of life to the people of northern New York and Vermont, which hugged the Canadian border. Lake Champlain, one hundred miles long, running due north and south, lapped across the border into Canada. On the southern end it was landlocked. Goods headed south to New York City had to be portaged to Lake George and carried over land to the headwaters of the Hudson River. It was nearly three hundred miles from Plattsburgh to the city and only fifty miles to Montreal, all by water. There was no contest for the primary marketplace—Montreal was everything to northern producers. In 1807, many of the roads were old Indian hunting trails that were often impassable. Federal customs officials patrolled the lake in shallow-draft brigs and sloops which bristled with guns. Goods seized were taken to Plattsburgh and placed in the warehouse of the chief federal customs officer, Peter Sailly. On the evening of November 3, 1811, citizens of Plattsburgh involved in the smuggling trade demanded that Sailly open the warehouse and give back contraband goods that his inspectors had seized. He refused and a gun fight broke out; one man was killed. At that time, the contraband was sold at auction and the money sent out of the north country, to Washington. The federal government's role in the society of the early 'nineteenth century was not well defined and the states considered themselves largely autonomous. The loss of revenue for the contraband goods was not condoned locally. Regardless, small lake warships were built in Vermont and manned with federal agents who felt allegiance not to the state, but to the central government.

Canada needed the timber, potash, iron ore, livestock, and grain which were plentiful in the bordering states. In turn, Plattsburgh, New York, and Burlington, Vermont, the only two towns of any size for a hundred miles, required finished goods such as furniture, machinery, and tableware, as well as sugar, rum, chocolate, medicine, and other refined commodities. To avoid capture, smugglers adopted many means to continue trading in the face of the federal restrictions. Cattle and pigs were driven through the forest, making their own paths to Canada off the patrolled routes.

The state militia was added to the enforcement when states passed a law supporting the embargo. A British army officer, buying beef for his soldiers, reported that he questioned a militia brigadier general, in full uniform, who was buying a herd of cattle that had been driven into Canada. "Don't you consider it treason to trade with the enemy?" asked the red-coated captain. The American militiaman replied, "While trading with the enemy was forbidden, I could not regard anyone who offered me such a good price for my cattle as really being an enemy." The New York State militia general, Jacob "Embargo" Brown, who later fought so successfully against the British, started out the war as smuggler.

The oddities of the situation were many. In one case a shack was built with a northern wall resting on the border. A farmer filled it with hams, bacon, flour, and the like, tipped it over so that it fell into Canada, and claimed that an act of God caused the contraband to cross the border. Boatbuilding took place on both sides of the border. All the timber had to come from New York. Spars and planks were put on boats at night and the crews attempted to run the customs pickets. This activity resulted in continuing gun battles and death to participants. John Jacob Astor, of New York City, had a long-standing fur trade with western Canada. When his supply was broken off because of the embargo, he appealed to political friends in Washington. He was advised to take advantage of the rules governing neutral nations trading on the high seas. Astor then chartered a boat and registered it in Sweden. From then on, a sloop flying the Nordic blue and yellow ensign plied the lake unmolested.[2]

Britain found it necessary to field a large army when Napoleon invaded first Spain and then Portugal. American merchantmen concentrated on supplying that army through the port of Lisbon. On July 4, 1807, over a hundred American merchant ships, discharging goods to feed the British army, celebrated in the harbor with lanterns and fireworks. Jefferson alternately tightened and loosened restrictions on trade with Britain, although the impressment of seamen continued throughout his time in office.

Sir James Craig, the governor general of Upper and Lower Canada, fostered illegal trade. Canada required American food for its population centers of Montreal and Quebec. In the embargo, the governor general thought he saw an opportunity to undo the American Revolution. Representatives of the New England states, at a meeting at Hartford, Connecticut, rankled over the embargo, which was strangling trade. Newspapers in England and Canada published stories on the conflicts over the embargo between the states and the federal government. To learn the true feeling of discontent, Craig sent an agent, John

Henry, to Burlington to ascertain the seriousness of the press reports. Henry's spying produced a letter dated February 12, 1809:

> The Governor General of Canada,
>
> Sir,
>   There seems but one opinion, namely, that they [embargo restrictions] are unnecessary, oppressive and unconstitutional. It must also be observed that the execution of them is so invidious as to attract towards the officers of government the enmity of the people, which is of course transferred to the government itself, so that, in case the State of Massachusetts should take any bold step towards resisting the execution of these laws is highly probable. It may calculate upon the hearty co-operation of the people of Vermont.[3]

Craig wrote to London of the ferment Henry discovered and suggested that there was a possibility that the northern portion of New England could be wooed into returning to Britain if the circumstances were right.

In this context in 1809, the new president, James Madison, took office. By June 1812 British interference at last prompted him to ask Congress for a declaration of war. In part his message to House and Senate read,

> Such is the spectacle of injuries and indignities which have been heaped upon our country, and such the crisis which its unexampled forbearance and conciliatory efforts have not been able to avert. It might at least have been expected that an enlightened nation, if less urged by moral obligations or invited by friendly disposition on the part of the United States, would have found in its true interest alone a sufficient motive to respect their rights and their tranquility on the high seas; that an enlarged policy would have favored that free and general circulation of commerce in which the British cabinet would not, for the sake of a precarious and surreptitious intercourse with hostile markets, have persevered in a course of measures which necessarily put at hazard the invaluable market of a great and growing country, disposed to cultivate the mutual advantages of an active commerce.

Other counsels have prevailed. Our moderation and conciliation have had no other effect than to encourage perseverance and to enlarge pretentions. We behold our sea-faring citizens still the daily victims of lawless violence, committed on the great common highway of nations, even within sight of the country which owes them protection. We behold our vessels freighted with the products of our soil and industry, or returning with the honest proceeds of them, wrested from their lawful destination, confiscated by prize courts no longer the organs of public law but the instruments of arbitrary edicts, and their unfortunate crews dispersed and lost, or forced or inveigled in British ports into British fleets, whilst arguments are employed in support of these aggressions which have no foundation but in a principle equally supporting a claim to regulate our external commerce in all cases whatsoever.

We behold, in fine, on the side of Great Britain a state of war against the United States, and on the side of the United States a state of peace towards Great Britain.

Whether the United States shall continue passive under these pergressive usurpations and these accumulating wrongs, or, opposing force to force in defence of their natural rights, shall commit a just cause into the hands of the Almighty Disposer of Events, avoiding all connections which might entangle it in the contest or views of other powers, and preserving a constant readiness to concur in an honorable re-establishment of peace and friendship, is a solemn question which the Constitution wisely confides to the legislative department of the government. In recommending it to their early deliberations I am happy in the assurance that the decision will be worthy of the enlightened and patriotic councils of a virtuous, as a free, and a powerful nation.[4]

Madison found support in both houses. The war hawks, members of Congress and their supporters from the western states, wanted war. Their westward expansion was being blocked by English fur trading interests and the Indians they employed. Britain continued to aid the western Indians in their conflict with the United States, offering the Indians a self-governed territory in what is today the Upper Peninsula of Michigan. Members of Parliament thought that the United States should end at the Mississippi and that Britain should take possession of all land westward to the Pacific Ocean. This only added to the tensions over the embargo and the impressment of sailors. The Orders in Counsel, passed by the king's government to stop trade with Napoleon, further restricted American freedom of action. Seen as a violation of neutral rights during the Napoleonic wars, the Orders were considered a sign of British arrogance, while Britain's failure to recognize the United States as a sovereign nation was considered intolerable.[5] In addition to these factors, Congress considered in its deliberations the intrigues of Governor Craig, further proof to many that Britain still regarded the loss of 1776 as an aberration. On June 18, 1812, war was declared on Great Britain:

DECLARATION OF WAR

BE IT ENACTED, . . . That war be and the same is hereby declared to exist between the United Kingdom of Great Britain and Ireland and the dependencies thereof, and the United States of America and their territories; and that the President of the United States is hereby authorized to use the whole land and naval force of the United States to carry the same into effect, and to issue to private armed vessels of the United States commissions or letters of marque and general reprisal, in such form as he shall think proper, and under the seal of the United States, against the vessels, goods and effects of the government of the said United Kingdom of Great Britain and Ireland, and the subjects thereof.

It would be the first of many such declarations in the history of the country.

AMERICA GOES TO WAR FOR THE FIRST TIME AS A PEOPLE

Former president Jefferson advised Madison in public, "The acquisition of Canada this year, as far as the neighborhood of Quebec, will be a mere matter of marching and will give us experience for the attack of Halifax next, and the final expulsion of England from the American continent." Henry Clay agreed with the declaration of war, but southern members of Congress were not in favor of invading Canada. They felt that if the expansion were to the north, that power would shift away from the southern states, who wished to acquire Florida. They encumbered the creation of a winning army by insisting upon the appointment of only good political party members as generals and commanders. This political interference extended down into the ranks of the junior officers in the local militia units, as well as in the emerging regular army. All were either in their sixties and veterans of the Revolution or had no real military experience. However, John Jay of Kentucky told everyone that his state militia alone could conquer Canada, a truly absurd statement. Many in the United States believed fervently that the citizens of Upper and Lower Canada were anxious to leave the grip of Britain, that given the chance, they would embrace the American army and join in the defeat of British forces in the provinces. Memories of the Revolution were confused. Many English-speaking Canadians had deliberately fled there during and after the Revolution because of strong attachments to things English. Americans believed that the militia system, the successor of the minutemen of Massachusetts, could defeat the might of the British regular army. Therefore, there was no need for a standing regular army. This belief was inaccurate and simplistic but had been passed down in legendary form. The truth was that the Revolution, which persisted over eight years, created a regular army, born after a harrowing gestation period nearly resulting in the death of the baby and mother. At the end of the war the army was disbanded. Yankees forgot that France contributed significantly, with both money and military forces. What remained, after the turn of the century, was a corroded, moth-eaten militia and a minuscule regular army that numbered just over a thousand. They were spread in garrisons to the west and dotted the coast. France, now under Napoleon, could not help this time; she was more at risk than America.

Perhaps French Canadian dissenters were on the minds of Jefferson and his war hawks, but like U.S. dissenters, they were a small minority. While Governor Craig, who favored the British settlers, had seriously oppressed the French-speaking community, which was the majority at that time, the prince regent in London had taken steps to placate the French Canadians. Fearing that Jefferson's words were directed at his French subjects, the prime regent carefully chose a new governor, Sir George Prevost, to replace Sir James.

Sir George was the son of a Swiss soldier recruited from the court in Holland in the 1760s. Major Augustin Prevost had been charged with forming the third battalion of the regiment of mercenaries prior to the American Revolution, while his brother James (Jacques) formed the 4th battalion. One of the original members of the 62d Infantry regiment, "The Royal Americans," Major Prevost formed his battalion of Germans and Swiss in the colonies.[6] Some of the four battalions of the regiment were recruited in Pennsylvania of men from the Palatine of Germany. During the Revolution the regiment, under Augustin's command, distinguished itself at the battles of Brier Creek and Savannah. Earlier in his career, at Quebec, Augustin had been wounded when a spent bullet struck him on the forehead. A steel plate, or trepan, was put on to cover the wound, which caused the family to refer to him as "old bullet head." After the campaign in Savannah, he and his family returned to England, where he retired as a major general.

In Hackensack, New Jersey, in 1767 a son, George, was born. Young George was educated at Lochee Military Academy in London and was sent on to the Military school at Colmar, France, near the border with Switzerland. He grew up speaking perfect

French, without a trace of an English accent. By his own merits, George attained a high rank in his profession, being first brought to the notice of his sovereign as a lieutenant colonel in a battalion of the 62d regiment, then serving in the West Indies. He distinguished himself at St. Vincent, where he was severely wounded, and for his conduct on that occasion, as well as in the subsequent operations in the West Indies, he was appointed brigadier. Soon afterwards George was made the governor of Dominica, which "was conferred upon him as a mark of His Majesty's approbation for his gallant and successful defense of that island and against a very superior force of enemy as well as for his conspicuous conduct at St. Lucia." In 1805, he was made a baronet, Sir George Prevost. Shortly after his return to England from the West Indies that year, he was appointed lieutenant governor of Portsmouth with command of the troops in that district. In 1808 he was selected to fill the important charge of lieutenant governor and lieutenant general commanding the forces in the province of Nova Scotia. In the autumn of the same year he proceeded with a division of troops from Halifax to the West Indies and was second in command upon the expedition at the capture of the island of Martinique from the French. He then returned to his government in Nova Scotia. Now, Sir George was called to the high and responsible position of governor in chief of Canada and commander of the forces in all British North America.[7]

It was feared in London that the heavy hand of Governor Craig had so angered the French-speaking Canadians that they might succumb to the temptation to throw off British rule and side with warring America. Sir George charmed such opposition with his French manners, and he instituted immediate reforms. He raised the pay of the Catholic bishop and moved French speakers into the government at every level. His courtship of the Francophones was regarded with acrimony by the dispossessed in the English-speaking community. The newspapers in Montreal vilified him on all issues and passed their venomous columns on to their colleagues in London's Fleet Street for publication. However, the throne of Britain supported his every move.

Sir George told London that the words contained in Madison's message to Congress, asking for a declaration of war, were filled with "Gun Powder." At the start of the war in the summer of 1812 Britain had in place in Upper and Lower Canada a small contingent of army and navy. They could spare little because Mother England was decisively engaged in the war with Napoleon. Though much weaker because of the purge of the aristocratic naval officer corps, the French kept the Royal Naval busy in the Caribbean. A provincial maritime force in Canada, under the scrutiny of the Royal Navy, was tasked with building and manning fleets on the Great Lakes and Lake Champlain. The British army supplied a few thousand regular troops and augmented them with Canadian volunteers. The Canadians were formed into fencible regiments, that is, established only for the defense of Canada. Unlike the American militia, which was at the disposal of a state governor for internal defense only, the fencibles could cross the border. From the French community, regiments of voltigeurs (Provincial Light Infantry Corps) and chasseurs took to the border as the first line of defense. The efforts of Prevost had been very effective and the citizens, no matter what the heritage, came to the colors easily. Jefferson had been mistaken, thinking that his hatred for the British was ubiquitous.

The American regular army just prior to the war numbered twenty-four hundred who were to be found in small groups within crumbling coastal forts or lonely outposts. Congress planned for ten thousand, but in 1812 the number was far less than half that. As an incentive to all recruits, the bonus was raised from twelve dollars to thirty-one dollars and a grant of 160 acres of land was offered.[8]

During the next two years of war, the entire regular army never reached the goal of ten thousand. A one-hundred-thousand-strong state militia was authorized to be paid for by the federal government. Though many were on the rolls, no effective fighting force neared that number. The spirit of 1776 was not there in 1812. The country was not interested in a standing army, regarding it as a European phenomenon and therefore not to their liking. They felt it was wasteful and dangerous. The young country was interested in nation building, agriculture, manufacturing, and trade. No outside threat was apparent. They knew the cost of a standing army and navy, which they believed outweighed its usefulness. The navy consisted of thirteen ships that were not prepared to take on the Royal Navy, which ruled the waves. A naval program began with the construction of frigates, the light cavalry of the ocean. A frigate was not listed in the three rates of men-of-war, since none carried sufficient guns to stand and fight. They would fight in hit-and-run engagements at sea, operating singly as a rule.

Following Jefferson's advice, the regular army prepared to invade Canada in the summer of 1812. Sir George Prevost intended to defend. There were five hundred thousand citizens in Upper and Lower Canada, the vast majority congregated from Montreal to the Atlantic coast.[9] Prevost was preparing to fight his neighbor, whose population was fifteen times larger. Under his command was a force of ten thousand foot soldiers, which included British regulars, the fencible regiments, and French volunteers, all of which he ensured were well trained. They were thinly spread along the northern bank of the St. Lawrence River and the Great Lakes of Ontario and Erie. The Canadian militia numbered eleven thousand, only four thousand of which were of any use. The provincial marine patrolled the watery border with twenty-two armed vessels, the largest of which was a twenty-two-gun sloop.[10] Armed American vessels were nearly nonexistent.[11]

AMERICA INVADES CANADA

The American invasion plan was concocted in Washington by Major General Henry Dearborn, secretary of war under Jefferson. It had been written in April and by early May, prior to the declaration of war, Dearborn was in Albany, New York, preparing. The war plan was simple for a well-trained and well-equipped army, which the United States, however, lacked. There would be four attacks into Canada. These were to be co-ordinated, to maximize their effectiveness, dooming the ambitious plan from the start. The more westerly attack was to be on Detroit, and was expected to occur simultaneously with one on the other end of Lake Erie, at Niagara, and a third near Sackets Harbor, New York. These attacks were to fix British troops and prevent reinforcement of Montreal, the objective of the main attack. The four victorious forces would meet at Montreal and then, their ranks swelled with grateful Canadians, proceed to Quebec. Without excellent communications over hundreds of miles of wilderness the plan was ludicrous.

Madison had appointed the governor of the Michigan Territory to command the effort at Detroit. No professional soldier, William Hull assembled a force of regular army and militia from Michigan, Ohio, and Indiana. In his youth, Hull had been an excellent field-grade officer during the Revolution. His command in 1812 totaled over twenty-two hundred and was nearly all infantry. Secretary of War William Eustis did not provide naval support, telling Hull he could convert the British fleet, once captured. Hull's army was nearly in place when war was declared. He hurried to the fort at Detroit, which had a garrison of one hundred twenty Americans that protected the five hundred citizens who were involved in the fur trade. On July 12 he managed to move the majority of his command across the

Detroit River into Canada and sent scouts out to find the British. English major general Isaac Brock commanded the opposition of little more than a thousand, which was augmented by Tecumseh's Indians. Brock, an experienced professional officer who had fought in India and in numerous engagements throughout the empire, was formidable. The British surprise attack at Mackinac Island, with a small force, drew the first blood of the land war. Hull got word of the loss after his units in Canada managed only a light skirmish. He then withdrew his command from Canada within days of crossing the border, and moved it to Detroit, fearing an attack there and along his line of communication to the south. Splitting off four hundred, knowing that the Indians were below him, he took the remaining fourteen hundred to the fort. He was losing troops to disease and desertion. The British bombarded the tiny fort with cannon from ships and gunboats in the river, while Brock crossed the river to the south of the American forces with his entire command. By the time the British prepared to attack Fort Detroit, six hundred of the Michigan militia had fled. Hull was offered surrender and accepted it on August 16. Knowing that the women and children would be slaughtered by the Indians, he obtained the necessary protection in the terms.

Immediately after the evacuation of the fort, the Indians rampaged through the nearby western territory. Major General William Henry Harrison, the victor over Tecumseh at Tippecanoe and future president of the United States, fought the Indian nations anew. With captains like Zachary Taylor, another future president, Harrison's troops tried to stabilize the frontier once again. No significant invasion of Canada in the west would be attempted for the remainder of the war.

Hull was court-martialed and found guilty of cowardice and neglect of duty, although he was acquitted of treason. The court, reportedly stacked with political enemies, recommended that he be shot, but Madison commuted his sentence and he was released due to his age and prior service. Court-martials were common when a defeat was suffered during the nineteenth century. Since the commander was responsible for all that happened while he was in charge, he could expect to receive the blame, just as he would the adulation if he were victorious.

General Dearborn seems not to have considered a coordinated attack in anything but his initial planning phase. Military thought in those days, on war on a national scale, was based on the campaigns of Frederick the Great of Germany and on the early campaigns of Napoleon. Neither offered an example of a coordinated scheme under the conditions of time, terrain, or troops that existed during the invasion of the Canadian wilderness. Not until August 3 did General Stephen Van Rensselaer receive the warning order to mobilize a one-thousand-man New York state militia for an attack on the narrow strip of land, the Niagara, separating Lake Ontario from Lake Erie. His mission was to cross the Niagara River into Canada and cut the portage road between the two great lakes, thus isolating western British army formations, prohibiting them from providing reinforcement against the primary attack by Dearborn on Montreal. But Brock had already arrived in the Niagara, his troops fresh from the victory in Detroit, and was preparing to attack America. Van Rensselaer would have had no choice but to run, since he had few supplies or trained troops. But he was saved from executing his mission by a truce proposed by the British government.

The British government took the idea of a truce seriously but Madison did not—he was determined to have this war. Britain did not want to be at war with America and repealed the Orders of Council, changing the trade picture. Lord Liverpool, who became prime minister in 1812, believed the two sides could find compromise over their grievances and avoid continued conflict. But Madison was determined, and so was his government, to conduct the war. The United States rejected the truce within weeks.

But the truce gave Van Rensselaer time to establish a military presence on the American side of the Niagara River. His command contained thirteen hundred regular infantry plus twice that in militia. A further sixteen hundred regulars were a few miles south at Buffalo, anchoring his line of communications. Major General Stephen Van Rensselaer was a gentleman from a prominent family and with a good reputation, but little military experience. America believed that in raising a citizen army in times of war, the natural and successful leaders would rise to the top. That would be true again in this the nation's second conflict, but that phenomenon would take time to play out. This war was still very young and in the meantime there would be many unnecessary casualties. The country would have to ask the question of whether it could afford such a lack of preparation or whether it would have to take on the traditions of Europe and maintain an officer corps of schooled and experienced professionals.

QUEENSTON

The amateurism of the American forces bloomed to full flower in the person of Brigadier General Alexander Smyth, a lawyer and political supporter of former president Jefferson who had appointed Smyth. Appointed colonel in 1805 he was promoted to general four years later, just before Jefferson left office. Taking command of the troops at Buffalo, he ignored his orders to work for Van Rensselaer and invoked his own plan, which was not coordinated with the main force at Lewiston, New York, preparing for invasion. Denied the services of Smyth's command, which remained near Buffalo, Van Rensselaer modified his plan on the fly and centered his force for an attack on Queenston, Upper Canada, across the river from his camp. This would accomplish his primary mission of cutting the portage road between the lakes. Just prior to the battle, within his combined command of regulars and militia, there were serious squabbles. Van Rensselaer named his cousin, Lieutenant Colonel Solomon Van Rensselaer, to command the strike force that was to cross the river and establish a beachhead on the Canadian side in Queenston. That formation was made up of six hundred regulars and militia men. Solomon Rensselaer was an officer in the New York state militia and junior to the regular officers who led their portion of the crossing. Lieutenant Colonel Winfield Scott refused to take orders from a junior and withdrew. Other regular officers complained but accepted the assignment in order to participate in the attack, and since the militia had experienced combat and the regulars had not. The crossing occurred in the darkness of early morning and was hindered from the start by the lack of boats and the ability to carry both formations and light artillery. The British were not caught unaware and poured murderous fire down on the little force that managed to get ashore. The Americans were racked by fire from British artillery batteries on two sides, and Solomon Van Rensselaer was killed. Regular captain John E. Wool, severely wounded in both buttocks, led a force behind the British and on to Queenston Heights, and then chased off the gunners and disabled the guns. British general Brock was killed in an attempt to retake the heights. The position of the Americans, with a foothold on the heights, was much improved and reinforcements began to trickle across the river. Scott was put in command of the force in Queenston, while General Van Rensselaer attempted to push more soldiers and supplies across the raging river. But the British were also joining in the battle with more regular troops, as the light of dawn began to flood the sky. The few American troops engaged fought like their forefathers had in '76 against the British. But the tide was turning to the redcoats now that they outnumbered the Yanks two to one. As the American wounded were evacuated in the returning boats, the militia refused to cross and left their ranks to join the civilians watching the battle from the American side. When Van Rensselaer pressed his officers, the New York militiamen said that they joined to fight in New York, not Canada. Scott and his struggling and gallant fighters were abandoned by their fellow soldiers. The Americans in Queenston withdrew to the boat landing but found that the boatmen would not come across to rescue them from the onslaught of the British. Scott was forced to surrender. Scott's militia, a force as large as the one that had surrendered, had gone to ground and were found hiding in the Canadian city after the battle. The colors of both the regular infantry and the militia were captured by the British and today hang high above the heads of the army pensioners in the dining hall of the Chelsea Royal Hospital in London. A painting of the battle is featured in the hospital's museum.

Over a hundred Americans were killed at Queenston, while nearly twice that were wounded and nine hundred were captured. The desertion rate on the part of the militia, cowed by the stories from the returning wounded, was high. The British suffered less than twenty killed and less than one hundred wounded. The Americans lost the battle due to a lack of planning; there never were enough boats to get the troops, equipment, and ammunition across the swift-flowing Niagara River. Although Smyth was called for, he never moved. After the battle, Jefferson blamed it all on Van Rensselaer, a political opponent. Madison had Eustis appoint Smyth as the commander of the remnants. Smyth called for more troops and by late November he had three thousand once again. He attempted two more crossings of the water into Canada in the next two weeks, and both sorties failed without engaging the enemy. Smyth's militia became mutinous as winter approached. By December the army of the center went into hibernation and Smyth wrote Dearborn requesting home leave. He never returned to military service.

Numerous skirmishes occurred across the border during this time. The most noteworthy was by Major Guilford Dudley Young of the Troy militia, on October 23. His command captured the colors and forty British soldiers at St. Regis on the Canadian side of the border. The colors were reportedly paraded in Albany and brought into the chamber of the state legislature to the strains of "Yankee Doodle" and "York Fusiliers." Young gave a speech presenting the flag to the people of New York and was promoted to the rank of colonel.[12] However, a Mr. Christe, a British writer, reported these events differently. He claimed the flag was only a Union Jack from the house of the resident interpreter that was usually hoisted on Sundays or holy days and was not a military standard. He also claimed that there had been no British troops present at St. Regis, only a border guard of a couple of men, due to a holy day. Yet the flag became known as the first foreign colors taken in the new war. There is no record of what happened to the "captured redcoats" and the flag no longer exists in the state archives.

NORTH TO MONTREAL

The long-awaited main attack into the heart of Canada, directed at Montreal, was finally launched on November 20, 1812, five months after the coordinated plan had begun so badly. Dearborn himself commanded the largest U.S. force since the revolution, six thousand blue-coated troops, the vast majority of whom were regulars. Dearborn deployed with not just infantry, but field artillery and mounted dragoons. The regulars were accompanied by New York State militia. Assembled at Plattsburgh, the troops set out on the twenty-five miles to the border, stopping for the night at the village of Champlain, near the shore of Lake Champlain. There, a small flotilla of U.S. Navy gunboats and sloops protected the waterfront. In the early morning, the Americans discovered that Major Charles Michel d'Irumberry de Salaberry was defending just across the border with a few hundred militia, Indians, and voltigeurs. Only a few miles inside Canada, on the Lacolle River, the enemy position was dominated by a small blockhouse. The American's formation began to envelop the guardhouse, manned by a few Indians and French-speaking troops. The defenders rushed out and broke through the American lines, escaping. One American column then mistakenly attacked another, killing and wounding their own. At this point the New York militia, which had hung back, refused to go on and returned to the southern side of the border. After some sporadic shooting, Dearborn determined that the attack should not continue. He ordered a countermarch and his command returned to Plattsburgh. In his account to Eustis and Madison, he cited the lateness of the year and offered to resign. Once back at Plattsburgh the formation split, some crossing the lake to Burlington and the remainder setting up winter quarters three miles from the lake on the Saranac River. No damage had been done to either army, but in Britain the aborted invasion only solidified the notion that Canada was in no real danger and therefore needed no more troops to defend itself. Dearborn's invasion force was dismissed at Horse Guards in London as a bunch of amateurs.[13]

The American navy, which had been contending with the Royal Navy since the Jefferson administration, had been in as poor condition as the army when the war broke out. While

Britain had 640 ships of the line deployed worldwide, America had limped along with a half-dozen sea-going frigates, which were not in good repair. The frigate was of a lesser class of man-of-war. By 1812, however, the American frigates had gained some fighting experience against the pirates in North Africa and had won minor victories against the Royal Navy. They had also tangled with the French. At the start of the war, Madison's secretary of the navy was Paul Hamilton, who before the year was out would be replaced by William Jones. Sailors and officers were easy to recruit because of the large American merchant fleet and the prize money offered for the capture of British trading vessels. At the opening of the war, the American navy abandoned the old hit-and-run tactics of single ships and created three squadrons: in the north Atlantic under John Rogers, in the Azores under Stephen Decatur, and in the South Atlantic under William Bainbridge. Each commodore (the title given an officer commanding a group of war ships) had one heavy frigate, one light frigate, and one sloop of war. This was in stark contrast to the Royal Navy, whose squadrons had numerous ships of the line that were far larger, in both guns and tonnage, than frigates. The American naval tactic was not to engage dreadnoughts, but to interfere with commercial shipping and interrupt trade, the lifeblood of Great Britain.

Many prizes were taken from the vast merchant stream that supplied England, as the American navy, though small, made its presence felt. The USS *Chesapeake,* repaired after its engagement with the *Leopard* in 1807, won revenge by capturing the largest prize to date, the merchantman *Volunteer,* worth $350,000. Over five hundred American privateers were commissioned with "letters of marque" that authorized them to roam the seas and nip away at Britain's trading empire. Although the British themselves supported privateering, they

called the American privateers "raiders"—no more than pirates—regarding them not as ships of war, but as totally outside the conventional rules of warfare. Along the eastern
seaboard the remainder of the American navy tried to protect
the major harbors and trading communities, but the vessels
were too few. For every blow to British commerce, the Royal
Navy sought retribution, continually raiding and causing havoc
at ports in New England and on the Chesapeake. Often shore
parties of British marines and soldiers, some of whom were
French Canadians, landed and plundered the towns.

On the Great Lakes of Ontario and Erie, Captain Isaac
Chauncey was charged too late (July 1812) to save Hull at Detroit. Prior to Chauncey's arrival, shore batteries and Lieutenant Malancthon Woolsey's gunboat *Oneida,* the only American armed vessel on the lake, defended Sackets Harbor, New
York, from destruction by the entire Provincial Marine fleet of
five ships. As on land, winter closed down the war on the lakes,
which were covered with ice and snow, giving the American
navy a chance to build.

Attempting to enforce the embargo, American naval lieutenant Sidney Smith, a young officer who had been on board
the *Chesapeake* in 1807, was charged with assisting the customs service in policing Lake Champlain. An experienced officer, Smith had served aboard the *Wasp* in 1810. At his disposal were several gunboats and sloops of war armed with a
few cannons that had been converted from commercial use.
The Canadian Provincial Marine guarded the upper end of the
lake with two gun boats stationed at the mouth of the Richelieu
River, the water route to the St. Lawrence and Montreal. The
river was blocked by rapids in Canada and a portage of ten
miles was required. Therefore Lake Champlain was locked out

of easy navigation to cities in Canada. A British boat-building yard was located on the southern side of the rapids at Ile aux Noix, the "island of nuts." By 1812 Secretary of the Navy Jones perceived that Smith was neither aggressive nor energetic enough to conduct proceedings now on a war footing.

NEW U.S. NAVY COMMANDER ON LAKE CHAMPLAIN

American naval lieutenant Thomas Macdonough was brought in from his duties defending ports along the Maine coast and put in command. As master commandant, the senior naval officer on the scene, he assumed the position of commodore of the small fleet of armed boats. Though only twenty-eight years old when he arrived, he was nationally known as a professional sailor with deep-sea experience, having had fought the Barbary pirates off the coast of Tripoli. Born in county New Castle, Delaware, his father was a physician and a major in the Continental Army during the Revolution. Thomas Macdonough entered navy service in 1798. With Decatur in the Mediterranean, he behaved with great gallantry. Later he gained notoriety from an incident in the harbor of Gibraltar, while a lieutenant on the USS *Siren,* which was moored near an American merchant brig. A boat from a British man-of-war went along side the brig and seized a sailor who was claimed as a British subject. Macdonough, whose captain was absent, saw the incident. He instantly armed, manned his gig, and gave chase. He overtook the boat under the guns of a British frigate, freed the sailor, and took him to the American man-of-war. The British captain, in a great rage, appeared on the *Siren* and inquired of Macdonough how he dared to take a man from his boat. The following conversation took place as reported in newspapers in the United States:

"What are you up to, sir?" shouted the British commander.

Macdonough stood fast. "That seaman was under the protection of my country's flag, and it was my duty."

Angered by the young officer's statement, the British captain's reply was strong: "You are a blaggard and a pirate like all your countrymen, sir. I shall lay my frigate along side and sink your ship."

Macdonough's next words went into American naval history: "While she swims you shall not have the man!"

The British captain blustered, "You'll repent of your rashness, young man. Suppose I had been in that boat, would you have dared to commit such an act?"

Macdonough: "I should have made the attempt, sir!"

Continuing, Macdonough's adversary countered, "What! Would you interfere if I were to impress men from that brig?"

Coolly, the young American lieutenant faced his enemy and replied, "You have only to try it, sir." The English officer wheeled about and left, but did not accept the challenge.

WINTER CANTONMENT

Secretary of the Navy Jones encouraged building of a war fleet, recognizing the threat to New York City from Lake Champlain. The boatbuilding yard at Vergennes, Vermont, provided Macdonough with both a home and starting point. During the winter of 1812–13 he improved on the boats that Lieutenant Sidney Smith had been sailing and "up gunned" for the coming spring thaw campaign. At Plattsburgh, Zebulon Pike put his army regiment into winter cantonment. In 1806, Pike's expedition to the west had mapped the edge of the mighty Rockies and gave his name to Pike's Peak. A resourceful and respected officer, Colonel Pike was about to fight his biggest battle. He took on the winter. His brigade of two thousand troops were satellited on the town three miles upriver. The area civilian population was nearly two thousand, all of whom were well sheltered and provisioned for the hard freeze and deep snow. The lake was frozen over. Pike chose his campsite on the swift-flowing Saranac River, which would supply his troops with fresh water. Cutting down the forest in an area one-half-mile square provided him with both building material for shelter and firewood. As a western explorer, Pike was an experienced woodsman, but since the campaign had lasted until early December, the camp was under construction during the worst of conditions. Before the permanent structures could be built the men lived in the few tents and lean-to's, exposed to the cold, snow, and wind of the north country. His officers lived in the town. Hunting parties supplied some fresh meat and limited supplies came from the village. The army supplies, stockpiled for the campaign, would soon be gone, and resupply from Albany, which depended on lake transport, was cut off when the lake was frozen over. By January, the troops were on half rations, while the rum and whiskey supply soon ran out. Fortunately, the troops could get food from farmers who had been supplying smuggled beef and grain to the British army in Canada. The British, however, paid higher prices in gold and were the preferred market over the federal troops, who paid in scrip and promises. Several Plattsburgh merchants were still trying to receive payment for services rendered as late as the 1840s. Pike managed to construct over two hundred miniature log cabins, each of which housed ten semifrozen soldiers. The rough structures were rectangular, ten feet by twenty feet, similar to those built at Valley Forge, Pennsylvania, during the Revolution. The cabins were low-roofed to preserve the heat, with clay fireplaces at the opposite end from the only door. The floors were frozen dirt, which soon to turned to a layer of slime that eventually covered everything. There were no windows and a draft was necessary, down the center of the open room from door to hearth, to keep the smoke from filling the room. Wooden pallets, stacked like springless bunk beds, became the living space for each man when he was not on duty. Work consisted of survival tasks, while guards were only required to protect the food and wood from thieves. There was no danger of attack from the British, who were maintaining themselves in little better conditions at Fort Chambley, twenty miles inside Canada.

The only contact with the redcoats came unexpectedly:

Cantonment, Saranak, Jany 18, 1813

Dear Sir,

Nothing of importance has transpired on the lines or at this Post since my last. An uncommon circumstance took place last week which for want of more interesting matter, I will detail to you.

A British deserter arrived here in a dashing state with a pair of grey ponies which he drove tandem to an elegant cariole in which he brought a beautiful young Canadian female with large trunks of clothing, buffelow skins and everything complete. His appearance not comporting with his story, Colonel Pike had him apprehended, and making a pretext of the event, dispatched Major Smith with a letter to Colonel Hamilton of the 100th Regiment, the commandant at the Isle aux Noix, to ascertain his real character.

Two days after the Colonel received a dispatch from Colonel Hamilton enclosing several letters sent to him by the officers of the battalion to which the deserter belonged, who represented him as one of the deepest, most consummate villains they ever met with. It appears that the man from a uniform series of good conduct for a number of years as sergeant of a company, had obtained the entire confidence of his Captain, and the good wishes of and favor of the officers of the battalion, and that upon their arrival at Chamblee from Quebec last summer he was appointed messman to the battalion. He was thereby permitted to suttle and retail to the soldiers, and obtained a standing pass to ride about the country to procure supplies for his table.

His Captain became his surety with several merchants of Montreal from whom he purchased his stores. They state that on the day he last set out for Montreal acording [sic] to his usual custom he gave the officers notice, who immediately crowded him with commissions. One sent for his gold watch repairing in town, another for clothing, lace, etc. A major gave him a fifty pound bill to get changed in gold and silver. A subaltern commanding a company sent a draft on the pay master for 60, being the subsistence of his company for one month; all of which he took care of, ran in debt to the amount of 5 or 600, and returning at night pushed on and got safely over the lines. He was taken up by Capt. Muhlenbergh at Champlain and sent down here.

Colonel Pike yesterday searched his trunks; he took the watch and the money he had stolen from the major and sent it by an officer immediately to Canada; after which he gave the gentleman a passport and suffered him to proceed with his establishment southward.

The British officers appear highly gratified with the attention paid them by Colonel Pike in this instance and no doubt will reciprocate this act of generosity and of justice.

With sincere esteem

Chas. W. Hunter[14]

The enemy was a home grown one that winter of 1813. The cold, wind, and snow caused men to huddle in the closely confined space. Illness and fevers were believed to be borne by gases from swamps and it was inexplicable to the medical men why disease should run rampant through the population during winter months. The summer uniforms were not replaced or augmented with warm overgarments. Exposed to the cold while on work parties, the men became vulnerable to airborne viruses. The dried and cracked inner surfaces of the noses and throats became hosts to all manner of pathogens for pulmonary diseases. Once the ever-present viruses were given a chance, they raced through the cloistered huts. That year a particularly virulent strain of pneumonia got a foothold in the cantonment. Visiting soldiers in the town spread it to the civilian population. There, the old and the children succumbed to the disease. Trade with the regiments at Burlington pushed it across the lake. It spread to the civilians there, and all around the edge of the big lake. In all, three thousand died, a large percentage of the population of the north country.[15] Pestilence naturally followed the lack of proper sanitary conditions at Pike's cantonment. Dysentery patients were treated with chamomile, opium, castor oil, and ipecacuanha. Every hut in the cantonment was home now to more sick than well. A hospital was set up, away from the camp and closer to the lake, where some communication existed across the frozen surface to Burlington, twenty-five miles east. Doctors and medics bled the fever patients, or burned their skin with heated cups applied upside down on the chest, leaving permanent scars to those who survived both the disease and the treatment. Men were moved outside into the cold in an attempt to kill the malady, which often killed the soldier as well. Colonel Pike lost 10 percent of his brigade to epidemic. The victims are buried on Crab Island, within sight of Plattsburgh, and a memorial marks the graves. It is believed that others were buried near the cantonment in unmarked graves.

SPRING CAMPAIGN

The year 1813 began with political change for the U.S. Army. Eustis had been replaced temporarily in the fall with James Monroe, and John Armstrong was eventually appointed to replace Monroe. Armstrong was a major during the Revolution and as ambassador to France in 1804 had seen Napoleon's army firsthand. He knew about war along the Lake Champlain corridor, since he had been present at the defeat of Burgoyne in 1777 at Saratoga, New York. In 1812 Armstrong was the brigadier general in charge of the defense of New York City. He had published a pretentious little book that same year, *Hints to Young Generals by an Old Soldier.* In that same spring, smuggling along the northern border had become epidemic due to the rich pickings from both armies. Odgensburg had been attacked by the British, and the American troops evacuated. This left the border open to illegal trade, leading Sir George Prevost to boast that much of his army was fed by the enemy. Troops stationed at Plattsburgh and Sackets Harbor spent a good deal of their time trying to prevent the smuggling of spars for ship construction, and cattle to feed the British forces in Canada. In Washington County, New York, customs officers aided by a pro-war vigilante mob fought with the local sheriff and war opponents over possession of illegally smuggled goods. The confrontation "was long and obstinately contested," reported the Lansingborough newspaper, "but ended in the complete discomfiture of Uncle Sam's party, who retired from the conflict with many a broken head and bruised limb leaving the men of New York in possession of the goods." Pike had to send troops when customs officials admitted they could not curb the illegal trade. On April 2, 1813, Lieutenant Lorinn Austin and fifty dragoons surrounded the New York village of Americus and arrested thirteen. But the smugglers soon were out of jail on bond and served a charge on Austin, who was arrested and sent to jail. Pike had to send bail money to Sackets Harbor. The Austin incident reflects the hostility of the citizens of New York toward the embargo.[16]

Armstrong suggested to Dearborn that that spring he attack in force at Kingston, Upper Canada, which was just across the bottom of Lake Ontario from the American base at Sackets Harbor. There he would cut off the western British army from Montreal and set the stage to take Prevost's most prized city. But even a good plan that was not of Dearborn's invention made little impression. Dearborn informed Armstrong that there were seven thousand British troops waiting in Kingston, which was an exaggeration of the five thousand that were there. Dearborn then launched a small excursion up the lake to York and further west, to eliminate the British army at Niagara. Commodore Chauncey would transport the troops and destroy the Provincial Marine boats being built at York. The operation did not address the possibility that Sackets Harbor would be open to a British attack that could thus destroy the only base of supply and naval forces on Lake Ontario. Nonetheless, Armstrong agreed, falsely believing that his field commander had the better judgment. Pike led a raiding force of two thousand toward York, which he attacked on April 22, 1813. The British succeeded in burning the only Royal Navy vessel in port, a sloop that was under construction, to prevent its capture. During the battle in the streets, Zebulon Pike was killed when the British arsenal blew up. Some say he was standing next to an ammunition wagon which ignited when the arsenal exploded.

Dearborn moved west to the Niagara while Prevost, along with his Royal Navy commander Sir James L. Yeo, attacked Dearborn's rear at Sackets Harbor. The British force very nearly took the base. Finding the Americans gone to York, Prevost pursued them to the western end of the lake, where Dearborn was defeated once again. The only positive outcome for the Americans was the establishment of Captain Oliver Hazard Perry's base of operations on Lake Erie, which would become the rock of the American defense in the Great Lakes. Sir George wrote to his boss, the head of the British army in London at Horse Guards, about Stoney Creek:

Headquarters Kingston Upper Canada 15th July 1813

To Field Marshal, His Royal Highness, The Duke of York

The enemy were completely surprised and after a short tho' severe action, driven from their camp with the loss of three Guns, and one brass Howitzer,—Two brigadier General's, the first and second in command, and upwards of 100 officers and men were made prison-

ers—our troops having returned to their cantonements with their prisoners and two, six pounders, all that they had means of bringing
away,—the enemy broke their encampment and retired with the greatest precipitation to the 40 mile creek, from whence I have the pleasure
of informing, your Royal Highness, they have since been driven, by
the appearance of the Squadron under the command of Sir James Yeo,
off that coast and by the approach of a body of 400 men, pushed on
in advance under Major Evans.

Your obet. Serv.

Lt. Gen. Sir Geo Prevost[17]

LAKE CHAMPLAIN WARFARE

When Pike moved off from Plattsburgh to his rendezvous with
death at York, he left Plattsburgh undefended. A small group of
regulars were left at Battery Park in Burlington under Colonel
Alexander Macomb and augmented by the Vermont militia. In the
spring of 1813, when Lake Champlain became free of ice, the
American navy aggressively attempted to sweep the northern end
of British influence. Macdonough dominated the center of the lake
with his brig, the *President,* accompanied by a dozen gunboats in
an attempt to interdict smugglers who were shipping timbers and
spars north to the Canadian boatbuilding yard at Ille aux Noix.
Macdonough suffered from a lack of sailors for both his vessels
and the gunboats. The boats were seventy feet long, powered by a
small lateen sail and oars, with a crew of thirty performing the un-
rewarding and backbreaking work of rowing. It is not surprising
that Macdonough had trouble finding sailors for the job. He called
upon the regular army and militia at Burlington to augment the few
lake seamen who agreed to join the small fleet. No prize money
was offered the crews, as with crews on the high seas. All seized
goods were given to the U.S. Customs Service in Plattsburgh. No
suitable leaders were found in the community to command the

gunboats, so the naval lieutenant appointed army officers to the positions. When Secretary Jones was informed of the shortage of men and leaders he replied,

> To the Master Commandant, Lake Champlain,
>
> Enclosed you will receive a copy of the joint regulations of the War and Navy Departments for the government of their respective Commanders, when action in concert.
>
> Regulation
> 1st. No officer of the Army of the United States, shall, on any pretence, command any of the Ships, or Vessels of the United States, nor shall Officers of the Navy of the United States, under any pretences, command any troops of the Army of the United States.
>
> Navy Department
> April 8th 1813
> (signed) W. Jones[18]

This was not the kind of help that the hard-pressed commodore was seeking. Jones's statement was ignored and several army captains were put in charge of gunboats. With respect to the arming of the burgeoning fleet, Macdonough and Jones were in agreement. Both saw the mission as an effort to fight smuggling, since the Royal Navy was yet to appear on the lake in any strength. It was known that they possessed only gunboats similar to the slow craft that clustered around the *President,* and that on the open lake the British boats were no match for the American sloops and brigs driven by sail. Macdonough and Jones never perceived that the British would build larger warships at Ile aux Noix, as they were doing on the Great Lakes. Reports from Peter Sailly's spies mentioned only gunboat construction. A letter from Macdonough to Jones in June 1813 states the case:

> "18 pound carronades I think are best for those kind of vessels, as they are light and carry a greater quantity of grape shot than long guns

of about the same weight, and it is likely they will be used principally against small vessels with many men exposed in them or against [merchant] sloops.[19]

It was therefore agreed that the American men-of-war would be equipped with carronades rather than the standard array of naval cannons. Only the gunboats would have a medium-size cannon, placed in the prow like an out-thrust stinger, while at the center they too could have a carronade-like gun, a columbiad, mounted on a slide that rotated in a full circle.

The "smasher," as the columbiad was known among the sailors, was an English invention. Carronades were named for the factory of their initial manufacture (Carron ironworks at Falkirk, Scotland) and were short, large-bore guns generally used for antipersonnel fire at short range and requiring a smaller powder charge. The shot traveled more slowly, thus inflicting more casualties by the production of splinters.[20] The cannon of comparable size, the twenty-four pound Congreve 7'6" gun, did not possess the punch of the carronade, but it had a range of one and a half miles, while the smasher had a range of only five hundred yards. Penetration of the wooden ships by cannonballs was a far different affair on the inland lakes of America than on the seas. Unlike sea-going ships, which were constructed of oak, the lake vessels were made largely of green pine. Cannon or carronade fire against the softer wood would produce massive splinters that could cut a man in half.[21]

Macdonough sent Lieutenant Sidney Smith, captain of the *Growler,* and Jarvis Loomis, sailing master of the *Eagle,* both sloops-of-war, to protect American shipping near the Canadian border, where merchant vessels had been attacked by Canadian gunboats. The Canadian marine's rowed galleys were armed with long twenty-four pounders, while the sloops carried the shorter-range eighteens. In pursuit of the enemy in June 1813, the *Eagle* and *Growler* left the lake and went down the Richelieu River until they were engaged by the guns at Ile aux Noix. British galleys closed in behind to block retreat. The winds on the river would not support the American sail-powered vessels and they lost steering. Three British boats laid off, out of range of Smith's helpless craft. Now the shore batteries fired in support of the gunboats, leaving Smith's two ships in the middle, unable to fight back. Smith could not withdraw and even the British infantry could reach his flotilla by musket fire. Sailing Master Loomis fired grape and canister into the troops on the nearby river banks, killing thirty British soldiers. *Growler,* racked by the shore batteries, ran ashore when her rigging was destroyed. After four hours of desperate battle, a Royal Navy cannonball penetrated the prow of the *Eagle* under the waterline, plowing straight through and out the other side. It was a mortal wound for the *Eagle* and she grounded on a shoal, out of action. The American crews were captured. One American was killed and thirty were held prisoner, while the nine wounded were returned on parole. The surviving Yankee sailors would spend much of the war interned in Canada, awaiting prisoner exchange. This action effectively wiped out the American naval strength on Lake Champlain.

To T. Macdonough, esq. US Navy

Quebec Prison, 28 March 1814

Having an opportunity of forwarding a Letter to the US, I think it my Duty to Enclose you a few lines to inform you that I am in very good health and also all of the American Officers that are held as hostages at this place. I shall inform you that field officers are indulged with the Liberty of a parolee, to a private house in Town with the liberty of the Garden and take the fresh air and that Lieut Smith being apparently on the Decline he has allowed the same indulgence and I heard this morning that he had [illegible] by recovered his health again.

I have not much news to write only that Col. Lewis and Major Maddison of the Kentucky [illegible] that were captured with Genrl Winchester leave this place for the US tomorrow on a parolee for [Troy?], but if the US [illegible] to send two of the same rank for their exchange they have the liberty to remain in the US. I shall inform you that on the return of Genrl Winder from the US he favors us with a List of the Navy which [illegible]. It appears that altho I have been unfortunate that the Government have not forgot me that they have been pleased to appoint me to the rank of a Lieut. which if it please God more I never Disgrace the appointment. Sir I would thank you if there is any Letters appear on the Lines for me to forward them by flag and also please to write me if you have heard any thing from my friend since I have been captured.

I Remain Sir Your obd Servant,

Jarvis Loomis[22]

But the bigger victory for the Royal Navy was the capture of the two American men-of-war, which they repaired and refloated as the Royal Navy's *Finch* and *Chub*. Refitted, the ships took to the lake on offensive operations against the United States, making the British the preeminent naval force on Lake Champlain. Macdonough reported the loss and requested to step up the warship construction program to make up for them. Pressed for time, for the most part he converted and armed merchant ships.

British lieutenant colonel John Murray began an expedition in July supported by the captured and renamed American fighting ships. The U.S. Navy was confined to the protected yard up Otter Creek at Basin Harbor, near Vergennes, Vermont. With a force of several hundred regulars and fencibles, Murray raided Burlington and Plattsburgh in the summer of 1813. Plattsburgh was undefended and hc looted Peter Sailly's customs warehouse as well as its shops, mills, and farms. Finding Pike's cantonment, which was nothing but two hundred empty log cabins, he burned the camp to the ground and destroyed all record of its existence, including the graves. Murray, aboard Captain Daniel Pring's flotilla, ranged the lake unmolested. Burlington's coast artillery at Battery Park warded off an attempt to capture the town.

A document left behind in June 1813 by Colonel Murray at Plattsburgh revealed that an American, spying for the British, led the English officer to the military supplies and informed him of the disposition of the troops around the lake's perimeter. Within days, the individual suspected was arrested and charged with treason. Such behavior was not uncommon. The question of loyalty was at odds with commerce and trade in the harsh north country, where many considered nationality to be of secondary importance to business. The majority of the people, however, opposed the antiwar protesters, who went underground as the war pressed on. Governor Martin Chittenden of Vermont did not help the American war effort, since he was at political odds with the federal government over their use of state militia. Chittenden demanded that the State Guard fight only in Vermont and under the direction of the governor.

While the discredited Dearborn was defending his actions in Washington, Major General James Wilkinson, politically well connected, was put in charge of the Army of the North and directed by Secretary of War Armstrong to conduct operations both in Ontario and toward Montreal. A former aide to General Horatio Gates at Saratoga in 1777, Wilkinson was described by his subordinates as old and imbecilic. Major General Wade Hampton, the new commander in the Champlain area, hated Wilkinson and only reluctantly agreed to follow his orders. Hampton's cavalier attitude toward the attack is revealed in a communiqué to one of his most able subordinates, Colonel Isaac Clark, a veteran of the Revolution now in his sixties. "What I am aiming at is tranquillity of the road, by kicking up a dust on the lines." Following that vague direction the venerable old officer on October 11, with only one hundred Vermont militia, surprised British major Powell's little command, who surrendered believing that Clark's force was the lead element

of a larger invasion force. Clark brought his one hundred prisoners back to Burlington to the delight of the local citizens.
Nonetheless, Hampton crossed the Canadian border with a
force of regulars and militia of four thousand and stabbed
north, at Wilkinson's and Armstrong's instructions. The first
day, the American army moved twenty-four miles. Six miles
later Hampton was fired upon by a substantial force that was
yet smaller than this own. Meanwhile, Wilkinson's effort at
Crysler's Farm disintegrated. As Hampton maneuvered for attack, he received a curious message that he was to establish
winter quarters for ten thousand. Confused by Armstrong's additional order and figuring that he was being abandoned for the
winter rather than reinforced by Wilkinson's larger force,
Hampton dithered. Armstrong, who had been with Wilkinson
coming up from Sackets Harbor, also announced that he was
leaving for Washington. When the troops of Colonel Charles de
Salaberry, commander of the Canadian voltigeurs, charged
Hampton, yelling wildly and cannons firing, Hampton withdrew and did not stop running until he was safely back on
American soil. Prevost's Canadian forces had suffered two
killed. The campaigning for 1813 ended in December and the
American army went into winter quarters with the words of the
governor general of Canada ringing in their ears: "the Americans had better behave themselves in the future, or else."
Colonel John Elting has said, "This is the lowest point in the
history of the American regular forces before Korea."[23]

By November Governor Chittenden had had enough of the
federal army requisitioning his state militia to fight outside of
Vermont and issued a statement in his annual message that "such
use of [Vermont's] troops was doubtful as to its necessity, expedience or justice." The governor had a point. Until then, nearly all
American military operations had been folly. But some of his

troops and their commanders ignored the governor. Lieutenant Colonel Luther Dixon took his men to New York to reinforce the garrison at Plattsburgh.

Colonel Murray's successful raid in the summer of 1813 only strengthened the Provincial Marine's interest on the lake and, when Macdonough, who was busy building new American warships, did not react to American losses on the lake, Captain Daniel Pring, the Royal Navy commander on Lake Champlain, began probing the American defense on his own. Pring, an aggressive officer, entered the naval service at an early age and when very young was a midshipman on the Jamaica station. In 1801 he served on board the *Russell* at Copenhagen. In 1807 he received his lieutenant's commission and, at the outbreak of the American war, was in command of the schooner *Paz* at the Halifax station. When Sir George Prevost required naval officers to take charge of the provincial navy on the lakes, Captain Pring was selected over others by Sir J. B. Warren for those duties.[24] Now he linked his flagship *Canada* with the *Chub* and the *Finch,* and went south to destroy American commerce and any craft he could find, in hopes of securing the lake as a British pond. But it was nearly November by the time Pring was met on the lake again by the Americans, and the ice forced major naval action to be postponed until spring.

WINTER 1814

The winter meant boatbuilding on both sides of the border. Pring constructed the *Linnet,* to that date the largest of his command at eighty-five feet. Macdonough had no trouble convincing Jones that the lake would be in British hands if a major effort were not made to counter. Noah Brown, a master shipbuilder from the navy yard in

New York City, and two hundred craftsmen were sent to Vergennes. The brig *Saratoga* and the sloop *Ticonderoga* were added to the *President,* along with ten rowed gunboats, allowing the U.S. Navy to once again stand out to battle, when the ships were fitted to fight.

SPRING 1814, AMERICA INVADES CANADA, AGAIN

It was the mission of Major General Wilkinson, the commander of the American Army of the North, to make true the boast made in November 1813 to the Marquis de Lafayette by Jefferson that "Our quarters for this winter will probably be Montreal." In March, with only a few calendar days of winter left, the major general attacked across the Canadian border once again. With four thousand troops in front of him, he proclaimed, "return victorious or not at all." They did neither. Confronted with deep snow at the mill in Lacolle, thirty miles north of Plattsburgh, loosely defended by 180 Canadians, they gave up the attack in confusion. It was the last attempt by the United States to conquer Montreal. There was one casualty: Wilkinson. He was relieved, never again to risk American soldiers in crude adventures. Afterward, he complained that, "I have been deprived of my sword in the dawn of the campaign."

Major General George Izard, his subordinate, was appointed to command the northern army. He gathered the troops at Plattsburgh and, with the help of newly promoted Brigadier General Alexander Macomb, began a rigorous training program. The attack in March had exposed the lack of discipline and soldier skills, which they would remedy before the force could be committed once again. Armstrong's interest now changed to Major General Brown's command in the center, which was to concentrate at Niagara. On Lake Champlain, Captain Pring was sent south by Sir George to destroy the American navy and its boatbuilding capability on the Otter River, south of Burlington. Tipped off by his spies, Peter Sailly wrote to Macdonough on April 6, 1814:

> [A] part of the British flotilla has been at Rouses Point since a few days. . . . We are apprehensive that they will pay us a visit in a few days and send us some of their heavy balls unless they choose to go first to the mouth of Otter Creek to block you up.

Macdonough's answer was short:

> It will do no good to growl, but I observe that we are going to be in desperate situation on the shores of this lake as long as the British can navigate it, stop all communication and plunder our shores.[25]

If Pring could block the entrance to the narrow channel at the mouth of Otter Creek by sinking barges filled with rocks, the American flotilla would be like a boat in a bottle. But the strong southerly winds kept the British on the northern end of the lake for a month. This blessing gave General Macomb time to move a battery of guns to the creek mouth and reinforce the Vermont militia, which were on the ground digging in for the British attack. The defensive positions of naval lieutenant Stephen Cassin and army captain Arthur Thornton on the point was attacked on May 14, in force, by the Royal Navy. In addition to the three men-of-war and row galleys, the British brought with them captured merchant vessels for scuttling up river. The 160 Royal Marines attempted to land under supporting gunfire from the *Linnet,* Pring's new flagship, but they were too late and the American position held fast. Unable to maintain the flotilla on station, Captain Pring broke contact, but not before discovering the exact intelligence needed on the new American fleet that Macdonough had been preparing for the spring campaign.

On May 26, Commodore Macdonough brought out the fleet, *Saratoga, Ticonderoga,* and *Preble,* along with six new armed gunboats. They were now the most powerful presence on the lake, and Pring went to Prevost for permission and funds to build a decisive vessel that could put a stop to the arms race on Lake Champlain once and for all. He wanted a real man-of-war, a shallow-draft lake frigate. He would get it, because of a major event in Europe that changed everything.

CHAPTER 2

All warfare is based on deception. Therefore when capable, feign incapable; when active, inactive. When near, make it appear that you are far away; when far that you are near. Offer the enemy a bait to lure him; feign disorder and strike him.

—Sun Tzu, *The Art of War.*

The conduct of the war in North America, known only in the United States as the War of 1812, had always been an annoying sideshow to the British government. They had tried to settle the war diplomatically ever since it began. It was a drain on troops that were needed in Spain and Portugal, where the British were decisively engaged in the field against Napoleon. While Napoleon called the war in Iberia his "Spanish ulcer," it was just as painful to the British. Wellington kept forty thousand combat troops in the field at any one time and was nearly always outnumbered. The logistical tail tied down much of the British merchant fleet.

Beginning in 1812, peace talks between Britain and America had been conducted in Moscow, under the tutelage of the czar's government. Sir George complained to his friend and mentor, the Earl Bathurst, who was conducting the war in Canada for the government, that the Canadians might desert the British cause if there was not an increased contribution of British soldiers. Bathurst rankled at the suggestion, saying that "Canadians could not be indifferent to the exertions which England was making for the liberties of Europe."[1] But Bathurst had missed the point, or perhaps he simply could not address it at that critical time. Citizens of the New World cared little for the Old.

The British allies, Russia, Prussia, and Austria, had been beating the French back to their borders ever since Napoleon's losses in the winter of 1812. The Russian campaign had nearly eliminated all the experienced members of the French army, who had won so many victories, and in 1813 they were largely replaced with inexperienced conscripts. While Napoleon's armies had won battles on all fronts, the overwhelming weight of the allies was steadily driving them back into fortress France. By the early spring of 1814 they were at the gates of Paris. In April the emperor was forced to abdicate. He accepted the new post of ruler of Elba, a small island off the coast of northern Italy, and retired there with a thousand household troops and the promise of money to sustain his diminished court life.

The peace mission in Moscow had broken down and the war in North America continued. A different kind of negotiation now began with the Congress of Vienna. There, war leaders from the allies gathered to restore the Bourbons to the throne of France and divide up the spoils. Wellington attended as the ambassador to France and to keep an eye on the disposition of the armies that were gathered in France as occupation troops. In London, the British government saw the opportunity to solve two problems together. The large British army was billeted in southern France and the situation in Europe was too delicate to disband it at that time. It was judged to be unwise to maintain such a large force intact at home. The war with the United States continued uninterrupted. Bathurst drafted a plan to end the War of 1812 on a high note. Rather than bringing all the troops back to Britain, he could send many of them to attack the United States, as well as to bolster British interest in the former holdings of France and

Spain in the Caribbean. A veteran army could crush the American army, of which Bathurst had a very low opinion. Realizing that the whole of the United States could not be conquered, he sought to stretch the southern border of Canada into New England. He remembered Governor Craig's communiqué suggesting that the citizens were dissatisfied with federal rule there. Governor General Sir George Prevost had been asking for more troops for the past two years to defend the colony. It was now possible to take him off the defense and assume the offense. Britain had the opportunity to finish the North American war and perhaps gain a portion of New England. Quebec was a frozen port in the winter, and a land route there across the northern portion of Maine would be a prime objective. Governor General Sherbrooke of New Brunswick had been campaigning to take the Penobscot River and had been quite successful in lopping off the northern corner of the Maine territory, which was under the protection of the State of Massachusetts. There were not sufficient American troops to hold Maine. In Upper Canada, a small group of British soldiers and merchants had enlisted the Indians for maintaining a hold on the northern Mississippi Valley, which was rich with promise. It was plain the peace talks were to be restarted in earnest at Ghent that summer. Wherever British troops were at the conclusion of the war would become the new border. There were members of Parliament who suggested that any new land secured in upper New England for the crown should be independent of Canada and become an autonomous colony, which they proposed to name "Columbia."

Lieutenant General Sir George Prevost had spent the spring of 1814 the same way he had spent every spring for the last two years: repelling invasions. He was becoming a master of defense, never really having the troops to do anything else. Through the expert use of terrain, and troops of various kinds, he and his field commanders had been able to maintain the borders of Canada. His spies told him that things were changing south of the border and that the old politically appointed generals were gone and new young and competent officers of all grades had taken over. The troops were experienced and supply lines were improving. The war was changing character in America and he feared what had happened to his father's army at Yorktown might be repeated again during his watch. He had lost some of his best commanders and Britain was not hearing his pleas.

Then in June a ship arrived with a secret order from London:

From Earl Bathurst 3rd June 1814

Reinforcements allotted for North America and the operations contemplated for the employment of them.

SECRET

Downing Street
3rd June 1814

Sir,

I have already communicated to you in my dispatch of the 14th of April the intention of His Majesty's government to avail themselves of the favorable state of affairs in Europe, in order to reinforce the Army under your Command. I have now to acquaint you with the arrangements which have been made in consequence, and to point out to you the views with which His Majesty's Government have made is considerable an augmentation of the Army in Canada.

The 2nd Battalion of the Royal Scots of the strength stated in the margin [768] sailed from Spithead on the 9th ulto. direct for Quebec, and was joined at Cork by the 97th Regiment destined to relieve the Nova Scotia Fencibles at Newfoundland; which latter will immediately proceed to Quebec.

The 6th & 82nd Regiments of the strength [as per margin, 980 8 /2. 8 37] sailed from Bordeaux on the 15th ulto. direct for Quebec. Orders have also been given for embarking at the same port twelve of the most effective Regiments of the Army under the Duke of Wellington together with the three companies of Artillery on the same service. This Force, which/when joined by the detachments about to proceed from this country will not fall far short of ten thousand Infantry, will proceed in three divisions to Quebec. The first of these divisions will embark immediately, the second a week after the first and the third as soon as the means of transport are collected. The last division however will arrive in Quebec long before the close of the year.

Six other Regiments have also been detached from the Gironde and the Mediterranean four of which are destined to be employed in a direct operation against the Enemy's Coast, and the other two are intended as a reinforcement to Nova Scotia and New Brunswick, available / if circumstances appear to you to render it necessary / for the defense of Canada, or for the offensive operations on the Frontier to which your attention will be particularly directed. It is also in contemplation at a later period of the year to make a more serious attack on some part of the Coast of the United States, and with this view a considerable force will be collected at Cork without delay. These operations will not fail to effect a powerful diversion in your favor.

The result of this arrangement as far as you are immediately concerned will be to place at your disposal the Royals, The Nova Scotia Fencibles, the 6th and the 82nd Regiments amounting to three thousand one hundred and twenty seven men; and to afford you in the course of the year a further reinforcement of ten thousand British troops.

When this force shall have been placed under your command His Majesty's Government conceive that the Canada's will not only be protected for the time against any attack which the Enemy may have the means of making, but it will enable you to commence offensive operations on the Enemy's Frontier before the close of this campaign. At the same time it is by no means the intention of His Majesty's Government to encourage such forward movements into the Interior of the American territory as might commit the safety of the force placed under your Command. The object to your operations will be, first, to give immediate protection. Secondly, to obtain if possible ultimate security to His Majesty's possessions in America. The entire destruction of Sackets Harbor and the Naval Establishment on Lake Erie and Lake Champlain come under the first description. The maintenance of Fort Niagara and so much of the adjacent Territory as may be deemed necessary, and the occupation of Detroit and the Michigan Country came under the second. Your successes shall enable us to terminate the war by the retention of the Fort of Niagara, and the restoration of Detroit and the whole of the Michigan Country to the Indians. The British frontier will be materially improved. Should there be any advance position on that part of our frontier which

extends towards Lake Champlain, the occupation of which would materially tend to the security of the province, you will if you deem it expe-
dient expel the Enemy from it, and occupy it by detachments of the
Troops under your Command, Always however, taking care not expose
His Majesty's Forces to being cut off by too extended a line of advance.

If you should not consider it necessary to call to your assistance the
two Regiments which are to proceed in the first instance to Halifax, Sir
J. Sherbrooke will receive instruction to occupy as much of the District
of Maine as will secure an uninterrupted intercourse between Halifax
and Quebec.

In contemplation of the increased force which by this arrangement
you will be under the necessity of maintaining in the Province directions
have been given for shipping immediately for Quebec provisions for
10,000 men for 6 months.

The Frigate which conveys this letter has also on board one hundred
thousand pounds in specie for the use of the Army under your Command. An equal sum will also be embarked on board the Ship of War
which may be appointed to convoy to Quebec the fleet which is expected
to sail from this country on the 10th or at latest on the 15th instant.

I have the honor to be
Sir
Your most obedient
Humble Servant
(signed)
BATHURST[2]

The tone of the communiqué is plainly informal and friendly.
Sir George had the confidence of the government and the Crown,
who paid no attention to the venomous campaign in the London
newspapers conducted by the anglophiles of Canada, who did not
like Sir George's pandering to the French speakers. To the many
citizens of Canada he had earned the title of "Savior of Canada,"
due to his defense of the region from the invasions conducted
over the past two years. Prevost showed great personal courage
at the battle of Sackets Harbor, though some questioned his actions. But the press never gave him credit. At age forty-six, the
governor general possessed considerable energy and strength of

will and was known for his graciousness and personal charm. He was described as a suave diplomat but was in declining health, a result of his years of military service in the tropics. A judge in Canada said of him that, "he was a tiny light gossamer man, cheerfulness of demeanor, with his simple unassuming manner and consideration of people of every rank."[3]

THE BRITISH TAKE THE OFFENSIVE

Now Sir George not only had the means to defend, but more importantly, he could attack. The master plan was most comprehensive. A diversionary force of considerable size was to be formed from London to deceive the American government and military into thinking that an British invasion of the eastern seaboard was imminent. President Madison knew that the great victory in France would allow Britain's mighty and experienced armed forces to be let loose on America, allowing them easily to revenge losses of the past two years. The American armed forces were still small and spread very thinly, no match for the veterans of the Napoleonic wars. If squadrons of the Royal Navy, embarked with masses of troops, appeared in New England and along the undefended shoreline of Delaware and Virginia, there would be little to contain them.

Prevost knew that such a diversion would keep reinforcements from appearing on the northern frontier. He need only contend with the enemy he had known. In the far west of Detroit and beyond, there were mostly militia, which were no real threat. At Niagara, there was little more, with the exception of some regular army units under Brigadier General Winfield Scott. At Sackets Harbor, the key support base for the American western forces, were only two thousand army and naval forces. The major force was at Plattsburgh, refitting and training after the abortive attack

of March on the border of Canada. Its new commander, Major
General George Izard, was a formidable officer who had six thousand regulars, as well as a burgeoning naval flotilla under Commodore Macdonough. In the summer of 1814, as the red-coated
regulars arrived, Sir George felt confident that the forces under
his command could fulfill the full extent of the instructions contained in the secret order.

His first inclination, and probably that of his boss in London,
was to continue the campaign in the Great Lakes. He could
overwhelm Sackets Harbor and move against Detroit. But his
experience told him that it was hard going on the shores of the
Great Lakes, and resupply of a large army would be very difficult, to say nothing of the transport problems. Admiral Yeo
could support a portion of the attack, but Prevost was not sure
that ten thousand reinforcements added to the burden of the
three thousand already on the ground would not grind to a logistical halt in that wilderness before winter. He could never
sustain them when the lakes and rivers froze. It was true that
the freeze might provided passable tracks, if the ice was smooth
and the snow was not too deep. But winter along the great
length of the Saint Lawrence and the shoreline of Lake Ontario
could be brutal. He might well repeat the folly of Napoleon in
Russia.[4] As a professional soldier, he had studied the New York
campaign of Burgoyne in 1777. If Burgoyne had used Lake
Champlain, Lake George, and the headwaters of the Hudson
River prudently, his campaign could have succeeded. The campaign had been well conceived because of the directness of the
route, which stabbed like a dagger straight at New York City,
the gate keeper for New England. The lesson that it now offered
seemed irresistible. The London order plainly called for the dis-
arming of Lake Champlain, which was only a few miles due

south of Montreal. The army could be more easily supplied because it had always been fed by the farmers of Vermont and New York, who had used the lake to smuggle goods north since 1807. There was no real threat to Prevost's rear from the American troops in the west, which he had contained for the past two years with formations that were still in place.

Prevost could add a bit of deception to his own plan by sending a small portion of the reinforcement west, making the American commanders believe that he was indeed going to attack Sackets Harbor, thus fixing them in place. Then, by launching a combined attack of army and navy straight south, he could break the American army at Plattsburgh instead, while his navy could destroy Macdonough's small fleet and secure the entire lake. There were no regular American forces between Plattsburgh and Washington, D.C. The state militias, modeled on the minutemen of Massachusetts from the American Revolution, were not the same force in 1814. Prevost had dealt with them on numerous occasions and found them skittish, ill equipped, and led by amateurs. After eliminating the front lines at Plattsburgh, he could winter on the edges of Lake Champlain a hundred miles south of the Canadian border and in spring continue down Burgoyne's old route toward New York City. He also believed that his predecessor, Governor Craig, may have been correct and that northern New Englanders, faced with the occupation of British soldiers, might give allegiance back to Britain. His military field position, with the treaty talks now underway again, this time in Ghent, Belgium, would result in the establishment of a new border for Canada at the point where his lines rested. It was a bold plan, and an old one that he believed would be well received by Bathurst. After all, had this not been the road to war in North America for nearly a hundred years?

BY LAND AND BY LAKE

While the British army gathered at Chambly, twenty miles south of Montreal and twenty miles north of the American border, Prevost turned his attention to the Royal Navy. Wellington had said that the key to control on the frontier was the waterways. The War of 1812 may have been the only war in which the front or battle lines and the lines of communications (logistical lines) were the same. Captain Daniel Pring requested to build a frigate on the lake that would be considerably more powerful than the whole of Macdonough's American fleet put together. Such a frigate could easily sweep the lake of the sloops, brigs, and rowed gunboats built and armed only to stop smuggling. While Sir George was in command of both the civil government and the military establishment in Upper and Lower Canada, Admiral Sir James Yeo, the senior Royal Navy officer in North America, answered directly to the Admiralty in London. Sir James was tasked to cooperate with, but was not commanded by, Prevost, thus clouding the lines of responsibility.

Commodore Sir James Lucas Yeo, RN, R.C.B., was the son of James Yeo, esq., formerly agent victualler at Minorca, who died in 1825. The younger Yeo was born at Southampton in 1782 and was educated at the Rev. Mr. Walters Academy at Bishop's Waltham, Hampshire, whence he embarked at a very early age on board the *Windsor Castle,* under Admiral Cosby. At the age of fifteen, Yeo was promoted to the rank of lieutenant. While holding this rank, he commenced his more public career. Dispatched to capture the enemy's vessels in the port of El Muros, Spain, in 1802, he stormed the fort in gallant style and afterwards succeeded in bringing out every vessel, armed and unarmed, lying in the port. He was promoted to the rank of commander and appointed to the *Confiance,* one of the vessels he had taken. Henry Morgan continues Yeo's story:

> He was the person who brought the first intelligence to England of the rising of the Spaniards against their French invaders and the consequent surrender of a part of the French army—an event that gave a new impulse to the people of Spain in all quarters, and at length, by the assistance of the British troops and their allies, finally drove the oppressive intruder out of the kingdom. His subsequent conquest of Cayenne led to promotion, the rank of post captain. The Prince Regent of Portugal, as a peculiar mark of his favor and high estimation conferred upon him a knight's commandery of St. Benito d'Asis (the only Protestant ever so highly honored) and the more gallant exploits and able service received the most flattering testimonials from Lt. Gen. Hunter under whom he served at the capture of Surinam. He was aide-de-camp to Lt. Gen. Sir Charles Green commander of the forces and was distinguished in his public dispatches as an officer of the greatest promise. In the year 1804, the committee at Lloyds voted him a sword of 100 guineas value, for their just appreciation of his talents and intrepidity in animating by his example the crew of the merchant ship *Fortitude* on board of which he was a passenger to a determined and valorous resistance against the united attack of two French privateers off the Island of Barbados, thereby successfully maintaining the luster of the British flag. He was severely wounded, his zealous and meritorious conduct was marked in the public dispatches as entitling him to the highest approbation. At Chippawa and subsequently in every engagement, he invariably exhibited the most eminent qualities of the soldier, and in private life his benevolence and urbanity were equally conspicuous.[5]

Admiral Yeo had concentrated on Lake Ontario, and Prevost had left him to deal with the maritime defense of that and Lake Champlain. But the two men did not get along and maintained separate headquarters. Sir James agreed that the building of a lake frigate was an excellent idea. He also supported Prevost's plan of attack, which hinged on cooperation between naval and land forces in the upcoming offensive. However, he did not believe that Captain Pring was the man to supervise the building of the large ship, nor that he was able to command the flotilla during the battle for Lake Champlain. While Pring was no longer to be the commodore of the tiny Royal Navy Lake Champlain fleet, he nonetheless knew the water and was retained as second in command and the captain of the *Linnet.*

Sir James selected Captain Peter Fisher in July to go to the Ille aux Noix and begin building the largest ship ever afloat on Lake Champlain. When the ship was completed he would also command the fleet, which would consist of four smaller sloops-of-war and a dozen gunboats. The new ship would be 160 feet over all and carry the new Congreve 7'6"-long, twenty-four-pound cannons, in addition to several carronades mounted in the bow and stern. The ship was counted as having thirty-seven guns. A third larger than any American vessel, it was armed with long-range cannon that could terrorize both ship and shore. The latest guns from England were the invention of the great ordnance designer William Congreve, director of the British Ordnance Board. The Department of Ordnance was a part of neither the army nor the navy, but was chartered to provide guns, projectiles, and powder for both services. This new gun could fire a twenty-four-pound solid iron cannonball over a mile and a half with great accuracy.

Construction on the frigate *Confiance* began in July on the Canadian end of Lake Champlain. Captain Fisher had become good friends with the entire Prevost family through frequent dinners at the governor's house. Such familiarity did not please Admiral Yeo, so Fisher named the new ship after the French vessel captured by Sir James, in an effort to get into the good graces of his mentor.

CONFIANCE DEPENDS ON SMUGGLERS

Time was now Prevost's enemy. Much of the materials had to be smuggled from New York and Vermont over the very lake that was patrolled by the U.S. Navy. Several illegal shipments were seized by Thomas Macdonough's vessels before enough spars, masts, tar, and timbers got through. Customs officers took to the American shipyard more than five thousand dollars worth of contraband that had been destined for use in the construction of the *Confiance*. The ship would not be ready before September according to William Simons, her master builder from Quebec, and by November the lake could be too treacherous for naval maneuver, much less a major battle. She required 270 sailors and Royal marines to man her. There was a serious shortage of sailors and few could be spared from the blue water Royal Navy ships that were anchored at Quebec. Prevost called on the 39th Infantry regiment, from Dorsetshire, to supply the crew. Strange-looking sailors they were, clad mainly in red crisscrossed with white belts, coats edged with pea-green collars and cuffs piped with yellow. They resembled the handful of Royal Marines on board, who were also in red coats, but with dark blue facings piped in white. The marines, however, wore more traditional naval wax-coated top hats, with the brims turned up on the left side and held in place by braided white cords.

Work was in progress to make the remainder of the fleet seaworthy and shipshape. *Linnet* was a new brig, crewed by ninety-nine, that carried sixteen cannons and was eighty-five feet long. Pring had been her captain for a year, and although he was no longer the commodore, he remained the deputy commander of the Royal flotilla. *Chub,* a sloop, was next in line at sixty feet and eleven guns, crewed by thirty sailors, with an additional one marine per gun. Last came *Finch,* a little longer at sixty-four feet and eleven guns. Easier to handle than the other ships, it carried a complement of thirty-two. Both *Chub* and *Finch* had been converted from the American vessels lost by Sidney Smith the year before. There were also a dozen sixty-foot gunboats powered by a combination of oars and a single lateen sail.[6] Like a pack of angry bees, they were to swarm close in near the hulls of an American warship and blast holes at the water line. While the Army could march at somewhat predictable rates, depending on the terrain, the winds on Lake Champlain were less predictable, which worried Sir George. Pring's experience earlier of beating against the prevailing southern gales suggested that providence could play a part in this venture.

The army too had its problems as far as Prevost was concerned. Regiments arrived as they had fought in Spain and France. Wellington was unconcerned with the appearance of his troops, as long as they could march and fight. Standing in ranks, on parade for their new commander in Canada, they were a motley group. Infantry uniforms were faded red, nearly to pink. Some soldiers wore parts of old French uniforms, since theirs had fallen to pieces. Cuffs and collars were worn and washed out. Normally faced and lined in the regimental color of bright blue for royal regiments, and the other regiments distinguished by buff, yellow, green, white, or crimson, all were now rather nondescript. Prevost castigated the men and their officers, who appeared no finer. The rebuke made him very unpopular. "How dare he criticize the heroes who defeated Napoleon?" was heard from the English population and press. The general officers, chosen personally by Wellington for this mission, were outraged by a man who had not seen active service in the real war that had just concluded in Europe. The three major generals, "Wellington's boys," were among his favorites and well known to Englishmen. Frederick Philipse Robinson, Thomas Brisbane, and Manley Powers were recently appointed to their rank as a result of extraordinary service. Sir George further ruffled their feathers by placing them under the direct command of Major General Francis De Rottenburg, Prevost's deputy commander. Because Provost's chief of staff, Edward Baynes, was only a colonel, he was quickly promoted to major general, so he would be on equal footing with Robinson, Brisbane, and Powers when transmitting orders. These maneuvers were designed to put the governor general in charge. As an old soldier, he knew he must make his impression as the boss of the coming campaign. Although grateful for the help, he would not hand over his command, no matter how able the new arrivals. He had fought this wilderness war for two years and knew the mission, enemy, terrain, and dangers. He had no time to school his subordinate commanders in the rules of this road. They were no longer fighting Napoleon: this was wilderness. The newly arrived commanders and soldiers had to shift their thinking to the New World. Provost was too direct in conveying this, not sensitive enough to the heroes of Europe, in the eyes of the newly arrived major generals. What Sir George needed was a disciplined force that would take the mission given them in their experienced hands and win. He authored the battle plan and expected them to carry it out as ordered.

At the end of the war in April, the veteran British soldiers rested in the wine cellars of southern France and recuperated. They expected to go home to their families and return to the regimental barracks, where they would be hailed as the heroes they indeed were. Now all they had to look forward to were blackflies, bad food, terrible roads, sleeping under the cold northern sky, and fighting for a God-forsaken spot most had never heard of before. On campaign there were no towns, no pubs, no women, and no shelter. Where they assembled at Chambly, there was only an old stone French fort and a surging river bank to keep them company. Most had come by troop ship to Quebec and by barge to Chambly. The 8th (King's) Regiment was landed on the Atlantic shoreline at St. Johns, New Brunswick, in March and demonstrated the need for a winter land route to Quebec by marching the distance. They were under the command of Major T. Evans, who also dragged 230 sailors along to help man the ships on Lake Champlain. The morale of this new army of Canada, not the enemy, was going to be the problem, thought Sir George.

He had his old army there to bolster the new troops. His regiments of Canadian fencibles had an outstanding combat record from previous campaigns. They stood honor guard in brilliant red uniforms with bright yellow facings piped in white cord and wide, white cross straps. Beside them stood both French Canadian voltigeur and foot chasseur regiments fresh from the latest victory against the Americans, in March at Lacolle, Canada. The Neufchatel Regiment of Colonel De Meuron, Swiss in origin, was raised in 1781 for service under the Dutch East India Company. When the company could not pay its wages, it passed into the British Army as one of the four mercenary units raised to increase the army's size.[7] Also waiting at Chambly, they were splendid in red coatees, the entire breasts of which were royal blue.

GUNS AND ROCKETS

In addition to the infantry, there was a considerable body of artillery. Five companies of field artillery were added to the Canadian army. The initial group was 536 men and forty guns from the army in France. Others were to come from the arsenal at Woolwich, only a few miles from London, the home of the Ordnance Board. At this time, the artillery was not a part of the army. Like the navy, they were a separate defense entity. The guns and crews were sent to the army in the field by the master-gunner of ordnances, who was equal to the commander of the army at Horse Guards, in London. Royal Artillery units, once in the field, were then placed in direct support of the infantry and cavalry. Once under the army commander's eye, they obeyed orders like any other unit. The technical and supply function, however, remained at Woolwich. It worked surprisingly well in combat, but the artillery commanders and units felt that they often did not receive the credit due them after a battle and that all the glory went to the army, which was primarily made up of infantry and cavalry. That was essentially true. The artillery were looked upon by the army as essential but still only support troops. This was a direct departure from the Napoleonic system, in which the artillery was the queen of the chessboard of battle, and central to the army battle plan. Napoleon, after all, was an artillery officer and proved the importance of massed guns at critical juncture. The gunners wore distinctive uniform coats. Cut the same as the infantry's, with long tails, the gunners' coats were never red, but dark blue with red collars and cuffs piped in bright yellow. The breast of the jacket was covered in descending rows of yellow braid, which made them look more like hussars. The hat, or shako, was a tall black cylinder, visor in front and topped with a six-inch white plume. In the field they wore light gray overalls with a red stripe down the side. The infantry wore white pants, which were kept white by rubbing clay pipes into the cloth. Often the infantry pants turned pink from red dye leaching out of the coat during downpours. Even when the clothes became shabby, the artillery cut dashing figures. But like the infantry they were not candy box soldiers. Their firepower on the battlefield was often decisive. In Canada, they acquired siege artillery as well, to be used in the attack on the defenses of Plattsburgh. Eight-inch mortars mounted on wooden slides and carried in wagons pulled by eight oxen would be dragged along with the expedition. The siege mortars were squat cylinders of black iron that looked more like an oil drum of today than a weapon. The mortars were short and stocky; the hole in the center of their barrels was only eight inches across, while the outer dimension was a nearly three feet. While field guns were relatively direct-firing weapons, like large rifles, howitzers and mortars could fire at a high angle and the cannonball or shell plunged onto the target. The round was often much larger and caused greater damage than did field guns.

Records of the Royal Artillery are nearly nonexistent regarding the movement and extent of support provided during the battle of Plattsburgh, which would be primarily an artillery slugfest of both naval and land guns. The company commanders of the 4th Battalion at Plattsburgh were S. Maxwell, P. M. Wallace, and J. S. Sinclair. J. Adams commanded a company supplied by 10th Battalion.[8] Major Francis Duncan writes:

> On 16 March, 1814, the company, with Captains Adams and King, 1st Lt. Day and 2nd Lt. Pickard, embarked at Portsmouth for North America, and disembarked at Quebec on the 30th of May. In July Captain King and Lt. Picard, with part of the company, were ordered to march to Chambly, where they were attached to a battery of 6-pounder field gun, for duty with that part of the army serving under Major-General De Rottenburg. In the beginning of August, this detachment, with two 6-pounders, and one 5½ in. howitzer, was ordered to the frontier to act with the army under the command of General De Watterville, and on the 4th September it moved forward with the army commanded by Lt. General Sir George Prevost to Plattsburgh, at which place it was removed from its field guns, and posted to a battery of four 8-inch mortars, for service against the American lines and gunboats.[9]

One other unit, a troop of Congreve rockets, was added by the leaders at the ordnance establishment.[10] The 172 rocketeers, all mounted, were the most mobile of the artillery elements. Dressed as Royal Horse Artillery, they sported a high-domed, derby-shaped, black leather helmet with a wide, full, black fur strip that was attached to the front visor and extended over the top to the rear brim, where it was again attached. It was known as a sausage roll, or Tarleton, and was embellished on the side by a blue-and-yellow turban wrap. The rocketeer's dark blue short-jacket breast was crossed with twenty-four rows of thin, yellow braid, while the pointed, Polish cuffs were red, piped in yellow. The light gray overall pants had two stripes of bright red. They were as striking as their modern weapons.

It is as surprising to us today as it was to opponents of the British army that there were operational rockets on the battlefield at Plattsburgh. Employed by the Ordnance Board for both the Royal Navy and Army, they were more than just a curiosity.[11] So extraordinary in 1814, they come down to us today in the very words of our national anthem, "the rockets red glare, the bombs bursting in air," written by Francis Scott Key on board a British ship two days after the battle of Plattsburgh, in Baltimore harbor. While the naval rockets could be as large as 320 lbs., the ones deployed in northern New York were from 20 lbs. to 40 lbs. The Royal Artillery Rocket Corps trooper had a bundle of four seven-foot rocket sticks attached to his saddle, and kept holsters for the projectiles in his saddle bags. The sticks looked like lances from a distance, since a single blue-and-white pennon was attached to the top. Within the troop were two-wheeled carts pulled by a single horse and rider. In the cart was a light gray painted wooden "A" frame that could be set up quickly. The stick would have a rocket warhead attached with two straps to one end, and the assembled weapon was leaned against the frame at an angle of about forty-five degrees. The point of the rocket was inclined in the direction of the enemy fortifications or massed troop formation, which could be as far away as two miles. A long fuse protruded from the back of the metal rocket, which contained both propellant and a charge packed with metal balls. After assembling the rocket, the rocketeer lit the fuse and took cover.[12] The rockets took off with a flash. The stick, about the thickness of today's

closet pole, went down range with the projectile to give it sta-
bility, much like the tail of a kite. These hellfire weapons were
fired in salvo of a dozen or more at a time. They were free
rockets in the broadest possible meaning of that term; there
were no guidance systems. In Spain, Wellington considered
them useful only for setting fire to a town or scaring horses.
They often boomeranged and came back into British lines.
They were also known to blow up on the launch frame or go to
ground and shoot along, ankle high, until stopped by some
solid object. Recruiting rocketeers was a problem within the
ranks of the Royal Horse Artillery.

The smallest contribution to the expeditionary army was represented by a single regiment of 340 troopers from the 19th Light
Dragoons, commanded by Lieutenant the Honorable J. B. R.
O'Neill. Never having served anywhere but England, where they
kept civil peace, they were forced to give up their horses, which
were requisitioned for transport wagons. The handful of mounted
troopers that remained were seconded to carry messages as the
signal corps for the unit commanders. Now they were infantry.
However, the 19th were the best-clad of the troops from the
homeland, dressed in the latest cavalry fashion of dark blue short
coats, with light yellow breast plastrons. On either side of the
chest was a rows of silver buttons. The pants were tight, white
deer skin. The men sat on blue blankets piped in two rows of yellow lace, astride matching bay horses. This, however, was forest
wilderness, and no place for cavalry charges.

The British army did have some of its own military transport
with the contingents of special troops. In addition to the engineers, artificers, miners, and sappers, the Corps of Drivers were
in very short supply in Canada. The actual movement of the army
was consigned to an assemblage of civilian teamsters under the
control of the Commissariat: men from the Treasury Department

and totally outside the control of the military. The formation of a separate army branch, the transport corps, was many years ahead. To invade America, an army so large would need a considerable number of horses and wagons. The force was assembled at Chambly, a flat plain near the edge of the Richelieu River, ready to move at the end of August.

There was now a formidable field army in North America that numbered nearly thirty thousand, a portion of which would band together in a three-brigade division of over twelve thousand for the invasion of New York.[13] Prevost's new army was the vanguard of Britain bent on ending the War of 1812. To ensure the governor general's success, the diversionary plan was nearly as ambitious.

CHAPTER 3

I must not be held responsible for the consequences of abandoning
my present strong position.

—Major General George Izard

Major General George Izard was getting reports of increased military activity in Canada from Peter Sailly, the customs collector for the north country. Sailly was a patriot and a
zealous spymaster. Born Pierre Maire on April 20, 1754, in the
Lorraine region of France, he was a member of a prominent
family that owned an iron works. Young Pierre grew up to serve
in the prestigious personal bodyguard of Louis XVI. But his father's business fell on hard times and Pierre was forced to accept the post of a minor tax collector, prior to the revolution. To
escape the family debt and the chaos that was beginning to grip
France, he left in 1784 for America and changed his name to
Peter Sailly. Once in New England, he looked for a place to
make a new start, and settled on a fledgling community at
Cumberland Bay, Lake Champlain, named Plattsburgh. Accustomed to prominence, he worked hard at becoming the town's
leading citizen. In his journal, he recorded impressions of the
land and people. He took note of the virgin forests and abundant fish and game. Hills and mountains suggested the presence
of mineral resources. Peter noted potential mill sites along
streams entering the lake. Waterways also provided a means to
float logs and transport goods to market. He surveyed the area

south of Plattsburgh and believed it prime for the cultivation of wheat. In a poignant passage, he writes of his new home,

> In general I have never in my life seen anything which approaches in beauty the borders of Lake Champlain, although they are uninhabited. On the east side of the lake there is a very fine plain, ten leagues in width. The Lake is as many miles at some places and sometimes a great deal less. We can see for fifteen leagues along the length of the lake. If this section is ever inhabited, it will be the finest in the world. The best lands are sold for fifteen to eighteen francs per acre. I would not hesitate to purchase if I was not afraid that in the first war with the English the inhabitants of Lake Champlain would be their first victims.

This fear for the future was recorded in 1785, twenty-nine years before the invasion. I have found no record of any other contemporary who ever indicated that there was a threat to northern New England from the British. Some wished that the inhabitants would choose to return to British rule, but none ever mentioned British military adventure.

In France, Sailly's young daughter, who had been left behind in school, was imprisoned by the Revolutionary government and did not join her father and mother until years later. Meanwhile, Sailly became a fur trader, traveled to western Canada, and interacted with businessmen in both Montreal and New York City. He soon prospered dealing in timber, furs, and potash, which was exported to Canada as fertilizer. Involved in civic affairs, he was for a time associate justice of the court, commissioner of highways, school commissioner, and town supervisor. The former Frenchman was elected to the state legislature, and went to the U.S. House of Representatives from the 11th district of New York in 1805. Returning to Plattsburgh in 1807, he arrived just in time to see the embargo go into effect. A more worldly man than his neighbors, Sailly recognized the restrictions as necessary. Peter considered New York an integral part of the nation-state and was in favor of Jefferson's measures. The incumbent customs collector, threatened with kidnapping by smugglers, resigned and Jefferson appointed Sailly to take his place.[1] When war came in 1812, Peter took his duties seriously and developed a spy network from his business contacts and customs inspectors. This network became invaluable as the British prepared to invade.

Ezra Thurber, a customs officer at Champlain, relayed word to Sailly in June 1814 from Ile aux Noix that the British were building a frigate bigger than anything seen on the lake. Other spies reported that there were so many troop transports in Quebec harbor that the estuary looked like a pine forest. General Izard, headquartered in Plattsburgh, hurried his training program. Secretary of War Armstrong had ordered his new commander in the north "to establish camps of instruction and to school the regular soldiers and officers in drill and hygiene." While they trained, new uniforms, supplies, and weapons arrived. This was in response to Izard's complaint that his forces consisted of inexperienced officers and green troops with too little time left in their enlistment to teach them essential skills.[2] First at Albany and then at Plattsburgh and Burlington, Vermont, Izard and his second in command, newly promoted Brigadier General Alexander Macomb, spent the spring and summer making ready to defend against an invasion. For the past two years these officers had been on the offensive; now the roles reversed. It was plain that redcoats on the waterways of Quebec and Montreal were soon to be found on Lake Champlain and headed south.

AN ALL-VOLUNTEER ARMY

The secretary of war could see that the army could not sustain itself as the early enlistments began to run out. His experience told him that militia were unreliable and never in the right place. They were untrained and equally unenthusiastic. He proposed to Congress that conscription be introduced. James Monroe vehemently opposed the suggestion, declaring that no such European practice would ever stain a free nation. But the recollections of Private Charles Fairbank suggest why it was difficult to maintain a sizeable volunteer army:

> A soldier when he enlists for one year receives a 16 dollar bounty. He also receives one cap, made of stiff hard leather, one neck stock, of the same material, four ruffled shirts, two red flannel shirts, two pair blue pants, one pair of white, four pairs of shoes, four pairs of socks, one blanket, one pair of blue gaiters, one coat, and one work jacket. Our rations consisted of bread, and salt beef; sometimes the beef was fresh, but usually salt, we also had salt pork, candles, soap and potato whiskey. I enlisted at Concord N. Hampshire with one companion, on the 16th of March 1813, in the N.H. Regiment of the United States volunteers, for one year. The first enlistment was one month previous to the time that we enlisted, and a promise was made to us that our names would be put with the first, but when we came time to draw our pay they said my companion's name was put back with the first, but mine was not, they asked him if he would give me half of his pay? but he refused to do this and [I] got nothing.[3]

Enlistments had been from one to three years and, in addition to the bonus, entailed the promise of a land grant of 160 acres. Veterans who had survived the disease and danger of their first term sought no glory fighting the British one more time. They left to settle new land in the territories. Deserters, who did not relish facing the men who beat Napoleon, melted away at night. Private Fairbank continues his saga:

> We left the "new cantonment" and proceeded down the lake 20 miles to Cumberland Head, at the entrance to Plattsburg Bay. While here two soldiers obtained a "pass" to get out of "camp". The oldest was about thirty-five, the other about twenty years of age. After they had got some

distance from the camp toward the Canada line, the older one told the younger, "that he was going to desert from the army", and wished him to go with him, but he declined. While they were talking, they were taken by a file of soldiers from the army. They had suspicion of the older, for, I think, he had deserted before. After being returned to camp, they had their trial, and both received sentence of death, although the younger one was proved innocent, the other confessing that he had urged him to go, but that he refused. Still, to frighten others from commission of a like offence, this young man must suffer the horrors of death for two long weeks. At the time of the execution, the army marched to a long field, the first brigade in front, then the prisoners in the center of the guard, they being formed into a hollow square, then all the drummers and fifers in the army, about forty of each, with their drums muffled beating a continual roll. Then the second brigade came up and formed a hollow square with the first, leaving a space on the north side for those to be shot. Then the prisoners marched out in the line about three rods, and faced about upon those that were to fire upon them, lastly, the music [was played] in the center of the square. The older one was now ordered to kneel beside his coffin, the soldiers fired and he fell dead. The younger one then kneeled beside his coffin, the cap was pulled over his eyes, the soldiers cocked their guns; then the reprieve was read, and thus ended the horrid scene.

Reinforced by Army Headquarters, Izard's complement numbered about six thousand by midsummer. Those numbers were lower when the sick, well over a thousand, were added to the hospital list and the military prisoners in the stockade of over a hundred were subtracted from the active ranks.[4]

It was said that the best of Izard's soldiers were equal to the worst of Prevost's. True or not, the Americans certainly looked like underdogs. The U.S. infantryman wore a dark blue long-tailed coat that buttoned down the chest, leaving no need for a waistcoat. The blue color was inherited from the uniform of his father or grandfather who fought for liberty from Britain. It contrasted with the red of the British soldier. There were no grand guardsmen or king's special troops to adorn the American ranks.

As the cost of uniforms drained the federal war chest, the colored facings were removed and one regiment could only be separated from another by the number on the buttons. The only colorful uniforms were worn by the musicians in each regiment. The drums, fifes, and bugles were the communications systems of the army and were found in each company. Additionally, each regular and militia regiment was authorized a band, composed of thirty players. Musicians played such instruments as sackbuts and serpentines. Clothed in the facing color of the regiment, they stood out in coats of red, buff, yellow, or green. Some wore extraordinary hats, such as polish *czapskas* or bear skins. There were no drummer boys, since the drums were now made out of heavy brass, rather than wood, and were man size. The brass gave a richer sound and carried further.

The American infantry was divided into regulars, federal troops under the authority of the central government, and the militia, under the authority of the state governors. There were two grades of militia: those that were formally organized and supported from federal funds and the backup militia, who were interested farmers who treated the work like a social invitation. When invited to attend, as militia troops were when the call went out, some came and some did not, depending on the time of year, crop conditions, and the danger involved. Generally speaking, the troops in the militia were as good as the men who led. In the case of the regulars, the men were better than the officers, political appointees who sought commissions and later regretted the boon when faced with the conduct of a war, for which they were untrained.

The standard weapon issued was the "model 1775" musket. For its day it was superior to the British Brown Bess. It was lighter, more accurate, and fired a slightly smaller ball. Loaded with "buck and ball," it could be more effective against dense formations. The weapon was designed for fighting the Indians in the wooded frontier. The Indians moved quickly through the brush and a clear shot was rare. At one time the muskets were loaded with nothing but buckshot. The paper-wrapped cartridge contained black powder, a small amount of which was poured into the flash pan of the lock. The remaining powder was poured down the front of the barrel. The torn paper and metal ball were then rammed down the barrel to form a tight fit. The American ammunition differed from the British in that, in addition to the musket ball, there were three pieces of rather formidable buckshot included to provide a lethal spray. The British army considered this to be a minor atrocity of war, along with the American habit of sniping.

Izard first had to teach his troops how to shoot the musket. Today we think of all early Americans as sharpshooters whose skills were honed from clearing the wilderness of Indians and hunting for the family table. But the reality in the War of 1812 was that most recruits were from the towns. Farm boys tended to be busy on farms. Many of the recruits had never held a firearm and had to be taught from the very beginning.

The musket was capable of being loaded and fired three times in one minute. The British soldier was famous for doing just that, in the teeth of a French charge. To attain that rate of fire the recruit must follow a twenty step procedure religiously. Skill only came with a great deal of supervised practice. And while no soldier of any era wants to spend his days on the shooting range, General Macomb knew it was the only way to ensure survival. Once recruits learned this skill, the officers worked to instill in the men the confidence that their muskets and formation could withstand a ground assault. This was going to be battle fought from cover, if the Americans had their way. A protected, static soldier in the defense could hold against superior numbers. The new commander knew he could not risk his force to the open field. Drill, or command and control of the forces on battlefield, was essential. In a day without radio, this could only be accomplished by packing men into formations that moved as a block. To maintain the integrity of a formation of fifty or more, and to direct them in conjunction with other blocks of troops from the same regiment, officers trained their men in simple voice and hand signals. Maintaining shoulder to shoulder lines that were twenty-one inches behind the line to their front had the effect of encouraging valor, or steadying up the skittish. It also made them a great target for artillery and cavalry. Musket fire, however, was highly inaccurate at anything over a football field away. Therefore, men in colored uniforms in the open were not in that much danger, since few weapons could reach them, especially if they were moving. The British were skilled at such movement, being trained under the drill regulation similar to General Von Steuben's *Blue Book* of 1779, which was upgraded under the French drill manual of 1791. But the northern army soldier of the United States did not have time for training needed for him to match the offensive skill of the British regular, who was eager to end the war and go home. Izard expected the red columns to come smashing down from the north with only one thing in mind, the destruction of the Yankee army in the field.

But it had been shown that not all infantry troops should fight from formations. The Royal Americans, Britain's 62d foot, founded by Prevost's uncle, were to become light infantry and armed not with muskets, but rifles. They had learned some of their modern tactics from fighting the American frontiersmen and switched from red uniforms with white belts to forest green with black belts. The American rifle regiment at Plattsburgh also wore green or gray and was armed with flintlock rifles with grooved barrels that placed a spin on the ball, which significantly increased accuracy. These light infantrymen were agile fighters who dropped their heavy packs prior to battle and ran in front of the main battle lines like rabbits, taking cover and shooting into the enemy formations at ever closing ranges. They were known as skirmishers or voltigeurs and had altered the character of the battlefield by 1814.

A company of black troops arrived with the reinforcements in the supply train from Massachusetts. They were expected to be trained as infantry, but the white officers declined to command them and the troops refused to serve with them. Macomb organized them into a segregated pioneer, or engineer, corps and set them to work on the earthen defensive positions along the perimeter of the American front lines. There was a great deal of digging to be done and, while they were relegated to menial labor, the black soldiers by providing trenches were making one of the most valuable contributions to the battle. Before long, all the American troops would be digging for their lives. But the presence of the black soldiers caused ill will and was used as an excuse for desertion, which was increasing.[5]

GUNS

There were five full companies of artillery gathered that summer at Plattsburgh. They employed a mix of cannon size. The primary weapon for the Americans seems to have been the French eight-pounder, which was actually 8.8 lbs., and therefore about the size of the British standard nine-pounder.[6] There were several pairs of twelve-pounders of French design. Although the Americans had no siege guns, they did have twenty-four-pounders mounted on fortification slides, of both French and British design. Supported on ten-inch wooden wheels, these guns could only be used in a fixed location. The brass barrels were copies made in American foundries from weapons leftover from the carnage of the Revolution. At Detroit, in 1812, British general Brock captured a six-pounder that had been one of Burgoyne's guns from Saratoga in 1777. While the American artillery used captured or copied English gun barrels, they built French-style carriages. Following the principles of Jean Baptiste de Gribeauval, the inspector general of the French army in 1776 who standardized the entire arena of artillery equipment, all American guns looked French from a distance. Guns were not thought of in terms of caliber in 1814. They were classed by the weight of the projectile. The problem was that cannon ball manufacturers often made eight-pound balls too large for the bore of the gun. Thus each gun had a metal ring the exact size of the hole in the barrel. Before an attempt was made to load a cannon ball, the ring would be dropped over it to ensure that the ball would not get stuck halfway down the barrel. Since these were not breech loaders, once the ball was logged the only way to get it out was to attempt to fire the gun. This could easily result in a burst barrel and death to anyone nearby. Unlike the British, the Americans had no school for training artillery officers. At West Point, officers learned infantry tactics and field engineering. They were familiarized with artillery but spent no time in the study of propellant, trajectory, or ballistics. Since the Academy had only been operational a few years, the officers trained there were still young and at the company level. Senior officers therefore had no appreciation for the "King of Battle" and often used artillerymen as infantry.[7] Also, guns, limbers, and horses were often in short supply and there were artillery units who went into battle for years without cannons, fighting as infantry.

Several squadrons of cavalry were with Izard. American dragoons could be effective in open country. The dragoon was heavily armed and expected to ride his horse to the battlefield and maneuver with speed. Once in place, he was to dismount and fight as infantry. A mounted man is very unlikely to dismount if he does not have to. As a result, cavalry were deployed with the intention that they would fire rifle muskets from the saddle. But the rifles were often impossible to reload while mounted, even though they were shortened versions of the infantry weapon. With the jolting from the horse, the powder would dribble from the pan of a preloaded flintlock. When it came time to fire, there was no flash in the pan. Therefore, once sent forward, the cavalry would stop at rifle range, turn their flank to the enemy, attempt to fire a volley, and then charge, with heavy straight swords swinging. This provided the shock action the tank would possess on modern battlefields, as the horses ran down the foot soldier. Most American mounted men were dragoons in name only. They were, in reality, light dragoons. Without muskets, they were useful only as scouts, guides, and messengers.

AMERICA ON THE DEFENSIVE

George Izard was a veteran who had trained in a French military academy, as had Prevost and Wellington, and was familiar with continental military tactics. He knew that he could not meet the British on the open field; his troops were not steady and, his forces being outnumbered, he used the convolutions in the land to multiply his force. The area north of Plattsburgh was virgin forest and small farms. The only road into town came from the north. Izard knew the enemy must take this road, since the Royal Navy's lake fleet provided no transports. Six miles north of town, the road split. At Beekmantown, the main road continued straight south and a western spur reached the lakeshore and

continued south again along Cumberland Bay and into Plattsburgh.[8] It was an easy and natural envelopment for the British,
one Izard could not hope to defend. The swift-flowing Saranac
River, which emptied the snow from the Adirondack mountains
twenty miles south, cut a gorge on the south side of town that
formed a peninsula. The river on the west and north and Cumberland Bay on the east made it a natural fortress. The lake was
both a vulnerability and a blessing. Izard would bring Macdonough's small fleet into the bay, not only to protect it from the
Royal Navy but to add their guns to his army artillery. Using the
land and the water, his force could be nearly equal to the British
if he dug in on the rivers edge and built redoubts with thick dirt
berms to protect his static guns. It was certain that Sir George
Prevost would occupy the town and attack Izard's front while
the British navy attempted to attack the American right flank,
which rested on the bay of Lake Champlain. The only certain
outcome was that the town of Plattsburgh, with its seventy-eight
houses, mills, stores, warehouses, churches, and courthouse,
would not survive this battle intact. The citizens began to slip
away as the forts and blockhouses went up.

Commodore Macdonough alarmed the secretary of the navy,
William Jones, with reports of both the raid by British captain Pring,
which nearly bottled up his entire complement for the duration of
the war, and the news that Yeo was building a lake frigate. Frigates
of this class had appeared on Lake Ontario and were feared. On a
lake like little Champlain, a frigate would rule. Jones sent his shipbuilder from the U.S. Navy yard in Brooklyn, Noah Brown, who arrived at Vergennes, Vermont, with two hundred carpenters. At the
Otter Creek yard, they built the twenty-six-gun sloop-of-war
Saratoga in forty days. Macdonough wrote in later life,

> Various reports reached me of their preparations—that the keel of a large
> vessel had been laid and a number of large gunboats or galleys were also

constructing. On our side, as I had directions at all hazards to maintain our ascendency, we were not idle. The keel of a ship was laid at Vergennes to mount 26 guns, also the keels of 6 large galleys, the latter to be 75 feet long and 15 feet wide. Went down to Albany and New York to arrange and forward the articles and supplies for this force. In the meantime rendezvous were opened along on the seabord at the different large places and all the necessary artificers sent to the lake from New York, from whence the guns and heavy articles were sent, though we had transported from Boston the sheet anchor of the Saratoga which weighed 3,000 pounds. Everything on both sides went on with all the dispatch which it was possible to apply.[9]

Brown also converted a steamboat hull into the seventeen-gun *Ticonderoga* and rehabilitated ten gunboats. The gunboats each carried a twenty-four-pounder cannon in the prow and an eighteen-pounder columbiad, which was a cross between a carronade and a gun and fired explosive shells. The columbiad is a heavy-shell gun, combining the qualities of a gun, howitzer, and mortar. Invented by Major George Bomford, it was named after the epic poem written by Joel Barlow, Bomford's brother-in-law.[10] The cannonball required the loader to light a fuse that was cut to a length so that it would explode over or just as it struck the target. Once lit, the cannonball was stuffed down the barrel and sent down range by the main charge in the bottom of the barrel. It was possible for the lighted fuse to set off the main charge prematurely, catching the crew exposed. The crew thought it so dangerous that they refused to fire the columbiads with fused ammunition.

When the full horror of the capability of the *Confiance* was passed on by the American spy network, Brown built, in nineteen days, the brig *Eagle,* a twenty-gun vessel complete with rigging and guns, ready for combat. Few lake men wanted to serve on the new American vessels, because there were no prizes to be had and lake fever made the work unhealthy. Only 250 seamen, most not able bodied, could be found in New York harbor to crew the new vessels. Macomb added another 250 soldiers. As the summer wore on, both sides trained, built, and supplied for the invasion.

In early August, Izard agreed with his boss, Secretary of War Armstrong, that his preparation of the defenses at Plattsburgh might not be necessary. Prevost was preparing to send troops west, according to the American informants in Montreal. Unknown to Izard and Sailly, Armstrong had a spy of his own who visited Canada, a lawyer who insisted that Prevost's entire force was starting to move west up the St. Lawrence. Caleb Nichols made numerous reports, which may be found in the National Archives in Washington. Some of his information has proven erroneous. And it appears that Armstrong received military advice as well as raw intelligence from Nichols. He enjoyed the confidence of the secretary, which Izard did not.[11] Why Armstrong put such great stock in Nichols's advice is unknown, since the spy had no military background. There was no grounds for Nichols's contention that the United States should have no naval presence on the lakes and should put all its money and might into a navy that could fight the Royal Navy on the high seas. Peter Sailly would have disagreed if he had known of Nichols. Sailly's spies reported a coordinated attack from the north aimed at Plattsburgh. Sailly predicted that the new frigate would lead and destroy the American fleet on the lake before investing Cumberland Bay and bombarding the town, while the British army attacked from the land. By mid-August Izard received orders to take the majority of his army, forty-five hundred, and go west to reinforce the Niagara between Lake Ontario and Lake Erie. Izard had second thoughts. His training at the military school in Europe nagged at him and he pored over the situation with his deputy commander, Alexander Macomb. He wrote to Armstrong in the strongest terms that he was certain the British would bring their whole strength down on Lake Champlain. Word came back that he was to go west immediately. It must be remembered that, due to the attack on Washington, the War Department was in some disarray. It had been burned out of its offices and the cabinet was on horseback in northwestern Maryland. Amid this confusion, Sir George's diversion, sending only one brigade west, had worked. Meanwhile, the London government put the diversionary portion of their strategic plan into action.

BRITISH DECEPTION

While John Quincy Adams, Henry Clay, and Albert Gallatin were locked in new peace talks in Ghent with representatives of the Foreign Office from London, the Royal Navy was bent on mischief. Vice Admiral Sir Alexander Cochrane in August 1814 sent his marauders to disrupt life and trade in small coastal New England towns. Following advice from Prevost, who believed that the New Englanders were ripe for revolt, Cochrane's attacks could demonstrate that the federal government was unable to protect communities from the might of the Royal Navy. The attacks would also mask Sir George's coming invasion. A former American sea captain, Richard Coote, now in the service of the British, took his ship unmolested into the harbor of New London, Connecticut, and with a company of Royal Marines set twenty-seven craft afire. He was paid two thousand dollars by the Royal Navy, which was widely advertised by the press. The Royal Navy raided in Buzzards Bay at Wareham, Massachusetts, burning and pillaging. When trapped by local militia, they hid behind hostages to make an escape. This was against the rules of engagement put out by Cochrane, who did not want civilians harmed. One attack was discouraged at New Bedford, Massachusetts, by the guns at Fort Phoenix, when H.M.S. *Nimrod* attacked the USS *Fairhaven*. The citizens of Nantucket Island were ordered by a British military force commander to give up their citizenship and become neutrals, which they did.

The governor general of New Brunswick, General Sir John Sherbrooke, had taken everything north of Penobscot and began to raid the coastal towns of Maine. Sir John took the recently arrived troops from England, a part of the secret order force, and captured the coast as far south as Bangor. Declaring the captured land as a part of New Brunswick, he required the people to become subjects of the king once again. Massachusetts, responsible for the defense of the territory of Maine, was unable to come to its defense.

During the previous year Royal Navy admiral George Cockburn had harassed shipping and costal settlements on Chesapeake Bay. It was believed in Washington that if the British were to invade, they would go for Baltimore. There were prize ships at anchor as well as privateers and three warships under construction, making it the principal port in the bay, as lucrative as Philadelphia or New York. Washington, D.C., housed a few federal government buildings and little else. The Potomac River was guarded by Fort Warburton, which was across the stream from Mount Vernon, Virginia.

As naval raids were planned all along the eastern seaboard, Major General Robert Ross was given the honor of the first major deception, a part of "operations contemplated for the employment in North America" (marked "Secret"). He sailed from Bordeaux, France, on a ten-week voyage, picking up four infantry regiments (forty-three hundred troops), a battalion of Royal Marines accompanied by a battery of six rocket launchers, and four six-pounders. His mission was "to create a diversion on the coasts of the United States in favor of the British army employed in the defense of Canada."[12] The raiders were not intended to remain, but to destroy and disrupt. These veterans of years of war saw that Washington was the perfect target. It was politically important, as seat of the national government, and lightly defended. The newspaper reports of the attack would resound around the world at little cost to the expedition, turning attention away from Canada.

Even the diversion had a diversion to hide where Cockburn's fleet was going. Other naval and marine elements, during the previous year, had been sent up the bay marauding at small villages on the shore and confusing the ineffective militia, which was nearly untrained and not accustomed to "call ups." On August 19, 1814 the militia was only capable of sending a warning to the commander of the military district around Washington, Brigadier General William Winder, a cousin of the governor of Maryland. Until recently, he had been a prisoner of war in Canada and had little experience in leading troops. Ross's command was landed on the banks of the Patuxent River at Benedict. Winder, with considerable meddling from President Madison, Secretary of State James Monroe, and Secretary of War Armstrong, managed to gather nine thousand militia. The majority were to defend Baltimore, since that was believed to be the main objective of Vice Admiral Cochrane's total force. Less than three thousand were gathered east of Washington at Woodyard. There was no preparation for the employment of the force and they lacked everything needed for life in the field. A brigade of thirteen hundred Maryland militia, clad in civilian clothes, arrived at nearby Bladensburg. Even though the numbers of men on either side were nearly equal, most of the Americans seemed nothing more than armed observers. There were less than five hundred American regular army, marines, and sailors broken up in small units. The British soldiers were from the 4th, 44th, and 85th regiments of foot-hardened veterans of the campaigns in Spain.

THE SO-CALLED DEFENSE OF WASHINGTON

Winder led a column of two thousand men, along with his unwanted personal adviser, James Monroe, right into Ross's column by mistake. He then turned his troops around and headed them back for Washington before Ross could engage. While Monroe went for help, Winder stopped to fight. At Woodyard, he mustered his troops and was visited by President Madison, who wanted to review the troops and give them an address to "buck them up." At five feet four, in the days before microphones, it is doubtful that he was seen or heard. Meanwhile, word came that Royal Navy captain Gordon was bringing a force up the Potomac River toward Alexandria. Winder had reinforced Fort Warburton with five hundred militia and told the commander to burn the fort if attacked in strength, and retreat to Washington. But the commander did so before the enemy appeared. Meanwhile, a pincer was closing on the capital.

By midmorning, after countermarching several times, General Winder, who was never short of presidential advice, readied his troops for the battle at Bladensburg. Uncharacteristically, the Americans fought from rigid formations, while the British took advantage of the terrain and woods and came at the Yankees from open order. Ross fired the field rockets, which had the desired effect, terrifying both the horses and the troops. The British swept the American militia down the hills, scattering them and the remnants of the president's entourage to the winds. Madison declared that the federal government should evacuate Washington and reconvene in Frederick, Maryland. The president left on horseback and crossed the Potomac River into Virginia, saying he was "leaving military movements to military men." Some felt that by this he meant the British. The redcoats entered Washington, which was undefended, and burned the capitol and the White

House and many government buildings. Ross's orders were to not harm civilians. However, when a sniper fired and killed the general's horse under him, he ordered that the house which provided the cover be burned. A British unit also entered the Washington Arsenal, which is Fort McNair today, and burned it to the ground. A soldier threw a lighted torch down a dry well where arsenal personnel had dumped the entire store of powder. The horrific explosion killed twelve officers and men and wounded thirty. The self-inflicted casualties were the most suffered by the British army during the entire action.[13]

Madison relieved John Armstrong as secretary of war and appointed James Monroe on a temporary basis. Everything was now on a temporary basis, since many of the cabinet did not appear at the meeting place at Frederick, and Madison moved on further west. Monroe, upon the withdrawal of Ross, continued meddling in the defense of the Potomac and the day after British Captain Gordon sacked Alexandria, Virginia, gave specific instructions to Colonel Decius Wadsworth on how to defend the city. The British forces had succeeded beyond expectations. The American government no longer functioned. The U.S. forces along the Canadian border were on their own. However, they did not know that the national capital had been practically abandoned and that the War Department was practically dissolved. Sir Alexander Cochrane took his fleet out of the Chesapeake and off to the Bahamas to refit and plan the next raid. He would be back in less than a month and continue to make history.

Too Late To Change Horses

Not aware that the secretary of war had been replaced in the third week of August, Major General Izard was now certain that

Prevost and the majority of his forces were going to attack Plattsburgh and sought relief. He held orders that required him to take a healthy majority of his northern army and depart. While trying to change Armstrong's mind, he threw his troops into the fortifications of the peninsula on the southern side of the remote town. He convinced Commodore Macdonough that the army needed the navy to guard its right and watery flank. It was not difficult to do so. Izard and Macdonough had always cooperated and the commodore knew he owed the victory at the mouth of Otter Creek to the cannon and troops sent by the army. The army had manned his boats for the last two years and would do so again for the upcoming battle, in spite of the orders sent him by Secretary Jones. Macdonough also knew that his flotilla had little chance on the open water of the lake against the new Royal Navy frigate armed with long-range cannons. He accepted the mission to bring his vessels into the bay and bombard the Royal Navy from one side of his ships, while from the other providing gunfire support against British army land targets. Unaware that the federal government and therefore the War Department were no longer functioning, George Izard waited for his change of orders in vain. On August 26 he began to move south to Schenectady, New York, in stages. Once all his troops were there, he waited another two days, hoping that Armstrong would rescind his orders. No message came. Izard's last communiqué before he faded from history was, "I must not be held responsible for the consequences of abandoning my present strong position." He wasn't. His correspondence was not a priority in the War Department office, wherever it resided after the loss of Washington. Brigadier General Macomb was left to command the troops remaining at Plattsburgh. They were a motley lot. They included seventy-seven strays from a variety of regiments, fifty from Captain Leonard's artillery company, one hundred from Captain McGlassin's company of the 15th regiment, and two hundred of Captain Sproul's company of the 13th. Remnants from the 6th, 29th, 30th, 31st, 33d, and 34th regiments of regular infantry brought the total up to fifteen hundred.[14] No dragoons were left behind and the rifle regiment marched off with General Izard. In addition to the fifteen hundred, there were the sick and military prisoners, who were more of a burden than anything else. The force that stayed behind was what Izard could spare. The coming battle had now dramatically changed character. Sir George Prevost's ruse, sending General Kempt's brigade of under a thousand to reinforce his lines in the west, had drawn off the bulk of the Yankee regular infantry. The odds on land were now twelve thousand red coats against fifteen hundred regulars, plus whatever the junior American brigadier general Macomb could muster from the militia. Major General Benjamin Mooers of the New York State militia was asked to mobilize his units in the northern counties. Mooers, a local man from Plattsburgh, was competent, but his troops were not. He called for twenty-five hundred militia to come to Plattsburgh in the last week of August. A meager seven hundred showed up. Governor Martin Chittenden of Vermont, a thorn in the side of the Army of the North, continued to hinder the use of his militia outside the border of the Green Mountain state. But Chittenden left this decision to his commander, Major General Sam Strong, who mustered twenty-five hundred of his militia, the Green Mountain Boys, on the eastern edge of Lake Champlain. Macdonough was prevailed upon to transport them across the lake on the lake sloop the *President* and anything else that floated. They all arrived the day before the main British attack.[15] While things looked very dark for the defense of the town of Plattsburgh, the odds on the lake, between the two navies, were no better for the Americans.

CHAPTER 4

Do what you can, with what you've got, where you are.
—Theodore Roosevelt

During the last week of August 1814, Prevost had one eye on the preparations of his invasion force and the other on the American army at Plattsburgh. For the past two years he had countered numerous cross-border excursions of his enemy and had stopped them all. No matter what he did, the anglophile critics in Montreal and London called him names and asked that a true Englishman be appointed in his place. But the prince regent and the government paid them no mind. Prevost was at last confirmed in his position and content with the army now under his command. British successes along the eastern seaboard convinced him that London's plan for North America was about to help him fulfill his destiny. Each day he waited for his spies to confirm that General Izard's army had gone west. The new British regiments had left Montreal with much pomp, with trailing clouds of dust that pointed west up the St. Lawrence, into the wilderness. The original brigade had been enlarged by troops fresh from the transports at Quebec, adding to the force's bulk. The new troops would slip away at dawn on the second day's march, and turn south to join the others at Chambly, just twenty miles north of the border. Only three thousand of the fifteen thousand would continue west. The boatmen of Quebec were busy

91

stockpiling the mountain of supplies at camp in Chambly, which was becoming a city of twelve thousand. The new army consumed forty-five tons of provisions a day. Its quartermaster general, desperately searching for horses and wagons to move the army along the march route, cast his eye on the horses of the 19th Light Dragoons to pull his wagons. To the cavalrymen, there was no greater insult than to have a charger hitched to a cart. But by the last week of August the three hundred dragoons were walking. Prevost had stayed away from Chambly to confirm to American spies that it was a mere gathering place, close to a branch of the St. Lawrence, a natural landing place for movement further west. He had spoken openly about Sackets Harbor and Niagara at social functions and government meetings. Delighted to use the hostile Montreal press for his purposes, he leaked that something big was going to happen in the Michigan Territory.

Even though the army was grumbling about life in the wilds of Canada, and their generals groused over being placed under someone other than their beloved Duke of Wellington, the preparations for the land battle were going along splendidly. While the troops complained, they knew that enjoying life was not necessarily a soldier's lot. The troops had complained about Portugal and Spain and the saying of the day was that "the British soldier would complain, even if you hung him with a new rope." The hinge to the whole affair was the Royal Navy and more specifically the new frigate, *Confiance*. She was the answer to Wellington's dictum that "naval superiority on the Lakes is the sine qua non of success in war on the frontier of Canada." Without control of the lake, the invasion was pointless. There were no south-running roads that could sustain an army as large as Prevost's. The water must be his for resupply and transportation. The Royal Navy must capture the American transport vessels if his army was to get to the southern extremity of the lake and there poise for a leap down the Hudson. The American navy, though small, was capable of stifling British progress southward and must be destroyed. The construction of the large frigate depended greatly upon lumber, which must come from the forests on the enemy side of the border. Surprising to us today, there was no shortage of smugglers willing to supply the timber for a British war effort that would take away their citizenship in a free society and make them subjects of the king once again. Prevost had sustained both his army and navy for the past two years by using smugglers and he did not fret that they would fail him now. In a letter to Lord Bathurst, Britain's colonial secretary of state, Sir George shows confidence in the reliability of the smugglers: "Vermont displayed a decided opposition to the war. . . . I mean for the present to confirm myself in any offensive Operations which may take place to the west side of Lake Champlain."[1] British commissariats paid in gold coin. Vermonters were paid with scrip when selling to federal government agents. "To not give a continental," a common saying of the day, reflects the confidence Americans had in their continental dollar.[2] Sailly's customs cutters captured contraband daily, arrested the perpetrators, and sent the goods to the yard at Otter Creek for use by Noah Brown's shipwrights, cutting the cost for the Department of the Navy. However, Sailly's boys only slowed the progress on the frigate. Prevost was interested in the smugglers for two reasons. Not only were they essential for raw materials, but they also acted as paid spies, doing double damage to their homeland.

Nearly Ready

During the last week of August, Sir George received very good and very bad news. The good news was that General Izard, taking the bait, and had gone west with the majority of his command.[3] Within a few days the northern army of the United States would be so committed to the rutted forest tracks of northwestern New York that they could not turn back and influence the battle planned for Plattsburgh. More good news for Prevost was that, in addition to their treachery, the smugglers had provided the last of the deck planks to complete *Confiance*. The very bad news was as unexpected as a thunderbolt. At the last possible minute, Admiral Yeo relieved Captain Peter Fisher, the commander of the Royal Navy on Lake Champlain and builder of the new frigate, whom Yeo personally had appointed only a few months before. Yeo, never a supporter of the governor general, confided to a friend, "one hot head [Prevost] was quite enough for the battle." The eighteen-year-old daughter of Prevost, Anne, records the event in her diary:

August 1814, Montreal, Canada.

During the summer, my Father was employed in frequently visiting the out posts, and he appeared to be greatly interested in the fitting out of a small Squadron in Lake Champlain. Captain Fisher was the Senior officer and he and my Father always appeared to be on the most cordial terms—he was several times at Montreal; but just as the Fleet was nearly ready, Sir James Yeo thought proper to supersede Captain Fisher, whose local knowledge must have been of value, and to appoint Captain Downie to the command. About 9,000 men were concentrated in the Champlain frontier and it was generally understood that as soon as the equipment of the Squadron was completed, an expedition would be effected into the Enemy's territory.[4]

Sir George, who only agreed to the replacement of Captain Pring because Sir James insisted that Pring could not handle the flotilla destined for the battle, was amazed when Fisher fell from grace and was also replaced. Captain George Downie reported to Montreal and was briefed by his governor general on the importance of the naval action within the overall strategy outlined from London. He understood the urgency of the situation and left immediately for the shipyard, where his new flagship was to be launched within days. Of Downie, Henry J. Morgan writes:

> This brave hero, Captain George Downie, was the son of a respectable clergyman in the county of Ross, Ireland. At an early period in his youth he entered the navy as a midshipman, and served on board the *Circe* frigate in the memorable battle of Camperdown. He acted in the same capacity for some time, in the Melampus, and afterwards in the Appollo frigate, in the West Indies for several years. In this station his uniform good conduct and strict attention to his duty received the most flattering approbation of his superiors and recommended him to the particular notice of Admiral Montague, the commander of the Jamaica station, who promoted him to the rank of Lieutenant. On his return to England for the recovery of his health, which had been much impaired, his promotion was confirmed by the admiralty and in 1804, he was appointed by Earl St. Vincent to the *Sea Horse* frigate, 36 guns, then commanded by the Honorable Captain Boyle. After seeing a good deal of service, he was promoted to the rank of commodore and placed in command of the fleet on Lake Champlain in 1814.[5]

Captain Downie was now the commodore of the Champlain flotilla and he arrived on a dead run. He was tasked to take over a new command of four ships, one of which, *Confiance,* was launched upon his arrival at the dockyards. His new boss called his portion of the invasion critical to the success of the plans set in motion at the highest level of His Majesty's government in London. Downie was the center of attention. It was plain to him that, if he failed, in spite of the fact that his force numbered only a fraction of the total troops committed by Britain, he would indeed have let his nation down. If forty-seven-year-old Sir George Prevost was worried about this late adjustment in the campaign, it was nothing compared to the concern of the thirty-three-year-old Royal Naval commodore. At Ille aux Noix, master shipbuilder

Simons took Downie around his flagship, whose bottom was wet for the first time on that day, August 25. She was like the other frigates he had sailed on the Great Lakes for the past two years. But there was simply no time to get to know her.

CONFIANCE, THE KEY TO VICTORY

Everything aboard *Confiance* was a third larger than her adversary, *Saratoga*. Longer, wider, and faster, she carried one third more sail on her three contraband masts. Not only did *Confiance* have more guns, they could shoot farther and were more accurate. There were four determining factors in the days of sail that rated warships. They were the weight of gun projectiles on target, the speed of the ship under sail, the competence of the crew to exploit both, and the ability of the captain to fight. The first two greatly favored the British. The crews on either side were equally inept. Each suffered from a lack of trained sailors and gunners. The British had an advantage, though, because Royal Marines were embarked on all the ships. They were trained gunners and drilled the 39th regiment of Foot at every possible opportunity. The masters of the fleets, Downie and Macdonough, destined to meet in combat, were equals. Each was professionally trained during years before the mast, in waters around the world. Each had been specially chosen for this very battle, taking the place of men thought to be not up to the task. A frigate, *Confiance* looked different—larger—to the casual observer. She was slightly longer than *Saratoga* at 147 feet, but sported additional upper decking fore and aft. This quarterdeck and forecastle provided extra gun space and elevated her high above her opponent. This great warrior, however, was not ready. Out on the lake she handled well, but on deck the carpenters were as numerous as the crew. Raw lumber lay in stacks near work benches, deep in shavings.

There was no magazine below and the gunpowder was tugged along behind in a series of small boats like a string of sausages. The gun crews would have two days that first week of September, to practice shooting the huge Congreve long guns. Mounted on wooden slides, supported by small, thick wooden wheels, the guns jumped back a dozen feet when fired. The decks were so rough from the green lumber that the wheels became stuck between the ridges. The ship's master, Mr. Brydon, declared, "The guns in general worked very heavy, owing to the decks being rough-scraped and a quantity of pitch on them; there were temporary locks fitted from carronade locks."[6] Guns had to be lifted and levered into place, rather than run up in the customary procedure. Moving twenty-five-hundred-pound guns tired the crews quickly. While a marine sighted the gun and energized the gun crew of ten, his work was checked by a junior officer or midshipman before he engaged the next target. Old hulks and unusable rafts were buoyed at a thousand yards as disposable bull's eyes. Downie was told by Daniel Pring that the American fleet carried carronades, whose maximum effective range was no more than five hundred yards. In addition to the cannon, Downie's vessel carried six carronades in the stern and bow, and he tested them as well. While *Confiance* tested her guns, her ships, *Linnet, Finch,* and *Chub,* were only a few miles away, within the Canadian waters of the northern end of Lake Champlain. Drawn by the noise, Sailly's spies observed from a distance. Nothing like the Royal Navy frigate had ever been seen before on the lake. It loomed up with white sails flying and drove powerfully in long racetrack circles before the tiny apertures of the spies' collapsible brass telescopes. Accustomed to watching darting smugglers on rickety rafts, the U.S. customs officials were transfixed by the grandeur of the flying flotilla.

While Commodore Downie coped with leaking seams and tangled lines, the news that Sailly provided to the American commodore Macdonough was threatening. The surprise that the British would build a vessel the size of *Confiance* drove him to the conclusion that both he and Secretary of War Jones had been very wrong about the intentions of the enemy on Lake Champlain. They never considered facing more than small, agile gun-mounted sloops or cutters, escorts for smuggler's barges. But then who could have envisioned that Britain would defeat Napoleon and turn her wrath on this little land-locked lake? The young commander of the American navy knew the power of a frigate, having served on board several. He knew that he could not match her on the open waters of the lake, which was known for strong southerly winds in September. Sailly's man, Ezra Thurber, relayed news of the change from Fisher to Downie. Macdonough did not doubt the skill of the flotilla's new master; British naval officers had earned their reputations the world over. Whoever commanded would be a worthy opponent. General Macomb's request that Macdonough defend the army's right flank, well within Cumberland Bay, reminded him of the accounts he had read about Admiral Nelson's exploits at Copenhagen and the Nile, where Nelson fought a fleet at anchor. His Royal Navy counterpart may have been a witness to those victories and could be lured into thinking that he could repeat Nelson's feat. Cumberland Bay appeared open, three miles across and nearly circular, with docks along the far shore which gave the appearance of fair sailing. But hidden by the blue water were shoals and sand bars, reaching out like long thin fingers, just under the surface, that would snag a keel and hold her fast. Additionally, the winds in the bay were very undependable. While the lake blew well, the bay suffered from swirling breaths of air, hardly able to sustain a ship's way. Macomb's mandate to bring the fleet into the bay for the sake of the army could be the Americans' best chance against the marauding British.

A PLAN WITHOUT A CREW IS NO PLAN

While Macdonough devised his plan, the American ships were made ready for battle. Macdonough lacked trained marines, but he was given nearly two months to turn his soldiers into sailors. Still short, he appealed to Alexander Macomb for more men to crew his gunboats and the brig *Eagle,* but the general had no more to offer. While Izard was still in residence, he had given 250 soldiers to the navy. In desperation, Macdonough asked for the prisoners in the stockade, men confined for drinking, disrespect, disruption, and desertion. Macdonough promised the general that they would not cause mayhem on a seventy-foot boat, powered by their own oars. Indeed, like galley slaves, they would have little energy left after rowing across the bay. Macomb, who had written the manual for courts-martial at West Point, felt that such duty was nearly cruel and unusual punishment, but he gave up the prisoners anyway. When Macomb's regimental band members heard of the appeal for oarsmen, seven of the thirty volunteered, as did the wife of one band member. A black sailor who had come up from Boston stepped forward to join the musicians. Charles Black had particular hatred for two things. One was digging holes and the other was the English, who first impressed and then imprisoned him in the hell hole of Dartmoor.

Meanwhile, time ticked down as the British naval commander turned to learning the lake. Downie had never sailed or ever seen Lake Champlain, which put him at a considerable disadvantage. Here the loss of Captain Fisher's experience cost Prevost dearly. Downie, focused on the destruction of the enemy fleet, was unaware of the water hazards on the long, narrow lake. He believed his movement would be independent of the British army. While the redcoats headed for Plattsburgh and the destruction of the American army, he would seek out the American navy, which according to his second in command was ensconced at the southern end and more inclined to defend Burlington, Vermont, or its home base at Vergennes. Pring had never seen the American army and navy act together until that spring, when the army drove him away from Otter Creek. Ann Prevost, who frequently witnessed military talk at the supper table when Fisher and, later, Downie dined, provides perspective in her solitary writing:

August 1814, Montreal, Canada.

The Principal object of the expedition, as I afterwards understood, was the destruction of the American Dock Yard at Vincennes on the opposite side of the Lake—and the capture of Plattsburg would be merely the first service effected by the Expedition on its way to an ulterior object. Of course it was first of all most necessary that the American Squadron should be defeated, and our command of the Lake quite established.

While the British commodore did his war gaming with the officers from his flotilla, the army was on the move. Sir George could wait no longer for Downie to become comfortable in his new job and he would coerce the commodore into battle, if necessary. September was the last month in the year that Prevost could count on good campaign weather. It would not be long before the Americans discovered his and Admiral Cochrane's deceptions, and their true intentions. Then the Americans could adjust their forces accordingly and all advantage would be lost. Sir George Prevost was no military adventurer. Unlike "Gentleman" Johnny Burgoyne, he took his profession seriously and was not a waster of men. "Prevost was not," as John Elting has said, "a death or glory boy." Furthermore, those three young strident major generals, Brisbane, Powers, and Robinson, wanted to be done and return to England in triumph. They had good friends in high places who could influence matters, if their carping letters home had time to ferment. Sir George was also a soldier who appreciated the importance of the lines of communication and supply. He called upon his commissary general frequently and listened to a litany of logistical impediments. Major General William Henry Robinson, not to be confused with the commander of the 1st brigade Major General Frederick Robinson, advised, "The roads are worse than you can imagine and many of our wagons are broken down—The road through the woods at Beatville [Beekmantown] is impassable therefore our only dependence is upon water communication."[7]

THE FINAL INVASION

Sir George gave the order to cross the border and invade the United States on September 1. He directed the deputy commander, Major General Francis De Rottenburg, to get the army moving and convene a conference of his field commanders at Rouses Point, New York. There, the first order of business was to issue the rules of engagement to his field commanders. No civilians were to be harmed and no property was to be destroyed that was not directly connected with combat conditions. There would be no looting and all items requisitioned for the campaign were to be paid for on the spot. These rules were not uncommon and mimicked those of the Peninsular campaign just concluded in Europe. In Spain, the rules had often been broken, especially after a fierce battle, when the men's blood was up. The violations often resulted in hangings, and Prevost wanted to avoid both the looting and the capital punishment. Here in America, though, there was a profound difference. Prevost reminded his officers that any ground taken could well become a part of Canada and that the people were to be treated not as prisoners but subjects of His Majesty, King George III. In fact there were politicians in London so certain of the success of the invasion that they already had plans for portions of New England that might fall during the invasion. They saw the new territory as a separate colony from Canada, to be called "Columbia," since it was culturally distinct from French-speaking Lower Canada. A proclamation to the citizens of New York was distributed as the army moved south. Posted on buildings, nailed to trees, and passed out by hand, it read:

> The peaceable and unoffending inhabitants can expect kind usage and generous treatment. It is against the government of the United States by whom this unjust and unprovoked war has been declared, and against those who support it, either openly or secretly, that the arms of His Majesty are directed.
>
> Lieutenant General Sir George Prevost
>
> Governor General of Canada.[8]

Sir George still believed that there was a considerable sympathy for British rule and that, once established, the British army would be favored by the surrounding communities as they moved ever south, if the army behaved itself and paid their way.

In her diary Anne Prevost, a young patriotic English woman, sets the scene at her father's departure:

> On the 30th of August I made breakfast for my Father and his suite at half past six, previous to their departure on the ill fated Expedition. I was most sanguine that something very brilliant would be achieved. I had often thought with regret that my Father had never yet been engaged in any bright affair—he had considered it necessary to conduct the defense of the Canadas with much caution,—defense, not conquest was necessarily his object. But now I thought the time had arrived when all murmurs would be silenced—I was delighted to think my Father was commanding some thousands of Wellington's Soldiers! I remember well my dear Mother saying to me one day, "I do not think your Father ought to go out of the Province—in his high situation he should remain on the frontier." No doubt her fears for his personal safety suggested this idea, but I could not agree with her.—Precious as was my Father's life, still I was so true a Soldier's daughter, I valued his renown even more. "But dearest Mama" I said in reply, "you must remember that every step he takes he turns Yankee Ground into our territory—its our King's at least, for the time being, whatever may

become of it afterwards." O how high the pulse of Hope beat at that moment. I do not recollect that I had any sort of fear as to the result of the Expedition. I looked forward to certain Victory.

On the 3rd September we heard from my Father that he should be within the Enemy's territory the next day. This day too we heard of the capture of Washington—I was delighted, and thought still better news would soon come.

News of the loss of the nation's capital arrived in Plattsburgh and Burlington as well. The reports were sketchy and provided a great shock. How could the nation be in the hands of the British once again? The people felt that they had let their grandfathers down by losing what had been won in 1781. The local citizens, many of whom had never taken the war seriously, began to rally to the cause. For the past two years, Eleazer Williams had opposed the war and refused to enter the militia, in spite of the destructive British raid led by Lieutenant Colonel Murray the previous summer. The frenzied construction on the field fortifications, combined with word that the invasion force had crossed the border in great strength, changed his mind. He went to Macomb, to whom he suggested a bit of skullduggery. On September 3, he crossed the lake to Burlington and procured from Colonel Elias Fassett, in Governor Chittenden's office, erroneous documents that announced the amalgamation of ten thousand Vermont militia with five thousand more from northern New York. Returning to New York, he headed for the northern border and planted the information for the descending British column to find. It was a noble effort, but there is no evidence that the documents ever reached anyone of importance in the British command. Two years of experience dealing with American militia held no fear for Prevost or the Canadian regiments, anyway. The regular British regiments regarded militia as armed civilians, undisciplined and ill trained. The invading force never hesitated, and no battle plans were altered, as they moved through forests and passed by farms.

While American commodore Macdonough waited on the lake, looking for signs of the Royal Navy, it remained thirty miles north, minus the flagship, protecting the British army's left flank as it took a toehold at Rouses Point, New York. The next few days would belong to the long columns of redcoats marching, route step and four abreast, with the southern sun in their eyes. There were no American formations at the border, not even a manned customs hut. Englishmen just walked across and made themselves at home. This veteran army had one advantage it had not enjoyed in Europe: they spoke the language of this land. Initially in the lead was the brigade of Major General Robinson, who was the son of Colonel Beverly Robinson, a loyalist New Yorker during the Revolution who was forced to return to England when the British lost on the field at Yorktown. General Robinson told his hostess, Mrs. Hubbell, that his father had told him that all Americans were small people. A well-mannered lady, she agreed and sent for Philip Hensinger to fetch the next course. The growing lad of six feet, seven inches and 260 pounds delivered the roast joint for the general to carve. In great humor, before his officers, the general remarked, "If the Yankees are all like him, the Lord deliver us from fighting them." The next morning, Mrs. Hubbell bid the guests goodbye. Though they were quite splendid in both manner and uniforms, and dispelling any thought that the family had been converted by the visit to the side of the king, she said, "Good-bye, Sirs, for a very little while, but I know you'll soon be back and hanging your heads as you come." Annoyed that she had not resigned herself to British rule, the general said, "If a man had said that, I would call him out, but since it is a fair lady that has been our charming hostess, I reply that when your prophecy comes true, every officer here shall throw his purse on your door step as he passes." During the retreat they stopped once again and gave up their money.[9]

REDCOATS IN THE WILDERNESS

The countryside that the British traveled through was so rough that not even the Indians had lived there, although their hunting parties had made paths through the region for untold generations. The track these parties made was now the road from Canada to New York, and had been little improved. The tall green pines, red oaks, black cherries, and golden-leafed aspens that lined the road provided fall colors that took the hardship off the minds of the plodding and hauling soldiers. Oxen were bought from the few farmers and loggers along the way for the teams, which struggled with the siege artillery and wagons filled with powder and cannonballs. This army was used to foraging in nearby communities to add to their rations of biscuit and salt beef. But the towns the army passed through, Rouses Point, Champlain, and Chazy, which were separated by wilderness and contained only clusters of houses where trails met, could barely sustain themselves, much less an army. Movement was so slow that it allowed the officers of the navy and army to convene at Chazy and buy an elegant dinner served on casks covered with boards and fine tablecloths. Most had their traveling kits, which consisted of a few wooden chests that contained, among other items, their linen, silver, china, and candlesticks. Borne on the backs of mules led by a servant, or batman, these luxuries followed the officers around the world and made for very long support columns. Also, the wives of one in ten enlisted men, sometimes with accompanying children, walked along with the baggage, a mile or two behind the brigade. In Britain, wives had been chosen for this role by lot. If the husband died on campaign, the wife often married another man from the regiment. The wives' duty was to keep house for the ten soldiers close to their husbands. This entailed cooking, sewing, fetching water, and setting up and striking camp. Since the medical corps was in its infancy, the women tended the sick and wounded and helped infirm soldiers keep up with the column. Women had been on the ships from Europe and Britain, numbering at least one thousand. Today they are called camp followers and often maligned, but if they had not been of real assistance to an army in the field, they would not have been there. The Royal Navy had women on board for the same reasons.

ENTER THE NEW YORK STATE MILITIA

Eleazer Williams was not far from wrong when he spoke of great numbers of militiamen that could be called upon in the first week of September to defend the land from all the king's men. Major General Benjamin Mooers, the commander of the New York State "minutemen" of the northern counties, called for twenty-five hundred to meet him at Plattsburgh. Many took their time and thought it over, some arriving after the battle. Sadly, only seven hundred showed up, and they brought with them nothing more than ragged clothes, native dirt, and large appetites.[10] The red tide was swallowing up the land and with it the courage of the people who watched them pass. Disappointed by the thin ranks, Mooers addressed them at the camp established near his home in Plattsburgh. "Attention and good order are expected by the Major General and he would feel mortified to hear of any depredations on the inhabitants or ill usage to any one, as the object in calling militia out is for the purpose of repelling the enemy and protecting the citizens in their persons and property." Delivered in the third person, as was the custom of the day, particularly in public matters, the speech got right to the heart of the matter. The militia was not a disciplined body of men and some joined for other than honorable reasons.

The first action by the militia was a bold one. Reconnoitering alone behind enemy lines, Lieutenants Matthew Standish and Roswell Wait of the New York State dragoons pretended to be British officers returning to their unit from a hunting expedition. This was a common practice in Spain, and on march officers often roamed freely about the country on their side of the lines, exploring and sometimes sketching or painting. During the march toward Plattsburgh, the infantry officers had horses and the time hung heavy, as the army had moved only ten miles in three days. The troop units were normally led by the senior enlisted men, sergeants and corporals who conducted drill and marksmanship, supervising the soldiers' every move. The officers lived apart and only joined their units on the march or when contact with the enemy was near. They were also often called upon by senior officers to act as personal aides or to carry orders and instructions when free from regimental duties. So it did not seem unusual for the two young American lieutenants, whose New York militia's red tunics and sausage roll hats were nearly identical to the dress of British cavalry, to be wandering among British formations. Since the force was so large, not all officers were known and anyone with a good Etonian accent could pass through any road control point. From their mission, Standish and Wait not only provided "order of battle" information, they identified the capability and positions of the British advance guard.[11]

SEPTEMBER 5, FIRST CONTACT

On the evening of the 5th, Standish and Wait, leading two companies of their New York State dragoons, struck the first blow since the enemy had crossed the border five days before. They attacked the British picket line and sent the picket fleeing to the rear. This brought the 3d Regiment of Foot to arms. The Americans were no longer elusive, but would they stand and fight?

A side road at Sampson's corners, eight miles north of Plattsburgh, offered Prevost an attractive opportunity. His men and supplies were strung out nearly nine miles. By splitting his force into two lines of march, he could relieve the traffic jam. Also, since the new spur road led to the edge of the lake and then on to Plattsburgh, he could envelop the town from two sides, while gaining gun support from his naval flotilla, which should now be on its way. Because of the overwhelming land force he led, he was not afraid that splitting it would weaken it. His intelligence agents informed him that there was nothing of consequence to his front. He sent Major General Brisbane's brigade to the left, along with the light brigade, which consisted of a dozen Canadian fencible battalions, the voltigeurs, chasseurs, militia, and De Meuron's Swiss regiment. An attached company of Indians was split, half to each column, to act as scouts, now that they were getting close to the American's lines.

On the 4th, Macomb had sent Mooers's seven-hundred-man militia farther north to intercept the British army. He was not expected to decisively engage, but to harass and delay the oncoming enemy, abatis the roads, and burn the bridges.[12] They were also expected to gather intelligence outlining the intentions of the invading army. Macomb wrote a letter on September 5 to General Mooers that included a sketch of the signaling rockets (modern sky or distress rockets used today for celebration or for signaling at sea) that Macomb was sending:

> I send you six rockets for signals—as it may not be understood in which manner they are set off the following is the way of using them
> A—is the rocket tied to the stick B
> C is the quick match that is to be touched by the fire which will set it off

D fire brand applied

The rocket is held perpendicular or set up against a fence.

Two or more of these Rockets set off we shall consider a signal for the certain approach of the Enemy. Tomorrow before day light I shall advance a Battalion of regular Light troops under Major Wool on the Beekman town road, also six pieces of Light artillery under Capt. Leonard, which pieces will also be supported by regulars and your troops must lend their aid.[13] The positions on the road are admirable & every way calculated for troops of the Discription you command— In Heaven's sake do not let the militia retire without fighting—the more they fight the better they will become & will soon get over the alarm of a few muskets.

Rockets will be fired at Dead Creek in like manner[14]

Historians differ on what the militia accomplished at this point. Early writings suggest that Mooers's men moved up the road to Sampson's corner to support the charge of Standish and Wait's dragoons.[15] Later writings state that, while moving forward, the militia, on foot, saw their dragoons coming up from behind. The dragoons were dressed as they had been since their inception after the Revolution, in bright red short coats and white pants. They wore the Tarleton helmets and so to the casual observer appeared to be British. The militia was not a trained force and was spooked at the site of "enemy" cavalry. In spite of General Mooers's assurances, the militia broke and ran. They did not stop until they were back at their camp, miles to the rear. General Mooers followed, nearly alone, paying the price for not having trained his troops in the very rudiments of military maneuver. Mooers sent a dispatch to the governor, their commander-in-chief in Albany, that evening. He did not speak of his own shortcomings that had caused the incident but of the men:

A portion of the militia have entailed an eternal disgrace on themselves, many of whom have left the ranks and gone home. The General regrets that there are some who are lost to patriotism and gone

home, after coming forward in obedience to his call, fled at the first
approach of the enemy, and afterwards basely disbanded themselves
and returned home; thereby disgracing themselves and their fellow-
soldiers an example of all that brave men detest and abhor.[16]

His outrage is understandable. But during the summer Macomb
and Izard resupplied, trained, and prepared for the attack, but
there is no evidence that Mooers did the same. The militia members were reluctant to undergo training, yet seeing to it that troops
are trained is the responsibility of those who seek officership. The
failure appears to have been with the leadership and not with the
courage of the soldiers. The battlefield is not the place to prepare.
Further evidence of Mooers's shortcomings as a military leader is
in the numbers that answered the call to arms. Putting a military-
looking force into the field in 1814 was far easier than training
one for war. Skill at arms and sustained training are the only
things that build in troops the confidence needed to steady them
in the face of the oncoming enemy. As the French would learn at
the start of World War I, it takes much more than élan, or the
spirit of the offense, to warrant victory.

General Macomb agreed with the assessment by Mooers but in
his report did not mention their commander. "The Militia, except
for a few brave men, fell back most precipitously in great disorder." But in the same correspondence he concludes, "the militia
behaved with great spirit after the first day, and the volunteers
from Vermont were exceedingly serviceable."[17] Here, Macomb
refers to the actions of a small band of New Yorkers after the first
day's desertion by much of General Mooers's militia. Macomb
refers to Vermonters as "volunteers" since the governor did not
allow their use. On September 5, New York State militia captain
Martin Aikin, age twenty-one, and Lieutenant Azariah Flagg,
age twenty, formed a platoon consisting of fifteen school boys of

under fifteen years of age and went to war. Following the main body of regulars, they went up the road into the face of the armed enemy, and stayed to fight. They remained until the battle was over, days later, "fighting every step of the way." They earned the thanks of General Macomb, who praised them in his official report of the battle. Macomb was inspired as he encountered them day after day on the ramparts. As a gesture from one warrior to another, and as a reward for their courage, he gave each a new army rifle. When his quartermaster officer pointed out to the general that he did not have the authority to give away government property, the rifles were recovered. Macomb petitioned Congress to reinstate the gifts. In March 1826, Congress presented the forgotten heroes with new Springfield rifles that carried a brass plaque on the stock engraved with the name, date, and deed of its recipient.[18] Other accounts of the action of the 5th credit individual fighting men from New York with taking a place within regular formations. Not all the militia deserted.

HELP FOR THE MILITIA

On the 5th, Macomb sent out a follow-up force, once he found out that the British column had split and that the militia was having difficulty. He sent Captain Robert Sproul and two hundred of the 13th regular infantry with two six-pound artillery pieces up the lakeside road to abatis and destroy bridges. They were to set up a defensive position at the Dead Creek bridge, less than a mile northeast of the town, where the creek enters the bay.

Lieutenant Colonel Daniel Appling, dressed in the field green of the rifle regiment, took his 110 riflemen and a troop of New York dragoons, led by Captain Stafford and Lieutenant Standish, up the lakeside road due north of town, directly into the path of the five-thousand-man red-coated column led by Brisbane. There were conflicting reports as to how much the militia had done to delay the enemy on the Beekmantown road. It is certain, however, that the first attempt to stop the British movement was made by the men under regular army major John E. Wool of the 29th Infantry regiment. Here it is best to use Major Wool's own words, which describe the action and give an account of the day. Historians have disagreed for years over the actions of the New York militia. Since history is usually written by the victor, no account has been written by the British. Official British army history makes little mention of the battle. Nearly forty years later, Wool responded to an inquiry about the disputed conduct of the New York militia:

Troy, New York,

May 10, 1860.

My dear Lossing,

In his account of the battle of Plattsburgh Mr. Dawson says, in page 379 and 380, that "the enemy on the 5th, continued his march, in the course of which he met serious obstructions from the trees which had been felled in the roads and from the removal of the bridges on his route—a duty which had been efficiently performed by General Mooers, of the New York Militia, seven hundred strong." General Mooers, on the 4th, as it appears from Macomb's report, "collected about 700 Militia and advanced seven miles on the Beekmantown road to watch the motions of the enemy, and to skirmish with him as he advanced—also to obstruct the roads with fallen trees and to break up the bridges." It is due to truth to say that the General, nor his Militia felled trees in the roads, removed bridges or skirmished with the enemy previous to, or on the morning of, the 6th when the enemy took possession of the village of Plattsburgh.

On the 5th, General Mooers with his Militia was encamped on the Beekmantown road, four or five miles from Plattsburgh. Majors Appling and Sproul were ordered on the direct road to Chazy with directions to obstruct the enemy's advance on this road. This service was performed by them on that, and on no other road was a similar duty performed. Up to the 5th not a shot had been fired at the enemy. It was this circumstance which induced me to call on General Macomb, when I remarked I thought we ought not to permit the enemy to reach Plattsburgh without some evidence of a determination to resist him and to defend our position; and requested permission to go out on the evening of the 5th with the troops under my command, the 29th regiment, only then 200 strong, when I would reach the enemy's camp before morning, beat up his quarters and perhaps take from him some prisoners from whom the General might learn the state of their forces. This he objected to saying I might be captured and he had no men to lose. In the course of the day I again called on the General and made the same application but with no better success. About sun down however he called at my quarters and directed me to go out the next morning at sunrise with two hundred and fifty infantry, and at the same time said Captain Leonard with his Artillery will go with you—the Captain was present and heard what the General said. Afterwards I induced the General to change the order from sunrise to 3 o'clock. Captain Leonard refused to march with me, because, as he said, he had not received orders to do so. The remarks of the General that he would go with me he did not consider an order. I halted at the camp of General Mooers when I learned the enemy was encamped at the junction of the two roads leading to Chazy, about four or five miles from the General's camp and nine miles from Plattsburgh. I recommenced my march and at daylight I met the advance of the enemy at Howes, seven or eight miles from Plattsburgh, and from this point I disputed every inch of ground. . . . I received no aid or assistance from General Mooers' Militia save about thirty men who volunteered to join my command and remained with it until my arrival at Plattsburgh. It is however due to General Mooers to say that he endeavored to bring his troops into action but did not succeed. They fled without firing a gun, and did not stop until they crossed at or near Pike's Cantonment, except a small party, which defended the upper bridge. These I am under the impression, were the twenty-five young men of the village, who formed themselves into an independent Volunteer corps for the occasion.[19]

An earlier letter from Wool written to Philip B. Roberts of Beekmantown, New York, challenges some of the folk myths that abound in Plattsburgh even today. The language is archaic and Wool refers to himself in the third person:

Troy January 6th, 1859

Sir,

Your communication of the 1st instant, relating to the "Battle of Beekmantown", which occurred on the morning of the 6th of September 1814, was received on the 3rd.

In reply to your request I would remark that on the evening of the 5th of September, 1814, Major John E. Wool, having volunteered his services, was ordered by Major General A. Macomb with 250 regular infantry and Captain Leonard with two pieces of Artillery, to march early next morning, the 6th of September, on the Beekmantown road "to support the Militia and set them an example of firmness" by resisting the advance on Plattsburgh of the British column on that road commonly reported to be 4,000 strong. The United States Militia under Major General Mooers, 700 strong, were encamped on that road about four or five miles from Plattsburgh.

Agreeably to the orders of Major General Macomb, Major Wool with 250 regular infantry afterwards joined by 30 Volunteer Militia, left Plattsburgh about twelve o'clock at night—Captain Leonard refused to accompany him, not having been as he said ordered to do so by General Macomb—and marched about seven miles when he met the advance of the British column under the command of Lieut. Colonel Wellington of the 3rd Buffs. From this point the command of Major Wool disputed every foot of ground until it arrived on the right bank of the Saranac in the village of Plattsburgh. On his reaching Culiver's Hill the Major made a stand and compelled the British troops to fall back—when Lieut. Colonel Wellington and a Lieutenant of the 3rd Buffs were killed—but the troops soon rallied and compelled the Major to retreat. On his arrival at the brook, some half a mile or more from Culiver's Hill, he made a short stand and tore up the bridge erected over the brook. From this position disputing every inch of ground, he again made a stand at Halseys Corner, a half of a mile or more from Plattsburgh, where he was joined by Captain Leonard with two pieces of Artillery, which were well served and did great execution. Being driven from his position he again made a stand in front of Judge Bayly's House, and again at Gallows Hill in the village of Plattsburgh. From this position he crossed and formed his troops on the right bank of the Saranac. The Major ordered Captain

Rochester with his company to tear up the bridge, which he promptley executed under a severe fire from the enemy. The British troops took possession of the stores and houses on the opposite [north] bank, from which they were driven by Major Wool's Infantry and the well directed fire of four pieces of Artillery under Captain Leonard, and from the fire of two block-houses near by. The enemy retired in the rear of the village, where the whole British force, 11,000 strong, concentrated, and where they remained until the 11th September, 1814.[20]

THE BRITISH BRUSHED THEM ASIDE

The leading British infantry unit was the East Kent regiment, the 3d Foot, or "Buffs." The name comes from the color on the facings, collar, and cuffs of their uniforms. The regiment was one of the first formed in the British model army of the seventeenth century and was distinguished on the field by the light brown color which edged the men's coats. When they encountered Major Wool's little force, they dropped their packs and charged with fixed bayonets. The charge was led by Lieutenant Colonel James Wellington, no relation to the Duke of Wellington. James Wellington had served as a captain with the regiment in Spain. He was with the regiment at Albuera, twelve miles from Badajoz, when the British army was attacked by the French and the "Buffs" became entangled in a fierce fight with the Polish lancers of the Vistula. When several lancers saw Lieutenant Matthew Lathum with the regimental colors, they attempted to take the standard as a prize. Lathum held on, even though his nose was cut off, his left arm was completely severed, and he was stuck through with a lance. After the action, Wellington was brevet promoted to major.[21] Upon his arrival in Canada he was again brevet promoted, to lieutenant colonel, several days before he was shot dead by Private Samuel Terry of Peru, New York, in the engagement Wool described years later. Beside Wellington, Lieutenant

West and Ensign Richard Chapman were also killed, along with twelve other British soldiers. They were buried by their comrades near Ira Howe's house in Beekmantown. Two Americans, Privates Goodspeed and Jay, were wounded and captured. When the two artillery pieces joined the running fight, many more redcoats fell. Lieutenant Kingsbury, also of the 3d, was wounded. He later died and was buried at Isaac Platt's farmhouse.[22] The bodies of all the slain British who had not been claimed by relatives were moved to the cemetery at Plattsburgh on September 11, 1843, by Captain Waite, commander of the Plattsburgh garrison and veteran of the battle.[23] This was done with considerable pomp and ceremony, as was the first hasty interment, just after the battle. Dignitaries from the United States, Canada, and Britain were present. Full military honors were accorded. Today, each year on September 11, a joint commemorative ceremony is held at the graves of both American and British, who lie side by side.

Wool's attempt to delay the British was futile. The formation never left its column, nor did it deploy skirmishers. They just kept coming. The speed of the British army was determined by its long tail, which slowed it down, rather than by the attempt of a few hundred Americans who risked their lives to impede the juggernaut from the front. On the lakeside road, Lieutenant Colonel Appling called upon the American fleet, which had moved into the bay on September 2. Along with the four men-of-war were twelve gunboats, each with two heavy naval guns and crewed by thirty men, most of whom were soldiers. At 10 A.M. of September 6, Major General Brisbane's brigade of nearly five thousand marched in an unbroken column along the road that hugged the northern edge of the bay. The town of Plattsburgh was well within sight, as was the American flotilla. The lead British regimental band played "The Girl I Left Behind Me," while over on the Beekmantown road the 88th (Connaught Rangers), played their regimental march on bagpipes. The noise of the drums and the skirl of the pipes reached across the water like a mailed fist and announced the arrival of the most successful army in the world. The British red line drawn along the shore was out of the range of the carronades that lined the decks of the American ships. Macdonough, therefore, ordered the gunboats to take on the mission of supporting Appling's defense of the bridge and attack the British column. The naval cannon flanking fire scattered the attackers and sent them to cover while they called for the Royal Field Artillery to come up the crowded road to their rescue. The gunboats had dropped their sails and half the crew rowed so they could point the guns, which were fixed in the prows. The rate of fire was slow. These seventy-foot-long whale boats were meant to attack smuggler's rafts. The gun was intended to be fired once or twice as the boat closed in for boarding a raft. Now the boats were called upon to act like men-of-war and take on a land target of moving men. At the narrow bow end of the boat it was difficult to clean out and reload the muzzle of the gun, which weighed over a ton. But the men worked at their task as the current drove them closer to shore. They came close enough to receive rifle fire and some of the crew were wounded. But they accomplished something that Major Wool had been unable to. They stopped the forward movement of the left arm of the British army and deprived Prevost of the simultaneous envelopment of the town. He and the remainder of his army were just then arriving in Plattsburgh, chasing Wool's men across the Saranac River, back into the arms of General Macomb.

Redcoats Fired on by the American Navy

The tricky winds shifted against the gunboats as the British field artillery's six-pounders took up the battle and found the range.

Macdonough, from his quarterdeck, saw that the flotilla near the shore would be destroyed and sent Midshipman Silas Duncan from the *Saratoga* in a gig with orders to retrieve the gunboats and place them behind the American fleet. Duncan was severely wounded as he ventured too close to shore in an attempt to gain control of the boats and lead them to safety. In spite of his wounds, he accomplished the mission and was taken to Crab Island, where a hospital had been established.[24]

C. S. Forester remarks that Macdonough, a student of military history, had in his possession a copy of *Nelson's Battles,* in which it is recorded how Nelson attacked fleets that were anchored, at both the battle of the Nile and Copenhagen, destroying the enemy totally. It also noted that at the battle of Algeciras the Royal Navy lost when the French rotated their vessels in place. Macdonough believed that the Royal Navy commander, who may have even been at those battles and most certainly knew of the tactics, would refight those engagements. Macdonough therefore fought from anchor and lured the Royal Navy into the seemingly safe waters of the bay. This strategy fit two additional conditions of the battle. First of all, the bay, where he had maneuvered during the previous summer, had perfidious waters. Secondly, he had been required by Macomb to provide fire support against the British land forces to increase the artillery fire of the army's cannons. A stationary position would suit both conditions. This battle was shaping up to be a duel of cannon. Macdonough anchored in a line nearly north and south and prepared to fight. He also deployed kedge anchors. These auxiliary anchors were placed both ahead of and behind his flagship. They were tied with lines, which were wrapped along and around the ship. Called "springs," such lines were commonly used to rotate a stationary vessel in place. Often used in port, they were known by every sailor for the ease they provided in moving a heavy vessel a short distance without having to put up the sail. By lifting the regular anchor and attaching the spring to the capstan, the ship could be wound around to expose the other side. Macdonough knew that whatever he did to prepare, it would be a hot fight and one he was very likely to lose. The worry came from the overwhelming power of the British fleet. Their ships were equipped with cannon that could outrange his by more than double. If the British stood off they could engage the Americans, who would be unable to return fire. After retrieving his gunboats, the commodore prepared to act in concert with Macomb and fire on the British army when they came into range on the streets of Plattsburgh.

THE LAND BATTLE IS JOINED

Macomb shared the same fear of the sheer mass of his terrestrial opponent. The British army had him nine to one on September 6. The militia that he had hoped for, ever since Izard left with the bulk of the regulars, had not materialized. The New York militia had left the field and there was still no word on the Vermont militia. But Alexander Macomb had not been idle. With the help of Major Joseph G. Totten and Lieutenant R. E. Darusie, Corps of Engineers, the entire command had labored all summer to construct field fortifications. Earthworks, easy to construct in sandy soil, were dug, taking advantage of the lay of the land on the southern side of town. The fastness was contained on a natural peninsula formed by the Saranac River and the bay.[25] Across the center of the peninsula were positioned three large redoubts to house the artillery, which could range any potential target in the town of Plattsburgh. Two blockhouses covering the two bridges were built near the water's edge. Trenches and laterals were dug the length and breadth of the line to protect the infantry. It looked very much like Yorktown or the more contemporary battlefield of Flanders. Large stockpiles of food, water, and ammunition were put into the dugouts for the troops so that they did not have to leave and expose themselves to enemy fire. Macomb was urged by members of his staff and townsfolk to abandon the position after Izard left. It was suggested that he go further south, perhaps as far as Albany. "If the British wanted to take another licking at Saratoga then we will do it again," one local businessman remarked. But he may have been motivated by the desire to save his shop. Macomb was concerned about morale among his men, especially now that the New York militia was gone. He told his troops that they "must defend to the last extremity." A general order was issued on the 5th, the day before the redcoats arrived in town:

> The eyes of America are on us, fortune always follows the brave. The works being now capable of resisting a powerful attack, the manner of defending them the General thinks is his duty to detail, that every man may know and do his duty. The troops will line the parapets in two ranks, leaving intervals for the artillery. A reserve of one-fifth of the whole force in infantry will be detailed and paraded fronting the several angles, which it will be their particular duty to sustain. To each bastion are to assign, by the several commanders of forts, a sufficient number of infantry to line all faces [in single ranks] of each tier. Should the enemy gain the ditch, the front rank of the part assailed will mount the parapet and repel him with its fire and bayonet. If the men of this rank are determined, no human force can dispossess them of the position.

He was correct. A good defensive position hugging the raging Saranac River, spanned with only two bridges that had had their flooring removed, could be held against a frontal attack of infantry for a considerable time.

Fort Brown, named for the American defender of the Niagara, was commanded by Lieutenant Colonel Huckens Stores, who put the 13th and 31st infantry in the trenches in front to ensure the safety of the guns. This was the most important of the three earthen forts because it sat on a high ridge that commanded the majority of the river below. Fort Moreau, the largest of the works, was two hundred feet square. It was armed with heavy artillery, eighteen- and twenty-four-pounders mounted on naval gun carriages, with the exception of six of the eighteens, mounted on field carriages. The fort was named by Izard for a French general exiled by Napoleon, and was commanded by Lieutenant Colonel Malancton Smith and defended by the 6th and the remnants of the 29th that had been out on the road with Major Wool. Fort Scott, on the lakeshore, was named for Macomb's old comrade, Winfield Scott. Major Thomas Vinson was put in charge of the remnants of the 33rd and 34th infantry. The blockhouse at the mouth of the river was manned by Lieutenant Fowler's artillery, while the other was garrisoned by the sick and some of the 1st Rifle Regiment, under Captain John Smith. Those too sick to fire or load were sent to Crab Island, in Cumberland Bay, to a hospital run by Dr. John Mann. By the start of the battle, Mann had nearly a thousand men in tents and lying on the open ground. With the help of the few who were ambulatory, he constructed wooden tent floors. Macomb sent two sixteen-pounder guns to be placed on the point of the island to prevent the Royal Navy from landing. The guns were serviced by invalids. Earlier, the diseased had been evacuated to Burlington. But now, with the battle near, all extra boats were busy moving supplies. Accounts of the weather vary, but it seems to have been rather wet the first two weeks of September, although some talk of bright, beautiful days. There is no indication that bad weather, a major concern to Prevost, ever materialized. Casualty lists for the battle vary widely at this point, as they do for all stages of the battle. Each side likely exaggerated the other's losses. It appears that the British lost about two hundred killed and wounded before the 6th and that the

Americans lost about fifty. The desertion rate was higher for the Americans, nearly seven hundred for the New York militia versus a hundred or so for the British. Posters were put up in all the border towns proclaiming that any British soldier presenting himself to local authorities with the desire to become an American citizen would be welcomed and given cash and one hundred acres of land on the western frontier. The British thought this was an unsporting way to fight a war.

THE BRITISH ARMY WAITS FOR ITS NAVY

On the morning of September 6, Prevost established his headquarters at the Allen farmhouse on the northeastern side of the town, barely out of range of the American cannon. While he waited for Brisbane to break through over Dead Creek bridge, he ordered the town cleared of enemy soldiers and reiterated his order not to destroy private property or harm the citizens. Being driven before the three enemy brigades, Lieutenant Colonel Appling and Major Wool continued to fight as they crossed the bridges, pulling up the planking as they went. Wool put his two guns into immediate action on the south side of Bridge Street bridge. At the inland bridge, nearer to Pike's cantonment, Appling managed to escape the soldiers of De Meuron's Swiss regiment, who boasted at the end of the battle that they had routed all the Americans from the town by dark.

By the morning of the 7th the battle lines were drawn on the banks of the Saranac River. Casualties were high as on the previous day as more carnage took place among the houses of the village. The killing was not as widespread as one might expect, because the fighting was infantry against infantry. The British artillery was not in place, and the American guns could not fire because Americans were intermingled with the British skirmishers in Plattsburgh, in a hit-and-run melee. Captain Noadie of the King's 8th Regiment took a scouting party of a hundred men west along the Saranac River looking for a crossing point. The New York militia, those that stayed, were allotted to the defense of the ford at Pike's old cantonment, three miles west, up the twisting river. Both sides of the river at this point were a convoluted wilderness of underbrush and maple trees. The red, gold, and rust color of the fall foliage helped to hide the red coats of the British soldiers, as they tramped noisily through the undergrowth. Militia captain Vaughan lined the south side of the stream with his riflemen. Some perched in the giant trees that nearly reached across the stream. Here, at a quiet point where the water slipped by in thin sheets over the solid rock bed, the militia was tested once more. The ford was of tactical importance: it was the chink in Macomb's armor. If it was not held, the British could roll up the Yankee left flank at will.

Benjah Phelps, eleven years old at the time of the battle, later told the story in a manner that recalled the excitement of a boy on a great adventure, nearly unaware of the gravity of the situation:

> My father was a Sergeant in the milishy [militia] and protecting the ford at Pike's Cantonment on the Saranac river. His company guarded the ford all day. The British did not know they was there, but they did pooty quick when they tried to cross. The woods was thick and the big trees and bushes came right down to the water on the other side, they shot them right down. Some of them dropped in the stream and was carried away by the current. Captain Dixon, he was cap'n of the company, was hit right on the brass plate on his sword belt where it crossed his heart. It made a big dent. I seen it myself.[26]

Two militia were killed in addition to several invaders, while others were wounded. Back in the town a company of Canadian chasseurs under Captain Mattley cleared the last Americans from the north side of the river.

Major Wool's letter to Lossing takes up once again: "In page 383 Mr. Dawson gives credit to Captain Leonard of driving the enemy out of the houses in the village with hot shot. This service was performed by Captain Brooks of the foot Artillery. Captain Leonard was with my command at the bridge." To the great dismay of the citizens of the town who stayed behind, General Macomb ordered the American artillery to fire hot cannon balls into the structures of the town and set them on fire. The British were using the houses, barns, and outbuildings for concealment and protection. They kept up a constant rifle fusillade, pinging away from niches on roofs and upstairs windows, at anything that was exposed. Cannonballs were heated on the cook fires behind the forts and brought into the battery at Fort Brown. The river, though swift and unfordable, was only thirty yards wide. The American trenches were dug on the very edge of the precipitous south side, so that the infantry could fire down at the other side, which was flat for miles. It was dangerous to shove a red-hot cannonball down a barrel that was primed with a bag of black gunpowder. Even the damp wadding, placed between ball and charge, began to smolder immediately. The gunner with the ram was afraid that the charge would be cooked off prematurely and that the hot shot, the ram, and he would go down range together. One of the townspeople describes the destruction caused by the hot shot:

Plattsburgh Sept. 20th, 1814

Dear Brother

I was in the village the morning the British came in and was every day in the cantonment during their stay. The first engagement commenced in Beekmentown, five miles from the Village. Our troops were driven in every direction, nor could they make a stand until they crossed the river.

How the enemy stopped and it appears made no trial to cross over that day, although a continual fire was kept up between the two armies on the banks of the river. Many of our men were either killed or wounded by the enemy's musketry from the houses where they had taken shelter. And in consequence of this our General ordered hot shot to be thrown into the buildings and burn them down. My house has shared the fate of many others. The whole block of buildings where it stood has been swept away by a single clash. Mr. Griffin's house and store and outhouses, Mr. Wait's house and store and Mr. Barker's house, also on that street, were burnt by our shot. The number of buildings burnt are about 30, with the courthouse. Such has been the conflagration and destruction of private property in this place caused by fortifications erected for the purpose of defending our frontier.[27]

The British slowly filled to overflowing the little town that once boasted seventy-eight fine homes. Prevost had two concerns: the establishment of the heavy artillery to bombard the American infantry out of their strong defenses and the location of his navy. To his surprise and delight Captain Downie would have to look no further for the American navy than Cumberland Bay. The Royal Navy could first destroy Macdonough's ships, which was the primary objective of Sir George's plan, and then turn their considerable guns on the American forts. Prevost relayed the good news to Downie on September 7 and categorized for Downie each ship in the American fleet and its capability. His letter goes on:

If you feel the vessels under your command are equal to a combat with these I have described, you will find the present moment offers many advantages which may not again occur. As my ulterior movements depend on your decision, you will have the goodness to favor me with it, with all possible promptitude.[28]

Anne Prevost, writing in her diary, relays her father's thoughts:

The 8th of September, we heard that my Father had established his Head Quarters within sight of Plattsburg—they directed red hot shot at the house he occupied. The Army were waiting for the Fleet, as the attack on the Squadron and the Fort was to be simultaneous.

There had been no word from the Royal Navy flotilla commander, Downie, in days. The last contact had been the visit paid by a staff officer who met with Captain Pring at Rouses Point, where Pring's vessel, *Linnet,* was in for provisions. Pring relayed that Downie was still struggling with the new vessel and training the crew. Through Pring, Sir George dispatched a message to his naval commander informing of the progress of the army and expanding Downie's instructions:

8th of September, 1814

Captain Downie, RN
Commodore of the Lake Champlain Flotilla.

I only wait your arrival to proceed against General Macomb's last position on the South Bank of the Saranac. Your share in the operation in the first instance, will be to destroy or capture the Enemy's Squadron if it should wait for a contest, and afterwards cooperate with this Division of the Army, but if it should run away and get out of your reach, we must meet here to consult on ulterior movements.

(signed) Prevost

It appears that Prevost was impressed with the stand the little American force was making. At Sackets Harbor, the previous summer, he had been repulsed by a similar but much weaker defense, and he did not care to repeat the humiliation. This time he would bring overwhelming odds by ensuring that the Royal Navy was not off chasing the American navy. After a successful attack on Plattsburgh by land and water, and the establishment of the army's winter cantonment, Downie could destroy Macdonough at will or bottle him up permanently at Otter Creek.

WILL THE ROYAL NAVY EVER COME?

Downie's reply was not what Sir George was expecting. The captain had been working with his new ship and crew and was unhappy with his progress. He promptly replied, the same day,

> Lieutenant General Sir George Prevost, Bt.   8th September, 1814
>
> I stated to you that the ship was not ready—she is not ready now, and until she is ready, it is my duty not to hazard the squadron before an Enemy who will even then be considerably superior in force.
>
> (signed)
> Your Obedient Servant
> Downie

Why Downie remarked that the enemy was "superior" is a total mystery. The following quote was found among the papers held by the family of Sir George: "The strongest confidence prevailed in the superiority of the British vessels, their weight of metal, and in the capacity and experience of their officer and crews; and as the commander of the forces was informed by an officer of the staff, who had been dispatched to Capt. Downie, that Capt. Downie credited himself with his own vessel alone a match for the whole American Squadron."[29] Naval statistics of the day show that the Americans could have come somewhat close to the throwing weight of the British, because carronades had heavier projectiles. But the British flotilla had the long-range guns to outstrip the Americans overwhelmingly.[30]

Prevost sent word again on the 9th that he had postponed his attack on the American army, but "need not dwell with you on the evils resulting to both Services from delay." Sir George could see in front of him a golden opportunity to destroy both the American army and navy in one stroke and did not want to let

Macdonough's fleet, his primary concern, get away. But Downie had been plagued with problems that all new ships face. Nothing worked properly on the series of shakedown cruises conducted in the safety of the northern waters of the lake. His crew of converted soldiers did not respond to the nautical life. He had kept the shipyard carpenters on board since the ship was launched, fixing leaks and reinforcing gun platforms.

Finally, on the 10th, he sent word to Prevost that, "I would have sailed on the 10th but the winds prevented it." He added that he would be in Plattsburgh as soon as the winds permitted. Sir George replied,

> I received at twelve last night your letter acquainting me with your determination to get under weigh about that time in the expectation of rounding Cumberland Head at dawn of day; in consequence, the troops have been held in readiness since six o'clock this morning to storm the enemy's works at nearly the same moment as the naval action should commence in the Bay. I ascribe the disappointment I have experienced to the unfortunate change of wind and shall rejoice to learn that my reasonable expectations have been frustrated by no other means.

Prevost instructed Downie to scale his guns when he intended to begin the attack, adding that he would then set the army in motion against the land fortification.[31] While the messages flew back and forth between the army and navy bosses, the army was assembling all eleven thousand in and around the village. The artillery, which was critical to the siege, was going into battery.

THE GUNS MAKE ALL THE DIFFERENCE

The British began digging eight gun positions on the north bank of the Saranac River and the bay side of the peninsula. The burning of the houses plagued the American gunners. The smoke from the smoldering town obscured the Royal Artillery activity as the British threw up dirt berms to protect the guns that would soon be registered. The Royal Artillery set up its headquarters at the Delord house at the north end of the line of six batteries near the mouth of the bay and extending to the south following the river's northwestern bank.[32] The house was abandoned and the officers laid their kit on the floors and put together additional boards for beds. The house was large, more than a dozen rooms with considerable outbuildings. It was next to Sailly's home, which was also an artillery billet. The officers were careful not to destroy any of the furnishings that had been left behind. Some of the valuables had been buried in the backyard garden. Major Francis Duncan writes

> The guns had started late due to the bad roads and weren't available to go into position until the 9th of September. Captain King, RA was separated from his company and sent to the two 8 inch siege mortars. Captains Maxwell, Wallace and Sinclair of the 4th battalion, were joined in the construction of the earthen batteries by J. Addams the commander of a company from the 10th battalion, who worked day and night to prepare for the battle.[33]

From these locations the heavier siege guns could not only hit the American forts, they could also menace Macdonough's anchored fleet, which looked like decoy ducks on a pond. The American commodore was forced to weigh anchors and reposition his entire fleet further to the southeast. Macomb watched with dread. He had just lost the ability to bombard the British army with naval artillery. Macdonough was also out of range of the friendly guns at Fort Scott. The simple move of establishing the Royal Artillery had split the American defensive plan without a shot being fired. It was now going to be two separate battles. Neither navy could be struck by, nor could they strike, the other side's army. Even though the civilian spectators, who lined the northern shore of the bay and spread blankets to picnic, could see much of the combined battle, they did not realize that the land and water conflicts were no longer connected.

To most civilians, though, the threat to their homes and property was more than they could stand. Dr. Beaumont described the scene in the village:

> The people are all frightened nearly out—out, did I say? rather into their wits—if they have any—moving everything off—under the expectation that all will be burnt or destroyed—poor souls. many of them love & uphold the British—censure & condemn our own Government—complaining they have no protection—neither will they take up arms to defend themselves—Indeed I pity their depravedty—but don't care much for their losses—if they should maintain, any.[34]

While the town smoked and the citizens scrambled to safety from the center, which had become a battlefield, Royal Artillery battery number one, across the river from Fort Brown, was nearly finished. An earthen pit half the size of a football field, and surrounded by a spoil which now reached twenty feet, was receiving the wagons containing the Congreve rocket launchers. Light gray, wooden "A" frames would be up by morning, and on the 10th the "rockets red glare," which would be commemorated in the American national anthem on September 13, 1814, in Baltimore, would ignite the defenses of Plattsburgh. Captain George McGlassin asked General Macomb for permission to attack the construction party. He was wished well by the commander. At two in the morning McGlassin put his plan into operation. A company of fifty men crept to the water's edge below Fort Brown. Within the British redoubt there were three hundred men working by campfire light. McGlassin's men had removed the flints from their rifles to prevent anyone from accidentally firing and thereby giving away their approach. Surprise was all-important. A pitched battle would be disastrous for the outnumbered American party. They waded across the Saranac River tied together with ropes, the dark, cold current tugging them downstream. Soaking wet, the men gathered at the stream edge and fixed bayonets. The captain split the detachment into two parties, to come in over the dirt revetments from either side. Terror was their tactic and noise the vehicle. With the first shout coming from McGlassin, "on the front and rear," the screaming Yankee soldiers rushed in, pointing and sticking. Laboring in the middle of the night, the work party was virtually unarmed except for shovels and picks. Disoriented, the three hundred redcoats ran for their lives, convinced that they were the centerpiece of a counterattack. McGlassin's men disabled the rockets with charges and blew up the launchers. He reported to Macomb that he had accomplished his mission and not lost a man. It took until the 11th to repair the damage. The following story enlivens this heroic incident:

A gentle man of Plattsburgh, some years ago, when visiting Canada was introduced to an elderly English Officer; and, on the officer's learning that he was from Plattsburgh, he inquired if he lived there at the time of the Battle, and if he knew the name of the officer who led the party that stormed the battery on the night of the 10th. The gentleman replied, that he was in Plattsburgh at the time of the battle, and that the officer that led the storming party he had named was McGlassin. "Will you be so good as to tell me," asked the officer, "what number of men he had with him?" "About sixty, I believe," replied the gentleman. The officer looked much astonished, and at last said, "Well sir, I was the officer in command of that battery, and I would give more to see McGlassin than any man in the world. It was the most complete thing," said he, "I ever saw or heard of, for we were quietly in our positions when the words, 'Charge the Front and Rear,' broke the death-like stillness as if a voice from the air had screamed, the men ran like mad. I tried my utmost, in the confusion, to bring them to some order, but without success for some time; at last I found a body charging in fine style. I placed myself at their head and, anxious to repulse the attack, urged them forward with all the energy I possessed, when, taking a more anxious look at them, to see what ones had stood firm in the surprise, behold!! they were a lot of damned Yankees who had charged up another way, and I was leading them. Then," said he, "was my time to run. Where my men had gone no one knew. But I rushed, pell-mell into the woods over logs, into the mud and water; then a straddle of some stump; then against a tree; over stones and into holes—up and down, sometimes on one end and sometimes on the other. I arrived in camp about the worst bruised, the worst scratched, the sorest and most frightened individual you ever saw. If you ever," said he, shaking the gentleman from Plattsburg by the hand, "meet Mr. McGlassin, give him my compliments and tell him that was the most gallant thing accomplished by any man."[35]

On the same night, September 10, Macomb allowed some suspected civilian spies housed in the American camp to overhear a false report that Izard's army was nearby and the woods contained ten thousand concealed militia, with more due the next day. After these suspicious fellows were observed crossing the river to the British side there was hope that the news might cause Prevost to be cautious. However, Sir George was well aware of Izard's location and so discounted the information. His spy network was very reliable throughout the campaign, due to the number of New Yorkers who were playing both sides of the border.

The lie turned out to be somewhat self-fulfilling. Shortly after the hoax was set, Major General Sam Strong, commanding general of the Vermont militia, strolled into Macomb's headquarters. He told Alexander Macomb that he would have twenty-five hundred of his "Green Mountain Boys" near Pike's cantonment by morning. Macomb was overcome with emotion. He plucked a sprig of pine from a nearby tree and placed it in Strong's hat as a mark of zeal shown by his men, who volunteered to serve outside their home state, against the desire of Governor Chittenden. Strong told Macomb several tales of his journey. At Horatio Seymour's law office in Middlebury Vermont, he said, men and boys worked all night making cartridges. Afraid of using candles, they worked in the dark and the next morning the floor was blackened with powder, leading one to exclaim: "We Certainly Have Been In More Danger Here To Night Than Any Of Our Volunteers Will Be In Plattsburgh." He also told about a Vermonter from one of his lakeside hamlets:

> He started for the lake shore, his zeal pushing him ahead of his companions, "Come on boys, lets kill some red coats," he shouted. Apparently he was scared by his own cry. Soon he began to hear heavy firing in the direction of Plattsburgh, across the water of the lake. Those whom he had outstripped met him in rapid retreat toward home. He explained breathlessly that, he had on his best Sunday shoes and his wife would feel dreadfully if he spoilt them, so he was going back to change. "I will catch you up."[36]

The man was not seen again in the ranks of the courageous Vermont militia. By early the next morning the Green Mountain Boys, successors of Ethan Allen's heroes, were on the ramparts of the peninsula. Benjah Phelps takes up the story:

> The British tried to get across in Plattsburgh, but they couldn't. Why, you see, all the Vermont milishy was there. I remember Uncle Colonel Tim Allen set in the grist-mill winder. He had a long rifle. The barrel was five feet long. The river was about 80 rods wide there. There he set in the winder and killed every soldier that come down for water. That was the morning when they was gittin breakfast. Colonel Tim stayed right there until he killed nine or ten of em before they stopped comin down.[37]

The morning of September 11 would prove to be more horrific than expected.

CHAPTER 5

What ought to be done, I know only too well. What is going to be done, only the gods know.

—Major General Gerhard von Sharnhorst

Late on September 9, Downie was determined to cooperate as best he could and sent Prevost a battle plan that could be disrupted only by the weather. "It is my intention to weigh and proceed from this anchorage about midnight in the expectation of rounding into the bay of Plattsburgh about dawn of day and commencing an immediate attack on the enemy, if they shall be found anchored in a position that will offer any chance of success. I rely on any assistance you can afford the squadron." It was however, not until late evening of the 10th before the wind swung around from the north and the anchors were pulled out of the mud off Rouses Point. Inky darkness greeted George Downie, the thirty-three-year-old captain of the Royal Navy frigate, when he gave in to Prevost's urging and set his flotilla into motion up Lake Champlain. As Yankee water passed under the black keel, the English commodore, who had never been south on Lake Champlain before, felt confident. The clouds blocked the stars and moon, leaving only a bobbing daisy chain of yellow lamp light as the Royal Navy fleet plowed south into history.

A red glowing sky greeted Commodore Thomas Macdonough, the twenty-eight-year-old commander of the little American fleet, early on the morning of September 11, 1814, standing on the quarterdeck of the *Saratoga*. He heard Downie's juggernaut scale her guns before he could see her. It reminded him of the old salt saying, "red sky in the morning, sailors' warning." But this time the hazard was not the weather. And that morning there was no need for his heavy brass-fitted telescope to find the British: they were all too close. Two miles north by east, around the point of land called Cumberland Head, as the rising sun silhouetted the black tops of their mastheads, yards spread and hung with puffy blankets of canvas, looming above the tree tops. Ominous, the tallest yardarms informed him that *Confiance*, Macdonough's nemesis, was all too real. He had read many reports about her birth and, from the height of her contraband mainmast, he could tell she was a giant. Sir George and his staff, eating breakfast together, were not in a position to see the Royal Navy arrive. Earlier, the pickets reported the sound of naval gunfire coming from the northeast. Rousing the British army, Sir George directed the brigades of Robinson and Powers to prepare to move and left Brisbane's to finish breakfast. The apparent inactivity of the British army brigade directly in front of the American position was expected to calm the alarm set off by the Royal Navy guns on the lake. That scaling of guns meant that Downie was coming, and the breakfast table talk was consumed by the refinement of the land battle preparations.

At first there was just *Confiance*, but within minutes other masts appeared on the horizon; by 7 A.M. there was a mass of naked pines scratching the damp dawn sky, beyond the finger of land that separated the combatants. Downie had started the passage with the fleet all in a bunch. The winds had separated the ships from the gunboats. All six principal ships, *Confiance*, *Linnet*, *Chub*, *Finch*, and the sloops *Icicle* and *Canada*, the latter two support vessels, dropped anchor above the point in the channel between Grand Island, Vermont, and the New York shore. They were waiting for the eleven galleys to catch up. Each of the gunboats was powered by a single lateen sail that looked like half a handkerchief, as the oarsmen saved their strength for the coming battle. Some of the sixty-three-foot-long wooden craft, which had once had pithy names like *Bloodletter, Blisterer, Deathdealer,* and *Dumbfounder,* were now more conventionally named for the historic battle. They bore names like *Prevost, Brock, Yeo,* and *Wellington.* Mounting a single twenty-four-pound cannon in the nose, which would be held until the last moment, then touched off at near water level directly into the pine planking from only yards away, the galley would punch great holes to let in the shimmering lake water. Then, cutlasses in hand, the crew would board like pirates and subdue the crew.

Downie Gets His First Look

While the other Royal Navy officers had fought on the lake and were familiar with the cut of the American ships, Downie was not. While the crew of *Confiance* stoked up the furnace and began to cook cannonballs, Downie and his sailing master, Bryden, took the gig and went to reconnoiter.[1] Bobbing around the point, Downie could not believe his good fortune. Just as Sir George had said, the entire American fleet was anchored and outside the supporting range of their own field artillery on the southern beach. His spyglass gave him a close-up view of the four enemy vessels. At the head of the line, which ran nearly north, was *Eagle,* her miniature deck crammed with twenty guns. From the glistening paint he could see she was new. Less than two hundred yards south was *Saratoga,* a name he had learned from his history books in school and probably the destination of Sir George Prevost's army. If he was successful that day on water, both the name of the ship and the old battlefield would take on new meaning. *Saratoga* was not as big as he had been led to believe, but at twenty-six carronades and cannon, she could do a great deal of damage within her limited range. Further along the straight line was the *Ticonderoga,* not just a ship of seventeen guns, but the name of his next port of call on the lake, where both British and American history had been written on previous military expeditions. Lastly, there was tiny *Preble,* whose eleven guns did not supply much of an anchor for his enemy's fighting line, although the ship was sufficient to maintain continuity with the tip of Crab Island and prevented him from sailing around the southern end. At the very edge, on the pale sand beach of the overgrown island, were two squat guns on naval carriages which appeared to be abandoned. Quick arithmetic told him that only a total of thirty-seven of the seventy-four guns could fire at once since the port-side guns were facing away. The flotilla at anchor posed little danger, he thought. The range of the American carronades meant that his plan would simply keep the fleet outside the five-hundred-yard marker. From a position of safety, he would bombard with broadsides until the Americans, unable to retaliate or maneuver, were shattered into matchsticks. Through his glass, he could also see that the Yankee gunboats lingered near the far shore. They were armed with cannon, but slow to close and more than likely reluctant to approach. He disregarded them as a threat. What made this battle so uneven was that the few twenty-four-pounders of the Americans were not equal to the new Congreve long guns on *Confiance.* Even if the Americans got too close, Downie's vessels were also armed with smashers. The Royal Navy generally did not count carronades because of their limited use and had them mounted in the bow and stern for employment when maneuvering in close. They were mounted not on wheels, but on slides that swung 180 degrees on a pin at the front of the carriage, making the guns much easier to aim. But although carronades were not highly valued in the Royal Navy, George Downie had great respect for the damage they could cause. After all, they were a British invention.

In addition to the standoff distance he planned, Downie would not anchor at first, but lead his ships in a race-track pattern before the Yankees, around the top of the bay. Firing the guns from one side and then the other as they reversed field would allow him to rest the crews and the guns, giving the gun captains time to restore any battle damage on the return trip. Range would not be a problem, he could shoot the length and breadth of the bay and, when the opposing navy was sunk, he would bear down on the American army, snug in their dirt forts, and reduce them to dust. It was all within his reach. The boast that he could defeat the entire American fleet with just his flagship alone was certainly true. It would make entertaining reading back in the London newspapers.

The Winds Are Everything

The naval tactics of the day were complex because of the wind. It was true that fleets often could see each other, but not engage in battle because the winds were unfavorable. This hound and hare chase could go on for days and lead commanders across seas, only to end in a loss of contact. Today, and indeed since the days of steam-powered ships, the battle formation often consists of big boats in the middle and little boats around the outside. The big boats fire over the horizon with any variety of weapons, while the little boats screen the big boats with their bodies. This no doubt is an oversimplification. But, in any case, in the days of wooden ships and iron men, things were very different. Then, the tactic was to subdue the enemy vessel by the cataclysmic capacity of a cannonade, deafen the enemy crew with noise, and frighten them with fire and blast, from only feet away if possible, before boarding. Then you would finish it all off with hand-to-hand combat. The sheer size of the cannonballs screaming down the gun deck and the terror of crushing yardarms, as big as tree trunks, falling on the crew, brought many a battle to a quick surrender. And the infliction of terrible ripping wounds on the ship was often followed by death from drowning. It is easy to see why men had to be pressed into service.

The British were the preeminent naval warriors of the day. All other navies copied their tactics. Admiral Lord Nelson rewrote the manual in his lifetime, which ended at Trafalgar in 1805. He had many great victories. At Copenhagen in 1801 he fought the Danes, who were at anchor, sending his ships up the channel, racking the enemy with murderous fire as they went. Later, when fighting on the open sea, he changed from the conventional attack of ships running in parallel lines to what he called crossing the "T." Attacking in two or more lines perpendicular to the enemy, who was in the traditional line-ahead formation, he would cut the line in several places and destroy the continuity of the enemy's firepower. It took a steady hand to maintain the approach. The enemy could only shoot at the prow and sails, the narrowest of silhouettes, but did so with dozens of guns at one time, while the British ship could only use the carronades in the bow to defend herself on the long "run in." After breaking through, and firing all guns on both sides at very close range, he still maintained his vessels' fire power in shortened lines, one supporting the other. Then he wheeled and took on the disrupted enemy formation, now smashed and burning.[2] Downie was a child of the Nelson school of naval tactics and had much to choose from in his "shot locker."

THE ROYAL NAVY FLOTILLA COILS

As his boat crew pulled him back around the point, Downie had a chance to see his own force gathered together at anchor. He had never seen it all at once before and, from the low angle of the gig, it was indeed formidable. Of course, *Confiance* caught his eye, with the sun shining brightly on her newly painted side. "He had a choice of color," said Mr. Simons, "black with white or deep yellow with black trim." He at once thought of Nelson's yellow-ochre *Victory,* a golden man-of-war, but perhaps too much for a frigate, which did not quite fit into the lowest rate for a real warship.[3] He noticed that the gun captains had run out the cannons, whose blunt noses formed a solid line of black, dotting the white band that ran from stem to stern on her black shiny hull. The barrels were bronze, but painted with a mixture of coal tar and saltwater to protect them from the corrosion of sea spray and foul weather. He had also painted the cannons this way because, if they had gone untreated, Yeo might have wanted him to have them polished.[4] Downie's other ships looked grand, clustered together and painted all in black, a ploy devised by the Royal Navy to make the vessels appear small and attackable. The last of the gunboats were now moored together ahead of the line, at the tip of the point, nearly within sight of the enemy. He could see that his order to feed the men was being carried out; the smell of breakfast filled the heavy air close to the water.

At sea, because of the gnawing grip of hunger, the crew always looked forward to breakfast, in fact to any meal. The Royal Navy food, salt pork and biscuits, was filling but not inviting. It was often accompanied by weevils, dead and alive, and the crew ate simply to live. Here, on an inland lake, fresh meat, fish, and vegetables were standard. The cooks, known as "idlers" since they did not man a station or watch, were safe from the wrath of the crew. And they were not the only idlers: carpenters, stewards, and cabin boys, in addition to women, filled out that complement. Women aboard ship were often officers' wives or the wives of some of the leading crew members. They were expected to assist with the chores aboard. The enlisted wives helped with laundry, sail mending, cooking, and cleaning. Officers' wives tended the sick and acted as chaplains when an Anglican priest was not available, or wrote letters for the ordinary seamen. There were only a few women as a rule, and they were all below this day preparing the infirmary. Wounded were cleared from the decks and taken below, where they were safe from gunfire and falling objects. Down below the waterline, in dark corners of the cockpit where the sun never shone, sailcloth was laid out for beds, and for shrouds, if necessary.

Puffed up with confidence after viewing both combatant fleets, the youthful Downie sat down in his cabin with his captains. Daniel Pring, his second-in-command, captain of *Linnet,* was not afraid of the Americans and had nearly put an end to their fleet the summer before. He had ranged the lake and been with Lieutenant Colonel Murray's raid in Cumberland Bay. Wary of the waters, he wished he had been taken on the ride with Downie, but it was up to him to make the fleet ready before the battle. Lieutenant James McGhie captained *Chub,* which was a cutter, very fast but short on firepower. Lieutenant William Hicks was the skipper of *Finch,* the smallest of all and, like *Chub,* a captured American warship. Downie took a chart and drew in the positions of the American navy and their shore battery at Crab Island and Fort Scott. He told them that the Royal Artillery was not going to be able to help, but neither could the American batteries. This was going to be a two-phased attack. The primary mission was the destruction of the American fleet. He would then take the Royal Navy in as close as possible to provide cannon fire support to the British army attacking the peninsula. He told Pring that, because of his knowledge of the shoals, it was up to him to position the line of ships for bombardment of the shore. He gave the only chart to Pring. Downie then read a message from Sir George that he had received on the 9th, while at Little Chazy. There, *Confiance* had stopped to take on the remainder of the crew and discharge some of the carpenters. Prevost wrote:

> I am happy to inform you that I find from deserters who have come over from the enemy that the American fleet is inefficiently manned, and that a few days ago after the arrival of the new brig [Eagle] they sent on shore for the prisoners of all descriptions in charge of the provost to make up a crew for the vessel."[5]

The message buoyed the spirits of the British captains, which had been running a little low as they observed the state of the flagship and her army crew. On board *Confiance,* impressions of her formidability faded, to a trained eye. Earlier, Downie had described the plan of attack from the intelligence gained on the 9th. In the communiqué to Sir George he laid it all out, never having seen Cumberland Bay:

> Should the enemy be attacked at anchor, it is the intention of the senior officers to confine the attack to their large ship, and the smaller vessels that may be moored on the windward side of her—Linnet, Chub and Finch—to go down in line abreast with the Confiance: the first division of gun boats on the opposite beam of the Confiance, and the second on the beam of the Finch.

THE ROYAL NAVY'S BATTLE PLAN

Now Downie finalized the instructions. The visit to view the enemy had enhanced the intelligence reports and served to confirm his earlier plan, with the exception of the role of *Finch. Chub* and *Linnet* would enter the bay abreast of *Confiance* and the three would attack the head of the line, *Eagle,* and broadside *Saratoga* as they passed by, out of American range. The three would make a turn about to starboard, exposing their starboard guns, and start back up the line. *Chub* and *Linnet* would concentrate on the destruction of the American brig, *Eagle,* while *Confiance* would continue across the upper bay, parallel to the American *Saratoga* and finish her off. *Finch* would be at the tail end, splitting off on the run in, and attack the American *Preble,* at the south end of the line, assisted by the British gunboats. Lieutenant Hicks would proceed with the gunboats and board *Ticonderoga.* Downie was confident that the first and second passes would do enough damage to allow the flotilla to anchor close in, so that his first three ships could complete the job of killing first *Eagle,* then *Saratoga,* from a standing position. From there, all the British naval guns could then reach *Ticonderoga,* if she had not already been taken by *Finch.*[6]

While the skippers returned to their commands, Commodore Downie inspected the progress of the oven. It was rare to have a furnace on deck to broil cannonballs in the Royal Navy, since fire was a prime danger on a wooden ship. But frigates were known to carry them. Since they were limited in armament, the hotshot gave them a capability that ships of the line in rates one, two, and three did not need, since they could carry as many as 120 guns. Battle damage inflicted by solid cannonballs rarely sank a vessel. It was nearly impossible at sea to punch holes in the hull below the water line that would be significant enough to endanger the survival of large vessels. The intended result of cannonballs was to dismount guns; kill, wound, or terrify the crew; and impair the running gear. If the sails, masts, spars, or rudder could be shot away, the ship must surrender. In addition to solid shot, the French had used hollow cannonballs with gunpowder inside, which was common to field artillery. Since these cannonballs were intended to fragment above the enemy and cause personnel casualties, they were not really suited for a moving target as small as a ship. The Royal Navy considered the hollow cannonballs too dangerous and attributed the defeat of the French at the battle of the Nile to their use. The hot shot, just as it did on land, could add another horror to war on the sea. A sizzling cannonball wedged into the structure could turn a vessel into an inferno. When hot shot hit, crew would have to abandon the guns and repeatedly douse the area hit with buckets of water or attempt to pry the shot loose and roll it overboard. If the fire took hold, the ship would soon be uninhabitable.[7]

THE BATTLE OF LAKE CHAMPLAIN, SEPTEMBER 11, 1814

At nearly 8 A.M. Downie brought the Royal Navy into harm's way, around the point and out of the lake. *Icicle* and *Canada* were the only vessels left behind. In their holds were supplies for the fleet, timbers to repair battle damage, and medicine to treat the wounded. *Confiance* hugged the shoreline and turned the corner with sails puffed out, driving the big ship at top speed, perhaps three knots. She needed to keep up with *Chub* and *Linnet,* which were quicker craft and abreast on her port side. Downie did not want to get too far behind after the turn, but planned to pass parallel to the Americans, in ships-in-trail formation, following *Chub* and *Linnet,* who were just off his bow and racing at full speed. The north wind kicked up the waves to white caps and the crews were sprayed as the bow bit in and tossed the water over the gun deck. Each ship would first deliver a broadside into *Saratoga* and then one into *Eagle,* before turning 180 degrees for the return bout. Careful to stay outside the range of the American carronades, each heeled over on the starboard as they plowed in a straight line nearly north by northeast. The British *Finch* lay behind. On either side was a horde of gunboats, or *bateaux*, since they were crewed mainly by French Canadians. *Finch* detached from the Royal Navy flotilla and headed straight for *Preble,* engaging her before the others hit their marks. Faster than the gunboats, *Finch* outreached the oarsmen, who were fatiguing. The long oars, or "sweeps," were fifteen feet in length and weighed fifty pounds. Even the drum, which beat out the pace, was beginning to slow after half a mile.

A young Teddy Roosevelt, author of *The Naval War of 1812*, describes the harrowing moment:

> As the English squadron stood bravely in, young Macdonough, who feared his foes not at all, but his God a great deal, Knelt for a moment, with his officers on the quarter deck; 'Stir up Thy strength O Lord, for Thou givest not always the battle to the strong, but can save by many or by few.' Then ensued a few minutes of perfect quiet, the men waiting with grim expectancy for the opening of the fight.[8]

A COORDINATED ATTACK: THE BRITISH ARMY MOVES

Prevost stood outside the Delord house, beside his guns, and watched the first naval cannonade, as did the civilian spectators all along the northern shore of the bay. The regimental bands on both sides began to play the men into battle, but were nearly drowned out by the roar of the field artillery. All six batteries opened up on the American lines at once, which added to the cacophony of the naval guns across the water. The rocket battery, which McGlassin had disrupted the night before, was in full glory. Their six- and ten-pound rockets lit the sky with contrails that took the breath away from the American infantry, who were about to receive them. Fired in salvo, the "woosh" could be heard above the guns. Twenty at once passed over the river and several impacted against the walls of the bridge blockhouse on the "first go." The house was set on fire and the invalids inside were killed. With the guns came a white smoke that consumed both the land and lake within minutes. The smoke provided an ominous sign that the English commodore was the first to notice. It hung in the air, swirled a bit, but did not dissipate. It obscured targets on both land and water, but more than that, it denied the British both speed and control of all their ships. No one on either side in the land battle paid the smoke any mind except the gunners at Fort Brown, for whom the smoke plagued their target acquisition. They could not see the red coats advancing, but were sure they were and continued to match the Royal Artillery round for round. Major General Brisbane was a little slow to get his men from breakfast, thinking that perhaps this day would be like the previous four, when they waited for the Navy, who never showed. But his troops were not critical to the plan at that moment. Their job was to put up a front and pretend to be the entire land force. They began to harass the American lines with musket fire, while bagpipes rent the air and men marched about in block formations, pretending to prepare for another frontal assault. Major Generals Robinson and Powers had combined into one column again and were about to strike out for the ford at Pike's cantonment, three miles upstream. With the naval battle going on loudly in the bay, the artillery keeping the American heads down in their trenches, and Brisbane parading, Macomb would be too busy to look for the other brigades. The battle was becoming a slugfest of land and sea artillery.

The noise of cannon was also of great tactical effect. One of the main criticisms leveled against light guns was that their noise failed to terrify the enemy, whereas the eight-pounder and, particularly, the twelve-pounder made a very frightening noise. Their effect in battle was materially enhanced by this, so it should not be assumed that the importance of firepower in Napoleonic battles could be measured entirely in terms of the number of casualties produced. Gunfire also spread confusion and hesitation in the enemy ranks by its intrusion on morale, especially in the case of howitzer fire, according to Paddy Griffith of the Royal Military Academy at Sandhurst, who studied the artillery used in this battle.[9]

FATE STEPS IN

The renowned military historian, Prussian General Carl von Clausewitz, wrote of his experience fighting Napoleon, "No plan ever survives the presence of the enemy."[10] At Plattsburgh, the enemy was found to be in the "direction of the wind." Just when the wind was needed most by the British aggressor to maintain separation between the two fleets, it failed them, and baffled, they fell away. With only swirls to flutter his canvas, which flapped like wash on a laundry line, Downie's plan fell to nothing. Unable to steer without the push of the wind, his three leading men-of-war drifted toward the motionless American naval line. Everything changed when the Royal Navy had to stop the progress of their attack and anchor three hundred yards in front of Macdonough's floating gun platforms.

The first gun fired by the Americans was sighted by Commodore Macdonough himself. Nearly on his knees, chin just above the breech of the short, fat, black iron tube, he waited until he had the prow of the oncoming *Confiance* resting above the front blade sight. His gun crew stood by breathless, the master gunner holding the smoldering match above the commodore's head. Macdonough cried "fire" and stepped aside. The fuse sputtered in the goose quill filled with powder, stuck in the touch hole, and set off the main charge. The twenty-four-pound cannonball emerged from the fiery blast of the muzzle, burst out of a white cloud of smoke, and went down range. According to British reports, the ball struck the bow of the flagship and careened along the deck, killing and wounding several British sailors and destroying the wheel. Not only did the remainder of the guns follow the captain's lead, but the entire American fleet opened up with a fusillade on the now precarious Royal Navy formation. In clearing the decks for action, the chicken coops on the American flagship were thrown overboard and the poultry left to run free on the deck. Startled by the report of the opening guns, a young rooster flew into the rigging, flapped its wings, and crowed. The men gave three cheers and considered the little incident a happy omen of the battle to come.

Captain Pring was quick to return the fire for his comrade, as *Linnet* drifted by, destined, she hoped, for her assigned station opposite *Eagle*. While cannonballs were indeed destructive anywhere, here on the lake they were more so. While at sea the guns were designed to take on ships made of oak, which quickly seasoned in the salt air and turned to a near-iron. All the vessels in this battle looked like ships of the line but were not. On Lake Champlain, ships were mostly constructed of unseasoned, soft pine planks seven inches thick, which were easy to saw and warp into shape. The effect of cannon was therefore much more devastating. Pring's shot splintered everything in its path and kept going right out the other side.

Before dropping anchor he poured a full broadside into *Eagle*. The crew became bewildered by the noise, and shocked by the sheer power of the shot. All the British ships had loaded double shot for their first round, sending two cannonballs with each blast from the port side guns. That would have been twenty rounds, counting the carronades in the prow and stern, that raked the eighty-five-foot-long hull and gun deck. The captain of *Eagle*, Lieutenant Henley, was wounded, along with much of the crew.

Plodding before the thin wind, *Confiance* stopped and anchored. It was her turn to fire from her array of ordnance, the most powerful afloat in the bay. *Saratoga* had allowed *Confiance* to close in without inhibiting her after Macdonough's first salvo. The uninjured members of the crew were taking the wounded below and busy clearing the deck of battle debris from the attack of the passing *Linnet*. Even though the advantage of long-range gunfire was lost, the sheer power of the Congreve cannon combined with the four carronades on *Confiance*'s upper deck was formidable. Downie had held his fire, even after the severe racking he had taken, ensuring that his ship was secure before fighting. He dropped the anchors and had them tied on with springs (lines), which were laid out by men in rowboats, in spite of the fire all around. George Downie stood behind his favorite gun, and prepared to send a broadside into the *Saratoga*.

BATTERING AT CLOSE RANGE

The effect of the double-shotted guns was terrible. The *Saratoga* trembled to her very keel, tilting sideways against her anchors. Nearly 40 of her crew's 250 were disabled or killed, including her first lieutenant, Peter Gamble, who was killed outright as he sighted a bow gun. He was kneeling down, checking the sights on the rear of the massive barrel, when a shot entered the open gun port, split the wooden quoin (a gun-elevating wedge, pronounced as "coin"), and drove a portion of it against Gamble's side, nearly cutting him in half. It is said that the survivors, caught up in the maelstrom on the open deck, carried on the fight with undiminished energy.

Macdonough himself worked like a common sailor, pointing and running a gun up into firing position. When a large naval cannon was fired, the cannonball went flying and the two-thousand-pound mass of bronze and wood went rolling backwards. Such cannons had no recoil mechanisms at that time to absorb the shock; the gun would come careening out of position and was arrested finally by restraining ropes attached to blocks in the deck, near the rail.[11]

On board the *Saratoga,* the full weight of the cannon was caught a dozen feet from the bulkhead by the restraining ropes. The bore was swabbed out with water to extinguish any remaining fragments of powder that might still be burning. A powder monkey, a light-weight sailor or boy who had run to the magazine below, brought the powder bag, which was rammed in first. The cannonball, taken from a stack in the center of the gun deck, was carried to the muzzle and pushed in with a rammer. In the meantime, the gunner would have replaced the goose quill primer. It took the crew of ten to get the gun, which rested on stout little wheels, back into position. With the gun fully forward, the muzzle stuck out through the bulkhead and cleared the side of the ship. When the cannon was fired, the fiery muzzle blast could ignite nearby wood. A fully fit and trained crew could fire the massive gun, which weighed more than two tons, three times in two minutes, if not distracted or reduced in number. That morning, in the heat of battle, one round in two minutes was the standard. Commands from above ceased now that both fleets were at anchor and gun captains fired to their front at their own pace. Coordinated firing at "one go," a true broadside, was not recommended, since the shock could break the spine of the ship.

A British cannonball from the first broadside of the *Confiance* split in two a spanker boom high up in the rigging of the *Saratoga,* the severed piece falling across Macdonough's shoulders and striking him senseless for several minutes. As he lay on the deck, the crew rushed to his aid. They picked him up and began to carry him to the safety of the medical station in the hold. Coming back to his senses before the men could carry him away, Macdonough had them put him down near to where he fell. He pushed them aside, stood unsupported, and sent them back into the fight. He then returned to his gun, which had been neglected during his brief absence. Gathering his reduced gun crew, he and the men began the wearying work again amid the fire, smoke, and noise. Over the deafening sound, only shouts could gain the attention of the man next to Macdonough. There was no longer a plan on either side; it was gun to gun, ship to ship. Well within the danger zone, Macdonough witnessed his ship being shot to pieces by the guns of the British frigate. Further along the gun deck was Midshipman Bellamy, a young officer who had shown much promise. Captain Macdonough was watching Bellamy's gun crew in action when a cannonball entered the ship, ricocheted off the metal gun barrel, and severed young Bellamy's head. The skull flew along the deck and hit Macdonough full in the face with such force that it knocked him to the opposing rail of his ship. Stunned again, he was missed by a cannonball that came careening along the deck, taking down a whole row of sailors. The crewmen wore no helmets or body armor. Only the officers wore shoes. The effect of the bouncing, raging, rolling cannonball was profound. History of that time is full of stories where men stuck a foot out to stop a nearly spent ball, only to have the foot taken off at the ankle. The commodore and his soldiers-turned-sailors fought on, surrounded by dead, wounded, debris, and hellfire.

LEADERLESS

The Americans were giving nearly as good as they got. "The firing was terrific," according to Julius Hubbell, "fairly shaking the ground, and so rapid that it seemed to be one continuous roar, intermingled with spiteful flashing from the mouths of the guns, and dense clouds of smoke soon hung over the two fleets."[12] Within fifteen minutes of the opening engagement, Downie found it necessary to assume the aiming of one of his big Congreve guns. A cannonball from *Saratoga* sought revenge. It struck the muzzle of Downie's gun and the force of the blow ripped the gun barrel, which weighed twenty-five hundred pounds, out of the wooden carriage. The tube flipped up on end, like a coin in the air, and was caught by Downie in the center of his chest. The two went to the deck together, the life crushed out of the unlucky commander of the Royal Navy fleet, fifteen minutes after the onslaught had begun. Downie was taken below by his gun crew to the makeshift infirmary, where it was found that the skin was not broken, but that a black and blue mark the size of a dinner plate was over Downie's heart. His waistcoat pocket watch had stopped at the precise moment of his death. The British flotilla was now leaderless.[13] Lieutenant Henry Robertson took command of the flagship but not the flag. He was unable to send word to Captain Daniel Pring of the death of the commodore. Not only had the captain's gig been shot away from the davits during the action, but in the confusion of battle, the signal book had been lost.

Most of the casualties were from splinters of all sizes. While missiles smashed men and ships, most casualties were the result of shrapnel, not of metal but of wood. A twenty-four-pound cannonball could penetrate three feet of wood at four hundred yards and this encounter was much closer. Giant splinters pierced the smoke-filled air, sliced through human flesh or stuck like untipped arrows. Those impaled usually bled to death, arteries sliced through. Captain Alexander Anderson, 1st battalion of the Royal Marines, was a fatality. The decks truly ran red with the blood, the loyal crews slipping barefoot at their stations, fighting blindly in the smoke and fire. There was a ship's doctor on *Confiance,* who with the help of the women on board applied tourniquets and bandages to stop the bleeding by lantern light in the bottom of the ship.

FLAWED GUN

Surprisingly, after the first horrific broadside from the British frigate, little personal injury was done on the American side. This was due, according to gun expert Captain Adrian Caruana, to the main gun of the *Confiance*:

> While Sir William Congreve was a brilliant ordnance inventor, he erroneously believed that the amount of the metal packed into the solid breach of the barrel would make the projectile go further. It did not. What it did do was to unbalance the gun so that too much weight was in the breech end. The gun swings freely from the trunnions, or stubby metal arms that stick out of the side of the barrel on either side and are used to attach the barrel to the carriage. The quoin is a wooden wedge which is stuck under the breech and shoved in against the frame of the carriage a little at a time. Its function is to elevate or depress the muzzle of the barrel and therefore effect the range of the projectile. The quoin is not fixed and is the responsibility of the gunner when directed by the gun captain, a midshipman or officer, to make a correction in the strike of the cannonball. The new twenty-four-pounder, Congreve six-foot, seven-inch-long gun jumped and recoiled when fired. The unbalanced breech of the barrel then allowed the quoin to move out slightly with each firing. Since the crew, who were green (army infantry as well), under fire for the first time, wounded, short handed, and eventually unsupervised due to the loss of leaders, failed to reset the quoin, thinking that since the target *[Saratoga]* was not moving, the gun need not be resighted. The result was that the gun continued to elevate and crept upwards on its own, shot after shot.[14]

Caruana's account explains why the entire rigging and masts of the American flagship were shot away, while the hull and main deck received no further damage after the initial broadside. The crew was saved from further direct fire; however, that did not reduce the casualties, since falling sail and split masts continued to maim. The red hot cannonballs appeared among the succeeding waves of fire from *Confiance.* Twice, the crew of Macdonough's ship had to break away from their artillery duties and concentrate on putting out the fires. The smoldering missiles set the port bulkhead ablaze, after they had passed through the starboard planking just above the waterline.

As the contest went on, the gunfire gradually decreased in severity. The guns were becoming disabled, one by one. The novice crews on both sides were the cause. Many officers were wounded and taken below. The fledgling seamen on the American ships overloaded the carronades, a gun not designed for double shot. A plugged barrel burst in a horrendous explosion, wounding the crew. Others, overwhelmed by the chaos of battle, crammed guns with shot until the last cannonball projected from the muzzle, which crippled the gun. On the *Confiance,* the confusion was even worse; after the death of her commander, some of the crew refused to resume their posts. Lieutenant Robertson, the new skipper, was able to restore order in the most heroic fashion. A frightened British gun crew loaded a cannon with double shot but forgot to precede it with powder, wrecking the gun. One gun was rammed with wadding before the powder was placed inside, thus preventing the firing of the main charge. On other British ships, haste caused a crew to recharge a gun that had not been swabbed out with water. The heat and embers fired the gun before the ball was seated, killing the loader. It was said that not a man escaped without injury from the morning's work.

At the head of the line, *Eagle* encountered both *Linnet* and *Chub.* But the American craft had some advantage, since she was moored and her fire not subject to movement. While attempting to maneuver, the *Chub* caught a broadside from ten carronades, the smashers, which ripped her gun deck asunder. Here are the words of her captain, Lieutenant James McGhie:

> When getting near enough for the carronades to the *Eagle,* the vessel I had orders to engage in support of the *Linnet* under your command, before I could choose a good situation for anchoring, my peak and throat halyards with the fore stay were shot away. This obliged me to let go an anchor in the way of the ship and brig's fire. We suffered so much from galling fire of the latter that it obliged me to strike for humanity's sake alone.[15]

There is evidence in addition to McGhie's description that *Chub* had absorbed such damage that she became uncontrollable. Her jib boom had been shot away, the head of the bowsprit was shattered, the forestay was gone, the foresail riven, half overboard and dragging, and the main boom, over the hatchway, damaged. She still spread some sail, but the throat and peak halyards were gone. As she drifted between the *Confiance* and the *Saratoga* the mainsail crashed. She provided a lull in the battle as she blocked the fire of the two flagships, slowly drifting into the American line between *Saratoga* and *Ticonderoga.* There, she was captured by Midshipman Charles Platt, who towed her to shore. Of her crew of forty-one, six were dead and sixteen wounded so badly they could not serve; not a man was untouched. There were only six men left on deck when *Chub* was taken.[16]

AMERICAN *EAGLE* DRIVEN OFF

The American *Eagle* was suffering as well. The prisoners who had been released to crew the ship were prominent among the dead and wounded. One of the three bandsmen killed was found by his wife as she brought gunpowder up from the magazine.

President Thomas Jefferson, whose prediction that the "acquisition of Canada this year will be a mere matter of marching" gained in notoriety with each successive American defeat.

President James Madison, who asked Congress to declare war on Great Britain in June 1812.

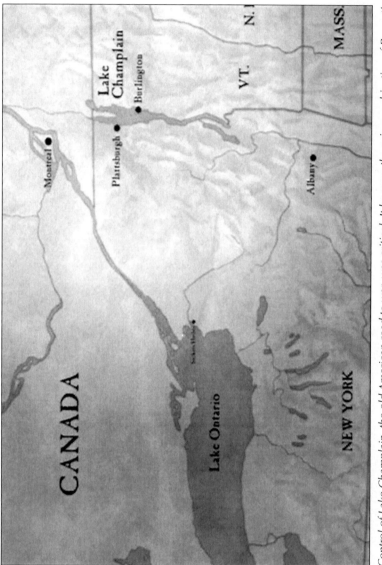

Control of Lake Champlain, the old American road to war, was critical. It became the primary objective of Prevost's invasion. A successful conquest of the lake would have given the British complete liberty of action.

Sir George Prevost, Baronet, Governor General of Canada, and commander of the British invasion force.

English newspapers in Montreal and London, always critical of Sir George Prevost, mocked the loss of his fleet on Lake Champlain and his efforts to build another expensive fleet, which he began immediately after the September 11 defeat.

"Reinforcements Allotted for North America, and the Operations Contemplated for the Employment of Them" was the title of Lord Bathurst's secret order that put Sir George Prevost's invasion force of 15,000 in motion.

The opening lines of Prevost's instructions from Downing Street. These secret orders were not revealed until 1922. The document was lost again in the depths of London's Public Record Office, until the author found a copy among the Prevost papers at Sir Christopher Prevost's villa in Portugal.

Lady Catherine Prevost, wife of Sir George, spent the rest of her life trying to clear her husband's name.

Anne Prevost, Sir George's eighteen-year-old daughter and diarist who maintained a vivid record of the changing tides of her father's fortune. The author, during research for this book, only recently discovered her diary.

Commodore Thomas Macdonough, U.S. Navy 1816.

Sir William Congreve, the original rocket scientist. The first salvo of unguided rockets destroyed an American blockhouse. A surprise to both sides.

Cameo of Sir George Prevost, done in 1805 after his victory in the West Indies.

Secretary of War John Armstrong, whose order compelled Major General Izard to lead 4,500 soldiers of his command away from Plattsburgh, just prior to the British invasion.

The Confiance under construction at Ile aux Noix, Canada. The frigate, the largest ship to ever appear on Lake Champlain, was the flagship of the Royal Navy.

Brigadier General Alexander Macomb commanded the 1,500 regular army soldiers at Plattsburgh.

General Macomb would become the commanding general of the United States Army in the 1830s.

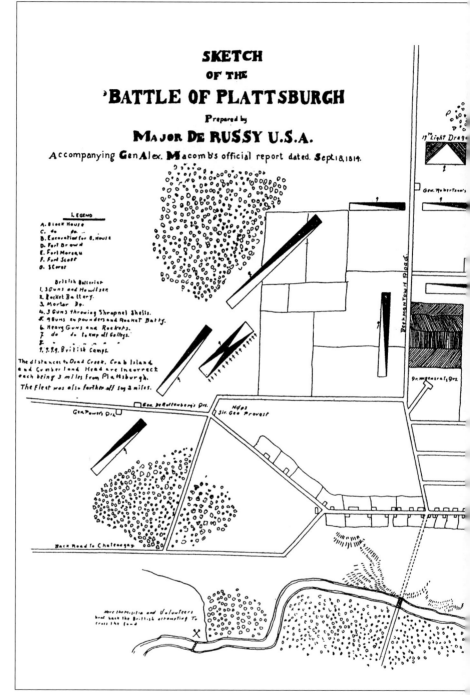

This map accompanied the official after-action report of the battle written by Brigadier General Alexander Macomb.

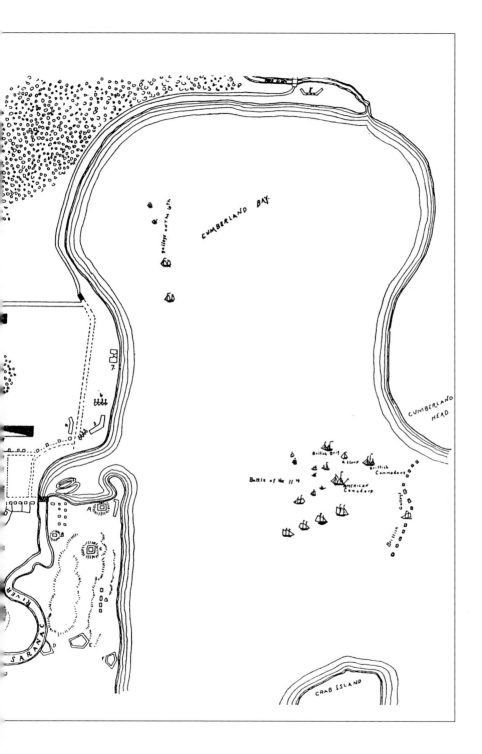

CUMBERLAND BAY.

Gallery 6 the 6th

CUMBERLAND
HEAD

British Brig
A Sloop
British
Commodore

Battle of the 11th

AMERICAN
Commodore

British Galley

CRAB ISLAND

SARANAC RIVER

A contemporary view of Plattsburgh, New York, and Cumberland Bay where the naval battle occurred.

Commodore Thomas Macdonough, U.S. Navy "Hero of Lake Champlain," appeared in most newspapers of the day.

British soldiers on the march. Prevost's invasion of the United States, calling for a joint effort by land and by lake, began on September 1, 1814.

American regular army infantry firing at the British invaders. (Print courtesy of The Company of Military Historians collection)

British redcoats in action.

American infantry re-enactors at the annual commemoration in Plattsburgh, New York, during the battle weekend.

Animation of the Royal Navy fleet with Chubb *(usually spelled "Chub") in the lead followed by* Finch, Confiance, *and* Linnet. *Gun boats trail as they cross the northern border and enter Lake Champlain.* (Scott Schuler, animator, taken from the documentary film *The Final Invasion*)

View of Lake Champlain as seen from Plattsburgh, New York. Cumberland Head is in the left background.

The Royal Navy's flagship, Confiance, in action.

Painting of the naval battle in Cumberland Bay. The British fleet is on the left in full sail, while the American vessels, on the right, are anchored.

Commodore Macdonough, commander of the American Navy flotilla, prepares to receive the Royal Navy attack. (Mural in the city hall of Plattsburgh, New York)

M'DONOUGH'S VICT'- ON LAKE CHAMPLAIN.

This print of "Macdonough's Victory" was circulated widely, which made him the man-of-the-hour after the burning of Washington, D.C.

Animation of the naval battle positions. The American Navy is on the left, the Royal Navy on the right, and the town of Plattsburgh in the background. (Scott Schuler, animator)

Print of the naval battle on Lake Champlain, September 11, 1814, between the Royal Navy and the American Navy. (Painting by Davidson, courtesy of the Battle of Plattsburgh Association)

Print of the naval battle. The Saratoga *is on the left and the Royal Navy's* Confiance *is on the right.*

Land and lake battle as seen from the north side of the Saranac River. On September 11, 1814, the sixth day of the land battle, the British army, on the left, attempted to seize the Bridge Street bridge from the American army.

Closeup of the Davidson painting. The Saratoga *fires a broadside from her carronades into the Royal Navy's* Confiance.

Saratoga, *rotated on her axis, fired the final blow that defeated the Royal Navy's flotilla.*

Below deck, the wounded are attended.

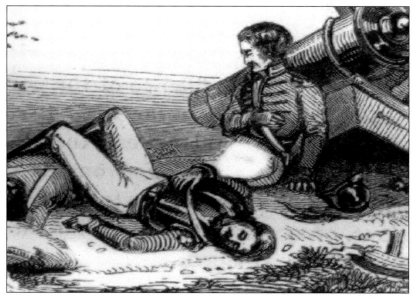

British soldiers, casualties from artillery counterbattery fire.

Heroic painting of the two major vessels, Saratoga *and* Confinace, *locked in combat.*

Chub *was smashed, and most of her crew were casualties. She drifted helplessly between the two battling fleets and into the hands of the Americans.*

The peace treaty, ending the War of 1812, was signed at Ghent, Belgium, on Christmas Eve 1814. Two weeks later, General Andrew Jackson, unaware that the war was over, repelled the British at the Battle of New Orleans.

In recognition of the splendid showing of the platoon of teenagers, Aikin's Volunteers, Congress presented new decorative rifles to each member.

Pictured is the cannon that was struck by an American cannonball, which ripped it out of its carriage and flung it into the arms of Royal Navy Captain George Downie, killing him. Today it rests in front of Macdonough Hall at the United States Naval Academy, Annapolis, Maryland.

A solid shot cannonball, a case shot and a grape shot from 1814. The flintlock pistol is shown to add perspective. The pistol once belonged to the Duke of Wellington. (Courtesy of the Royal Artillery Rotunda Museum, Woolwich Arsenal, England)

Both remaining British ships at the head of the line forced her to pull up her anchor and slide behind *Saratoga.* Only two guns were functioning and her crew was wounded and dying. *Eagle*'s commander intended to leave altogether, but when the brig was released from the grip of battle, the captain and crew rallied and she took up a position between the *Saratoga* and *Ticonderoga.* There, with the port side guns exposed, *Eagle* fought the battle once again.

The British *Finch* accomplished half of her mission. Taking on the American *Preble* at the start, she had swept her aside without the assistance of the gunboats which had lagged behind. Coming about, she changed course and charged *Ticonderoga.* Some galleys pursued and veered close enough to *Preble* to fire grapeshot. The little American, with only four of her seven nine-pounders operational, could barely range *Finch* as she laid off and fired both cannon and carronades. *Preble* turned away, out of line. Here are the words of Lieutenant Charles A. Budd, captain of *Preble:*

U.S. Sloop Preble off Plattsburg

13th Septr. 1814

Sir; I have the honor to express to you the satisfaction which the officers and men of the U.S. Sloop *Preble* under my command afforded me in the late action of the 11th inst. When the enemy's fleet were standing in for the purpose of laying their larger vessels alongside of those of ours, the sloop Finch of 11 guns with several galleys outside of her made for my sloop with her peak down and tack triced up. When within shot the fire was opened on her from the *Preble* with coolness and deliberation, the galleys having taken in their sails and lying at long gun shot. The Finch continued edging down on my starboard quarter with an intention of getting a raking position which I prevented with my spring, which proving too short in consequence of the wind having shifted 2 or 3 points to the Easwd, was obliged to let it go entirely and keep her broadside to bear with 2 sweeps out of her stern ports. About this time my boatswain Joseph Rose was killed on the forecastle. I could now perceive confusion on board the Finch, when wishing to avoid the incessant and well directed fire of the Preble she endeavored to go about but failed, which gave me a chance, and I did not miss it, of raking her. At this instant 4 galleys were coming down on my weather bow within grape distance with a visible intention of boarding me and which the officers commanding those galleys have since assured me when I was down to the lines with the flag of truce was actually their intention and that 'in five minutes they would have been along side of me,' which is the fact, to prevent which, as each galley had more men than my whole crew, I thought it best, with the concurrence of all my officers, to get under way, more especially as my having been obliged to slip one of my cables when the Saratoga drifted on board of me in consequence of the sudden shift of the wind from south to north the preceding evening which occasioned me to be so far to leeward that no assistance could be afforded me from any of the rest of the squadron. I accordingly cut my cable and wore round under my jib toward the Finch, who at the same time wore from me and stood out of the bay. In the act of wearing I manned my larboard broadside and gave the galleys its contents of grape, which, from their short distance from me, must have had good effect. At this time Sailing Master Rogers Carter was severely wounded with a grape shot from one of them, of which he has since died. I then got my mainsail on her and brought her by the wind, the galleys pursuing me closely and firing immense quantities of grape, which fortunately being directed too high did no other damage than cut my sails very much. I made one stretch in shore, then stood off.

Closing in on *Ticonderoga, Finch* cornered hard astarboard to bring her guns to bear. The same wind that defeated the other three Royal Navy vessels stopped *Finch* in her tracks as she attempted to sail to the northeast. When *Finch* drifted within carronade range of her target, she got a face full of shot and shell. Nearly locked together, *Finch* along with her escort of gunboats attempted to board *Ticonderoga.* The Americans changed from solid shot to canister and leather bags filled with rifle bullets, turning the carronades into giant shotguns. When the fighting was at its hottest, the enemy attempted to board once again. Light swivel guns on the rail, meant more for signaling, were pressed into action against the intruders. Elevating the breech to its highest setting, the carronade discharge went down into the gunboats near the hull, killing the crew and blowing holes in the bottom of the boat. Many of the new flintlock firing devices installed on *Ticonderoga*'s recently manufactured carronades were defective. Midshipman Hiram Paulding, an American lad of only sixteen years, fired the four guns of his division by the flash of his pistol for two hours.[17] When the enemy boarded, he fired at them with the same pistol. Captain Stephen Cassin put out fires on the deck started from the hot shot that they received from the carronades on the bow of *Confiance*. One of the American gunboats under Midshipman Conover attempted to support Cassin's vessel and attacked the British gunboat crew that was attempting to board. Three of Conover's crew were killed.

BRITISH GUNS DUMPED

In the middle of the engagement, Royal Navy lieutenant Hicks's vessel, *Finch,* received five wounds below the waterline and attempted to maneuver away, but grounded on a sandbar near Crab Island. They came under immediate fire from the invalid soldiers manning the two-gun shore battery. *Finch* fired grapeshot at the guns in an attempt to silence the position. Hicks attempted to free the ship by lightening, throwing overboard four six-pounders and all her ballast. He sent a boat crew out with a line from her stern to pull her free. But it was too late; she had two feet of water in her hull and Lieutenant William Hicks struck his colors. U.S. Navy Lieutenant Charles Budd, captain of the *Preble,* describes the action of the *Finch* at the close of his after-action report:

> In the meantime the galleys had left me to assist the Finch, who I afterwards understood was aground. Whether she was got there accidentally

or purposely I will not pretend to assert. After the ship Confiance had struck and the galleys left the vicinity of the Finch, who had her colours still flying, I prepared for lying longside of her and bore up for that purpose, which she, perceiving, struck her flag. I still stood down for her and discovered she was ashore. She has 4 nine pound shot below the surface of the water which impressed me very forcibly with the opinion that she was in a sinking condition when she grounded. The Preble I have the pleasure to state is not materially injured. She has got 2 eighteen pound shot through her hull about a foot from the water; her larboard wales considerably started; 1 eighteen pound shot lodged in her stern, having carried away the head knees and shattered the stern; one 24 lb shot through her quarter bulwarks & the dents of two 18 lb shot from the Finch's columbiads.[18]

The other combatants had fought to a standstill. The absence of *Eagle* at the head of the line exposed the American flagship to the cannonades of both the *Linnet* and *Confiance,* which were shooting away the remaining rigging, which continued to fall to *Saratoga*'s gun deck, crushing, maiming, and killing in furious proportions. A cannonball from *Linnet* struck the one remaining gun on the starboard side of Macdonough's ship and sent it careening down the main hatch into the deck below, taking the crew with it. The decisive moment had arrived. Neither the *Confiance* nor the *Saratoga* was capable of defending herself. The *Linnet,* though heavily damaged, was still operational and she continued to pour hell fire onto the defenseless decks of the *Saratoga.* Of the 250 members of the *Saratoga*'s crew, less than 100 were still fighting.

THE MASTER STROKE

It was then that Commodore Macdonough played his trump card. During the preparation for battle, he had secured his vessel by the bow and stern. Additionally, he positioned kedge anchors, which had been rowed out to either end and dropped. Now with all his guns gone on one side, he was able to cut some anchor lines and pull in others and thus rotate the stricken ship in place and expose the port side, which bristled with a fresh battery. While the maneuver took place, he sheltered most of his crew below deck from the fire of the *Linnet*. Mr. Brum, the sailing master of the *Saratoga,* had his clothes torn off by splinters while he supervised the turning of the capstan, which wound the ship around. The Royal Navy lieutenant commanding *Confiance* tried to duplicate *Saratoga*'s maneuver, but was unable because of tangled lines, succeeding in only moving forward a few yards. It was as if a new ship had suddenly taken the place of the shattered combatant *Saratoga.* Now a dozen fresh guns were trained on both the remaining British men-of-war. When Macdonough spun the *Saratoga* around and fired, the *Confiance* lost over half of her remaining crew. There, on the rude deck that was strewn with the wreckage of war, 140 lay either dead or wounded. Most of the guns on the engaged side were dismounted and *Confiance*'s stout masts had been splintered, looking like bundles of matches strung together with knotted string. Her sails had been torn to rags, which hung limp in strips above the heads of the exhausted sailors. A midshipman on the *Confiance* later wrote:

14th September 1814

Dear Mother

   The havoc on both sides is dreadful. I don't think there are more than five of our men, out of three hundred, but what are killed or wounded. Never was a shower of hail so thick as the shot whistling about our ears. Were you to see my jacket, waistcoat, and trousers, you would be astonished how I escaped as I did, for they are literally torn all to rags with shot and splinters; the upper part of my hat was also shot away. There is one of our marines who was in the Trafalgar action with Lord Nelson, who says it was a mere Flea-Bite in comparison with this.

Midshipman R. Lea,
Royal Navy, aboard H.M.S. Confiance.[19]

In fact, Lea was counted among the wounded, but failed to tell his mother. The carnage aboard the defenseless British flagship under the renewed cannonade was terrible. It was no longer a battle; it was a shipwreck and slaughter. Blood poured from *Confiance*'s scuppers as would water after shipping a heavy sea. The dead so littered the decks that they had to be thrust through the shattered ports for burial in the bay. One woman was among the victims. She was a steward's wife working with the surgeon in the shelter of the lazarette, one of the "idlers" who was tending to the wounded. A wretch lay writhing by the companion ladder, one leg mangled by a cannonball. The woman stooped, tore off the folds of her skirt, and began to bind up his wounds. A solid shot plowed through the bulwarks, struck her in the chest as she knelt, and hurled her, a crumpled corpse, clear across the ship's deck.[20]

A midshipman of Captain Pring's was sent in a gig, through the boiling water, to Downie on the flagship for instruction. He returned through the maelstrom of musket balls, shot, and flaming splinters with the news that Downie had been killed at the beginning of the battle and that Pring had been in charge of the action since 8:15 that morning. It was nearing 10:30 and Robertson further informed Commodore Pring that he could no longer sustain the action and intended to strike his colors. *Linnet* was in no better shape. Her masts were shattered and her spars and sails lay on the deck, mere debris of battle. There was no hope for her to escape unless the gunboats could tow her from harm's way.

The spectators, British and Canadian men and women watching from a private vessel out in the lake, could see little of the fleet through the smoke, but it was apparent that the ships had become nothing but hulks.[21] None of the eight ships were capable of moving under sail. *Confiance* had 105 holes punched in her side when she lowered her white ensign crossed with red, which had the union jack in the upper corner.[22] Mr. Simons, the shipwright who had put her in the water only two weeks before, was still on board and was killed trying to keep her afloat. At the moment that *Confiance* struck her colors, with the *Finch* and *Chub* already prisoner, the *Linnet* followed her flagship's example. The British gunboats pulled away from *Ticonderoga* when *Finch* was disabled and clustered together in the center of the bay, licking their wounds. An idler on the *Confiance* accidentally fired a gun on the starboard side when he brushed a primed lock spring.[23] Apparently, it was a prearranged signal for the gunboats to move off. They were the only serviceable Royal Navy vessels on the bay. Robertson attempted to signal the boats to come to the rescue of *Linnet,* but because of the missing code that was kept in the lost signal instruction, he could do nothing to stop their progress out of the bay to the safety of the support ship *Icicle,* moored above the point.

The American galleys, which had done little after their action against the arriving British army, attempted to pursue the *Icicle,* but were recalled by Macdonough, whose ship was in danger of sinking. The exhausted Americans gathered together all remaining ships, British and American, and everyone gave a hand with the salvage work. Wounded on both sides were put into the gunboats and taken to Crab Island for treatment. The surviving commanders from the Royal Navy were conducted, when all was secured, to Commodore Macdonough, who received them on what remained of the beleaguered quarterdeck of *Saratoga.* Captain Daniel Pring, Macdonough's adversary for the past two years of hit-and-run warfare, presented his commanders, Lieutenants McGhie, Hicks, and Robertson. The British officers drew their swords and presented them, in the presence of the victorious American crew, to Thomas Macdonough. The young American commodore graciously declined to accept their arms, the symbol of command and authority, and said, "Gentlemen, your gallant conduct makes you worthy to wear your weapons; return them to their scabbards."

In the wake of the battle, a wounded midshipman, Lee of the *Eagle*, recounted an anecdote of a sailor who survived the engagement:

December 14th, 1814

Dear Brother,
Mr. James Sloane of Oswego informed me that a few days before the battle, he gave one of the seamen a very nice glazed hat. After the battle was over the sailor came to him with the hat in his hand, having a semi-circular cut in the side and crown made by a cannon shot while it was on his head. "Look here, Mr. Sloane," said the sailor, "how the damned John Bulls have spoiled my hat." He did not seem to reflect for a moment how nearly the cannonball came to spoiling his head.

But it was not only sailors who weathered the battle. The commander of the army troops whose men made up the bulk of the crew of the American squadron records the event:

U.S. Ship Saratoga, Lake Champlain,
September 12, 1814

To: Com. T. Macdonough
    Sir, I have the honor of enclosing to you a list of killed and wounded troops of the line [regular army soldiers] in action of the 11th instant.
    In attempting to do justice to the brave officers and men I have the honor to command, my feeble abilities fall far short of my wishes. First Lieut. Morrison, 33rd infantry, stationed on board the U.S. brig Eagle, was wounded but remained on deck during the action, animating his men by his honorable conduct. Second Lieut. James Young, 6th infantry, on board the U.S. schooner Ticonderoga, merits my warmest thanks. I would particularly recommend him to your notice. Second Lieut. William B. Howell, 15th infantry, in the U.S. ship Saratoga, rendered me every assistance. Notwithstanding his having been confined for ten days of a fever, yet, at the commencement of the action, he was found on deck and continued until the enemy had struck, when he was borne to his bed. I would also recommend him to your notice.

The conduct of the non-commissioned officers and privates was so highly honorable to their country and themselves it would be superfluous to particularize them.

I have the honor to be, sir, your obedient servant,

White Youngs,
Capt. 15th. com'ing detach.
        of acting marines

Macdonough attaches the above to his own letter to Macomb.

U.S. Ship Saratoga, off Plattsburgh
September 13, 1814

Dear Sir; Enclosed is a copy of a letter from Capt. White Youngs and a list of killed and wounded attached to his command.

I beg leave to recommend Capt. Youngs to your particular notice. During the action his conduct was such as to meet with my warmest approbation. I feel much indebted to him for his personal valor and example of coolness and intrepidity to his own men as well as to the sailors. He volunteered in a sinking boat to carry my order to the galleys for close action in the hottest part of it and supplied the guns with his men as fast as the sailors were disabled.

I am with much respect and esteem, your obedient servant,

T. Macdonough

MEANWHILE, ON LAND

Sir George Prevost had dispatched the two brigades off to flank Macomb shortly after Downie entered the bay. The force of seven thousand marched in a column four abreast to the southwest, heading for the river ford where the Vermont militia of twenty-five hundred waited. Both sides of the river were choked by tangled forest and underbrush. The only cleared area was the old cantonment that Zebulon Pike had clear-cut in 1813. The militia formed up for battle in straight lines, some dressed in fragments of uniforms. All were armed with issued muskets, but had no artillery to back their play. The red-coated column was accompanied by field artillery, in addition to the overwhelming strength of veteran regiments. It was going to be a short fight there in the open field and General Sam Strong decided, after taking a look at the lines of amateur soldiers, to break them up and withdraw most of them into the edge of the forest, on the southeastern side of the clearing. The others he put in reserve block formations, which he could shift as needed. The British force was led by a staff officer, from the quartermaster general's, who had been at the ford two days before. If Macdonough had been blessed by the winds, Macomb was about to be saved by the "fog of war." Carl von Clausewitz writes, "Action in war is like movement in a resistance. Just as the simplest and most natural of movements, walking, cannot easily be performed in water, so in war it is difficult for normal efforts to achieve even moderate results." Writing years after his experience in the war against the French, as a professor at the German War College in 1832, he called this theory the "friction of war." His writing goes on, "such actions bring about efforts that cannot be measured, just because they are largely due to chance," which seems to describe the events at Plattsburgh exactly.[24] The misguided five-mile-long line of anxious British soldiers tramped west for an hour without finding the river and its vital ford. During that valuable time, between 8:30 and 9:30, the naval battle could be heard in the distance. Lost, the column reversed itself to the starting point and struck out once more. Later, back in England, Major General Frederick Robinson said, "a full hour of precious time had been irretrievably lost by the unfortunate mistake." Not until nearly 10 A.M. was Robinson able to send his first line across at Pike's cantonment. The first to cross were all from Major General Manley Powers's brigade, who were supported by Royal Artillery six-pound field pieces.

Powers waded into the militia and immediately dislodged them. He pursed them through the thickets for four miles, taking so few casualties that there is no record of losses. The retreating Vermonters headed south for the Salmon River, where perhaps they could make a stand. This left Macomb's left flank wide open. Robinson, trailing Powers, crossed the Saranac and turned ninety degrees to the left with his brigade of thirty-four hundred, led by the 27th infantry regiment, the Inniskillings, in red with pale yellow facings and white cross belts. The Irish were most aggressive, crashing through growth on the southern side—the American side—of the Saranac. It was less than a three-mile trek. Topping a wooded ridge, they gained the road, closing Macomb's main supply and escape route. Robinson could see the backs of the regular American infantry defending the upper bridge less than a mile away. The British were behind American lines in great force, primed for the final and fatal assault.

DISHONOR RATHER THAN DEATH?

But time had been wasted that could not be reclaimed. Following the path beaten by the marauding redcoats, an aide from General Prevost, Adjutant Baynes, caught up with General Robinson and delivered a message. Seated on his bay charger, he pulled up the black "sabretache" piped in gold, which hung on three white leather straps behind his sword scabbard. The item was made of heavy stiff leather and used to keep maps and writing paper dry. Breaking the wax seal, stamped with Lieutenant General Prevost's coat of arms, he was shocked to read, "I am directed to inform you that *Confiance* and the Brig having struck their colors in consequence of the Frigate having ground, it will no longer be prudent to persevere in Service committed to your charge, and it is therefore the Orders of the Commander of the Forces that you immediately return with the troops under your command."

In a letter home, Robinson's feelings are revealed, "Never was anything like the disappointment expressed in every countenance. The advance was within shot, and full view of the Redoubt, and in one hour they must have been ours. We retired under two 6 pounders posted on our side the Ford in as much silent discontent as was ever exhibited."

In the letter to Lossing, at Troy, New York, dated May 10, 1860, Major General John E. Wool, who was a major during the battle, fills in the details:

> On the 11th on the approach of the British Fleet to attack McDonough, the troops on land opened their batteries upon the works of General Macomb, but without much effect. Their fire was briskly and efficiently returned from Forts Moreau, Brown and the block-houses. The enemy formed in two columns preparatory to an assault intended as soon as the anticipated victory obtained over the fleet of McDonough [sic]. One column moved near the bridge in the center of the village to be in readiness to cross, and the other crossed the ford at Pike's Cantonment without resistance from the Militia, who retired as the column advanced, the head of which halted within a short distance of the rear of our works and remained there until the engagement of the two fleets was decided. This being in the favor of the Americans, Prevost recalled his columns of assault and immediately commenced preparations for retreating to Canada. The column in rear of the American works recrossed the Saranac without interruption, excepting the company in advance which not receiving the order to fall back and after waiting some time for the main column, went back to learn the cause of the delay, when they came in contact with General Strong's Vermont Militia, who killed and took prisoners the greater part of the company. Thus ended the battle of Plattsburgh, excepting on the retreat of the enemy some of the Militia followed and picked up as prisoners 250 or 300 deserters.

The unit that failed to get the word to withdraw was a company of the 76th regiment, one of the few British regiments not to have an affiliation with a geographic county or royal distinction. Captain Perchase, the commander, was killed attempting to get his unit through the swarm of militia moving north for the first time since the beginning of the battle. The majority of his company was captured and returned to Canada after the battle, during prisoner exchange.

Even though the battle was over before noon, the Royal Artillery continued to fire until after 3 P.M. This was done for two reasons. First, covering fire was needed to allow the British army to pick up and move out. Infantry units were pulled out by brigade, Robinson's and Powers's first. Breaking contact is always tricky, and if the enemy is allowed to pursue, real killing can begin. There was little danger of pursuit that day, though. Macomb's men were exhausted and had taken thirty-seven killed, sixty-two wounded. There is no count on the militia, but their casualties were believed to be higher. The wounded figures do not include all those injured, only the ones who were hospitalized or given medical pension.

On a war game board or in a classroom, pursuit is always desirable. Napoleon preached it as dogma, Rommel lived by it, and Patton demanded it. But anyone who has been in a battle will tell you that the exhilaration of victory is soon absorbed by fatigue, mental and physical. Thirst dominates and the adrenaline that drove the mind and body forward is opposed by weariness and relief. Besides, Macomb was not equipped for the offense; there was no American cavalry and his infantry could only match the retiring British pace. Also, the British artillery did not want to move all those heavy cannonballs back across the border. They could shoot them up or carry them home. They are still picking up cannonballs on Plattsburgh Air Force Base, even today.

Commissary General William Robinson now reversed his operation, which had taken over a week. He had brought down a mountain of material, not only to support the army in battle but to set up winter camp. There were not nearly enough wagons and much of the supplies had to be abandoned, much to the joy of the local population. It is even said that a quantity of gold was left in a well or hidden in a cellar. But that ranks among the many fairy tales that surround this invasion. It is true, however, that a number of sick and wounded were left in the care of the town ladies, who set up hospitals and cared for the enemy with the same degree of kindness they gave to their own. Prevost accepted this, since it was better not to move the wounded over rutted roads in unsprung wagons. The war was fought in an age of military chivalry, although there was little chivalry in this war.

Words attributed to Sir James Henry Craig nearly echo those of Clausewitz: "It may be considered as one of those misfortunes incidental to warfare which human prudence can neither foresee nor prevent."[25]

CHAPTER 6

The war was practically ended by Prevost's retreat. What remained was purely episodical in character, and should be so regarded.

—Arthur Wellesley, Duke of Wellington

The battle was over. Commodore Macdonough now attempted to save his beloved *Saratoga,* the other two American vessels, and the remnants of the Royal Navy's *Confiance* and *Linnet.* Midshipman William Boden writes,

US Schooner Ticonderoga
off Plattsburgh, Lake Champlain
Sept. 14th, 1814

Dear Mother,
The anxiety is over. By the blessing of God our arms are victorious. On Sunday the 11th I was at 5 in the morning rowing guard when I discovered the British Fleet. At 9 the British consisting of 1 frigate, 1 brig, 4 sloops, 13 gallies came round Cumberland Head. Our fleet were at anchor in a line of Battle. The action continued an hour & 40 minutes when the frigate, brig & 2 sloops struck to us. The frigate mounts 37 guns, 28 long 24pds., 13 32 pd. carronades & was manned by 260 seaman & marines besides some soldiers. They had 135 men killed & wounded besides some that were hove overboard as I heard an officer say he hove 3 men from one gun to clear it so it could work.
The brig mounts 16 guns, the sloops 11 each. The Enemy mounted 103 gun, [our?] mounted 88. We lost a sloop some days by striking a rock, so that we were much [hole in paper] 75 guns struck [illegible] 28 guns escaped. We lost [illegible] Stansbury our Lieut. killed &

16 men killed & wounded on board the schooner, besides some men slightly wounded by splinters. I got a [illegible] by a splinter the first part of the action. The British army have retreated from before Platts-burg. They lost about 100 prisoners. Above as many deserters came in yesterday.

The Dead were buried yesterday with the honors of war. The people around are very generous. They gave as many as 50 bushels of potatoes, onions, & corn to our crew yesterday.

I have been much hurried as I am the oldest midshipmen & our Lieut. is dead or I would have written before.

Your Son,

(signed) William Boden

PS. Give my love to all my acquaintances. Tell Mrs. Lindsay her hus-band is well.[1]

Silas Hubbell went aboard the *Saratoga* shortly after the British surrendered to help with the evacuation of the wounded to hospitals that were set up in the homes of local citizens. The women of the village, with the help of Dr. Mann, nursed both American and British soldiers. Hubbell knew that there must be many more on board those smashed ships. Together with a party of militia that had returned to town after the retreat of the British army, he manned a barge and sailed it alongside the American flagship. He wrote that, "the Confiance was absolutely torn to pieces. and mutilated bodies lay in all directions." Simons Dory, a militiaman, confirms the scene and could scarcely believe that anyone could have survived. Benjah Phelps, eleven-year-old son of a militiaman, accompanied the Hubbell rescue. Benjah's memories appear in a book published in 1901: "Blood, blood was everywhere. The decks was covered with arms and legs and heads, and pieces of hands and bodies all torn to pieces. I never seen anything in this world like it. Seemed as if everybody had been killed. The Yankee ships was badly damaged too and lots of our folks was killed too."[2] Not every citizen was helping to restore life and property. In a letter to his brother, Dr. Michael Freligh, George Freligh, whose house and business were destroyed during the battle, writes, "The militia after the enemy retreated broke open stores and houses which the enemy left untouched and plundered them of everything that could be carried away. They even went so far as to pick up hooks, hinges, door latches and nails where buildings had been burnt. Mr. Green's house was set on fire twice and was extinguished by the enemy."

NO ONE WAS KEEPING SCORE

The naval casualties were hard to determine, since the British simply threw the dead overboard during the fighting, and bodies surfaced for days afterward in the shallow bay. Some Americans as well went into the water, as crews attempted to clear the way for the guns. The Royal Navy did not record the number of crewmen lost, so all we have are estimates. It appears that 25 percent were killed and nearly all the survivors were wounded to one degree or another. The American navy recorded that 14 percent were killed and give very conflicting figures as to the wounded.[3] There seemed to have been two degrees of wounded: those who required hospitalization and pensions, since they could no longer report for duty, and the walking wounded, whose wounds healed. Walking wounded were not recorded. There were no Purple Hearts given in those days, so there were no accompanying medical records.[4] There are many opinions about the army losses. The American injured appear to have been one in every eight men, but there is no mention whether that includes militia. The term "casualties" means both killed in action and wounded to the point of hospitalization. The British army recorded thirty-seven killed and fifty wounded in the left division. In addition to that figure, a letter of inquiry that was sent to the War Office in London in 1894 revealed that in the same division there were three officers killed, eight wounded, and four missing. There are no figures for the other units in the British army. The missing in action were put down to desertion and those figures for the British army are very sketchy, since they did not want to admit that the U.S. program that offered deserters land and money was effective.

The *Naval Chronicle,* London, December 1814 records:

> The rumored defeat of our naval squadron on Lake Champlain turned out but too well founded—it has been taken or dispersed—and its gallant commander slain! On the heels of this disastrous intelligence came the news of the retreat of our Army from before Plattsburg, attended with circumstances peculiarly galling to the feelings of the nation. These defeats and disasters in America excited most rapturous applause from the friends of that people in Paris. The most alarming feature is the desertion of our forces, particularly from the Army, to the Americans. It has been offered in Congress, and scarcely a doubt remains it will pass into law, to bestow 100 acres of fertile land upon every military person who would desert from our Army. This measure will, of course, extend to our seamen.

The official British figure was three hundred, while the New York papers reported one thousand new citizens. The American papers were silent as to the desertion from their own lines, but if the militia were counted it would be substantial.

William Dent, a medical student in London, had been sent that summer to serve with the British army in Canada as a part of the expedition sent by the earl of Bathurst. While he never left Montreal for the front lines, Dent nonetheless made revealing comments on the operation in a letter home:

> the whole of the Army now regret very much our ever having left France, the people are very uneasy and everywhere imposition is attempted to be practiced upon us. You must have heard before this of the affair on Lake Champlain, and the retreat of the Army before a handful

of Americans which caused about five hundred British soldiers to desert; everything is carried on in a very different manner to what we had been used to in Europe, and everyone is discontented. Only the Irishman of the Connaught's Rangers resisted the temptation of free land, and did not loose a man.[5]

Commodore Macdonough, professional to a fault, wrote the following communication to the secretary of the navy, relating nothing of the struggle he and his men endured.[6]

To: The Honorable William Jones   11 September 1814
Secretary of the Navy

Sir:

The almighty has been pleased to grant us a signal victory on Lake Champlain in the capture of one Frigate, one Brig and two sloops of war of the enemy.

I have the honor to be
very respectfully,

Sir, your ob't Sere't

T Macdonough, Com.

Lieutenant Cassin, captain of the *Ticonderoga,* was dispatched down the lake with this and another communiqué, written two days later, and the captured flags of the Royal Navy fleet. The second letter read,

United States' ship Saratoga
at anchor off Plattsburgh, Sept. 13, 1814

Hon. William Jones, secretary
of the navy, Washington

Sir,

By Lieut. commandant Cassin I have the honor to convey to you the flags of his Britannic majesty's late squadron, captured on the 11th inst. by the United States' squadron, under my command. Also, my despatches relating to that occurrence, which should have been in your possession at an earlier period, but for the difficulty in arranging the different statements.

The squadron under my command now lies at Plattsburgh—it will bear of considerable diminution, and leave a force sufficient to repel any attempt of the enemy in this quarter. I shall wait your order what to do with the whole or any part thereof, and, should it be consistent, I beg you will favor me with permission to leave the lake, and place me under the command of commodore Decatur [sic], at New York. My health, (being some time on the lake,) together with the almost certain inactivity of future naval operations here, are among the causes for the request of my removal.

I have the honor to be,
Sir, with much respect,

Your most ob't servant,

T. MACDONOUGH.[7]

Cassin's arrival in New York City was heralded by Mayor Dewitt Clinton, before Cassin proceeded to Philadelphia by sloop-of-war. It was tradition in the military to send victorious news by a noble participant in the battle, an honor richly deserved by the young naval commander of the *Ticonderoga*. Stephen Cassin passed through Baltimore on the 15th and learned of the battle that had taken place there on the 13th. While he and his comrades had been fighting the invasion force on the 11th, the British fleet had disgorged four thousand troops, many of them sailors who were firing muskets for the first time, and attacked the city. The Royal Navy pressed hard to enter the harbor and raid the shipping. But Fort McHenry, a little red-brick-covered, earthen star fortress, in the French style, had prevented the passage of the warships into the inner harbor. The battle was joined on the 13th. Eager to make amends for the defeat they took at Bladensburg, and in spite of "the rockets red glare," the twelve thousand militia and six hundred regular army prevailed. Francis Scott Key, an American lawyer aboard a British vessel negotiating prisoner exchange, was inspired to compose a poem that would become the U.S. national anthem.

The news that Cassin carried to the secretary of war was more than could be hoped for and the newspapers declared the double victory was a sign that God was indeed looking out for the future survival of the United States of America and her radical form of self-government. At noon on September 18, the victorious citizens of Baltimore fired the guns of Fort McHenry as a salute to the heroism of their comrades at Plattsburgh. No evidence suggests that anyone in America realized that the attacks on the U.S. capital and ports were intended to draw interest away from the invasion from Montreal. Those in Washington and Baltimore considered that they had beaten off a serious attempt by Britain to seize the government and once again rule over all of the new United States. Of course, they never saw the secret order.

THE STAR-SPANGLED BANNER WAS NOT WAVING IN LONDON

"They took the news hard in England. The London *Times* wept, 'A lamentable event to the civilized world.'" The *Naval Chronicle* wrote:

> There are rumors of a most unfavorable kind; namely, of the total destruction of our fleet on Lake Champlain, and the retreat of Sir George Prevost, with considerable loss from before Plattsburg, these disastrous reports are unhappily confirmed, although the official accounts have not yet appeared. The effects of the failure of our attack on Baltimore and the events in Canada, have already produced consequences in America very different from those calculated upon by the advocates for this unnatural and dangerous war, whilst at home the public feelings are vehemently and variously agitated. Some of our leading journals are for crushing the United States at once, by sending the Duke of Wellington and 50,000 troops there![8]

Only six months before, the same force had driven the French out of Spain and into southern France in a campaign that had lasted from 1807 to 1814. The people of Great Britain could not understand how they could fail when confronted by former colonists and frontiersmen without the traditions of a great country. An Englishman, William Corbett, wrote a letter on the lost battle which was published in London:

Pro-War sentiment against the Americans is outraging the Prince Regent to fight on. A battle is to be fought now between the whole of our army and navy and those of the republic of America. She will not shy the fight. She is ready for us. The world is now going to witness the fall of the last republic, or the decline of the Naval power of England. There will be no medium after another year of war. We must completely subjugate the Americans; or openly fall before them. We must beat them, or they must beat us. The battle will be a famous one. A great kingdom, the mistress of the sea, and Dictatress of Europe, on the one side; and the last of the republics on the other. Not only the question of maritime rights to be decided, but the question of the nature of governments. The world is now going to see whether a republic, without a standing army, with half a dozen frigates, and with a chief magistrate of five thousand pounds a year, be able to contend, single-handed against a kingdom with a thousand ships of war, and army of two-hundred thousand men, and with a royal family whose civil list amounts to more than a million pounds a year. Nothing was ever so favorable as this spectacle. May the end be favorable to this country and mankind in general.[9]

At home in Montreal, a devastated eighteen-year-old Anne Prevost writes in her diary:

Monday 12th, the mortifying news arrived that our Squadron was defeated, captured, and Captain Downie killed. The scene of our hearing the news is now before me. Mr. Brenton came into the drawing-room much agitated and told us first that sad fate of our little Fleet, which was, by the way, quite as large as the American Squadron. I was breathless till I heard what the Army was about; the loss of the Fleet seemed to me a secondary consideration, and when Mr. B. went on to say the Army is to retreat, it seemed to me I heard a death's knell ringing in my ears. The news had a different effect on my Mother with perfect confidence in my

Father's right judgement, she seemed only to deplore the loss of our vessels and Captain Downie's death. I never was much given to shedding tears, far from it—but I now wept bitter tears not for poor Captain Downie or his Squadron, but because the Army was to retreat without having first destroyed Plattsburg! I felt certain that however necessary this determination might be, it would bring the greatest odium on my Father—it would not be tolerated at a period especially when our troops were so perpetually victorious. O how My heart ached that day, and often, often afterwards! It was a secret sorrow too—for not even with Miss C. did I ever like to talk on this painful subject.

My Father's idea on the subject seems to have been simply this:—Here are 9,000 men, all I have for the defense of Lower Canada—the Squadron is lost—the principal object of the Expedition cannot be effected—I shall therefore retire within our own territory and there wait for the Enemy. If my Father's life had been spared his Brother Officers would have decided whether this decision was what accorded best with the good of the service. He must have known that not one individual in the Army could be blamed for the retreat but himself; he took upon himself all the odium which he knew would be excited by an unpopular measure, and acted as he thought best. As the Fleet was lost, Plattsburg must have been abandoned as soon as captured,—I never heard but one opinion on that point. The weather was very rainy and the difficulty of moving artillery, stores, etc., is increased every hour. The American Militia were coming forward—General Burgoyne's Army was surrounded and captured not far from hence—Saratoga is only at the extremity of Lake Champlain,—But it is useless to dwell on this most painful subject. Military fame cannot be rescued by argument—like woman's honour it is sullied even by the breath of calumny. And I know too well that not even the gracious approval of my Father's services, which George IV, granted to his family, is sufficient to raise his memory to the estimation which it merits.

Sir George Prevost gives us a glimpse into his own thinking in his first dispatch to the man who sent the forces and wrote the operations order, Lord Bathurst, a friend and supporter:

11 September 1814

. . . Notwithstanding the intrepid valor with which captain Downie led his flotilla into action, my most sanguinary hopes of complete success were, not long afterwards, blasted, by a combination, as appeared to us, of unfortunate events, to which naval warfare is peculiarly exposed.

Scarcely had his majesty's troops forced a passage across the Saranac, (the attack at Pikes cantonment) and ascended the height on which stand the enemy's works, when I had the extreme mortification to hear the shout of victory from the enemy's works, in consequence of the British flag being lowered on board the Confiance and Linnet, and to see our gun-boats seeking their safety in flight. This unlooked-for event deprived me of the co-operation of the fleet, without which the further procecution of the service was become impracticable. I did not hesitate to arrest the course of the troops advancing to the attack, because the most complete success would have been unavailing, and the possession of the enemy's works offered no advantage to compensate for the loss we must have sustained in acquiring possession of them.

I have ordered the batteries to be dismantled, the guns withdrawn, and the baggage, with the wounded men who can be removed, to be sent to the rear, in order that the troops may return to Chazy tomorrow, and on the following day to Champlain, where I propose to halt until I have ascertained the use the enemy propose making of the naval ascendancy they have acquired on Lake Champlain.[10]

The next day he sent the following message:

To, The Colonial Secretary
The Earl Bathurst   12 September 1814
Ministry of State for Colonial Affairs
London

Your Lordship must have been aware from my previous dispatches that no Offensive Operation could be carried out within the Enemy's Territory for the destruction of his Naval Establishment without Naval Support. . . . The disastrous and unlooked for result of the Naval Contest by depriving me of the only means by which I could avail myself of any advantage I might gain, rendered a perseverance in the attack of the Enemy's position highly imprudent as well as hazardous. Under the circumstances I had to determine whether I should consider my own fame by gratifying the ardor of the troops in persevering in the attack, or consult the more substantial interest of my country by withdrawing the Army which was yet un-crippled for the security of these provinces.

I remain your Obedient Servant
(signed)
Prevost

Sir George Prevost believed that the war was not over. He was still receiving more troops every day by ship from Europe. The government in London appeared to be determined to continue the fight until a favorable outcome could be obtained. By the first of the year he would have over thirty thousand regular army. He expected to rebuild the fleet, knowing that the Americans would have to do the same, since all the vessels that participated in the battle on the bay would require extensive repair. Indeed, before the year was out he received a proposal, by a New Yorker loyal to Britain, to burn the whole American flotilla. General Prevost knew that he would be fiercely criticized by Canadians, Parliament, the army establishment, and the public at large. But he hoped that His Majesty's government would take a longer view of the matter and stand by him, as they always had during the past two difficult years. The Duke of Wellington agreed with Prevost's decision to withdraw the army after the loss of the naval engagement. But he wrote publicly, in defense of the generals he had sent on the expedition, that "the campaign had been managed as ill as possible and that [Prevost] had gone to war about trifles with the general officers I sent him, which are certainly the best to their rank and the Army." Privately, to the prime minister, he responded to the offer to replace Sir George Prevost as governor general of Canada and continue the battle:

To: The Prime Minister   9, November, 1814
Paris, France.

My Lord,

    If you remove me from hence, you must employ me elsewhere. You cannot, in my opinion, at this moment decide upon sending me to America. I told Lord Bathurst that I had no objection to going, though I don't promise him much success there. I believe there are troops enough for the defense of Canada for ever and even for the accomplishment of any reasonable offensive plan. . . . What appears to me to be wanting in America is not a General, or General Officers and troops but a naval superiority on the Lakes. Till that superiority is acquired, it is impossible according to my notion, to maintain any army in such a situation as to keep the enemy out of the whole frontier, much less to making conquests from the enemy. . . . The whole history of the war proves its truth. The question is whether we can obtain this naval superiority on the Lakes. If we cannot, I shall do you but little good in America: and I shall go there only to prove the truth of Prevost's defense and to sign a peace which might as well be signed now.[11]

In another letter to Bathurst, Wellington relates that the plan was good, but the execution flawed and unlucky. He continues, "It may, therefore, reasonably be said in favor of Prevost that the capture of a position which he was unlikely to be able to hold would have been a needless sacrifice of life which he was justified in avoiding."

BRITAIN HAD NEED

As ambassador to France after the defeat of Napoleon, Wellington attended the Congress of Vienna. There the victors carved up Europe among themselves, believing that the "ogre," Napoleon, was caged for good on his new kingdom of Elba. The duke watched and listened all summer long and he believed he saw something sinister approaching. With the power vacuum created by the defeat of imperial France and the restoration of Louis XVIII to the throne of a now disenfranchised Continental System, the small German states, recently allied to Napoleon as the Confederation of the Rhine, were up for grabs. Wellington believed that Russia and Prussia, which had grown closer over the years, would both play prominent roles in Europe. It was in Great Britain's interest that no new coalition be formed that could dominate the European continent and potentially shut off trade for Britain. The duke so believed that the threat was real that he informed his government that he may come in urgent need of the troops that were being squandered in a vain attempt to wrench chunks away from the United States. Wellington foresaw a new war in Europe in which Britain would be allied with France and Austria to maintain French sovereignty.

At Vienna, the czar, the emperor of Austria, and the king of Prussia chided Wellington, Lord Castlereagh, and the prime minister over Britain's showing in its war with one of its own former colonies. The United States was not considered a power, and the humiliation the British had suffered cut Wellington deeply. The European leaders disregarded the Royal Navy's exploits against the French at Trafalgar, referring to Napoleon's navy as a moribund fleet. They also pointed out that Napoleon had been absent during Wellington's defeat of the French army in Spain.

The British were still seething and wanted the affair at Plattsburgh resolved; they insisted on fixing blame. *The Naval Chronicle for 1814 of the Royal Navy of the United Kingdom* continues its harangue:

To the Editor   14 December 1814

[T]he American war was very popular at first, because we thought to chastise them without difficulty, but now we find it not so easy a task as it appeared, and have met with a few reverses, many of those so eager at first, are crying out lustily for peace, and blaming everything that is done, of this whining I am ashamed: let us put our shoulders to the wheel and have determined, active war, or none. If we have not the firmness to struggle with difficulties—better to give it up at once; grant them all they ask, give them Canada, dismantle our navy, become a nation of shopkeepers, and leave it for posterity to say, that the English people having risen to the highest rank among nations, had not the courage and talent to keep their situation, but fell before a people without a Treasury, Army or Navy

I remain your humble servant

T. C. (anonymous)

The Anglo-American peace conference, conducted under the tutelage of the czar in the imperial city of St. Petersburg, had failed after a more than a year. It reconvened in August 1814 in Ghent, Belgium. Britain wanted to enter the talks from a position of strength. The British operation in North America was intended to produce concessions concentrated on the northwestern border with Canada. Britain's aim was to set up an Indian territory between the two countries in what is now northern Michigan. The boundaries were to be generally the Ohio, Mississippi, and Missouri rivers, which would have denied the United States most of what is now Ohio, Indiana, Illinois, Wisconsin, Michigan, and Minnesota.[12] The United States would not be allowed to have a military presence on the Great Lakes. This meant that Britain would maintain sovereignty over everything to the west of the existing state borders. The British made no mention of the Louisiana purchase or the western frontier.

Henry Goulburn, Ministry of State and head of the British delegation in Ghent, submitted the new British terms on October 21—just as the first details of Baltimore and Plattsburgh arrived. It was a bad day for asking Americans for anything.[13] "The news is very far from satisfactory," he wrote to Bathurst that night. "We owed the acceptance of our article respecting the Indians to the capture of Washington; and if we had either burnt Baltimore or held Plattsburg, I believe we could have had peace on our terms which you have sent us in a month at least. As things appear to be going on in America, the result of our negotiation may be very different." Wellington wrote to the British delegation at Ghent, advising, "no claim for territorial cession could be considered to exist, and that the basis of 'Uti Possidetis', upon which it was proposed to treat, was untenable." The great duke was blunt, and told them to settle with America without further haggling.[14] Britain's earlier demands had been that the territory in northern Maine, taken earlier that year by General Sir John Sherbrooke, remain in British hands. Now, with the military defeat at Plattsburgh, even the straightening of the Niagara border was no longer viable. The Americans were in a strong position to have the prewar boundaries restored and demand that Britain no longer interfere with American shipping. The talks dragged on until December 24, 1814, Christmas eve, when the Treaty of Ghent was signed. The treaty called for the status quo of 1812. Nothing was gained and nothing was lost except the lives of soldiers and sailors on both sides, which did not seem to matter. Britain would never again attempt to interfere in the affairs of the United States and the American government ceased to think of absorbing Canada. Canada was the only gainer. Its staunch defense by its French and British citizens convinced the Crown that they were indeed to be trusted as loyal members of the empire. From that day forward Canada was considered a nation and not a colony.

TREATY

The Treaty was ratified by the British government on the 28th. Two days later, the London *Times* wrote, "We have retired from combat with the stripes still bleeding on our backs with the recent defeats at Plattsburg and Lake Champlain still unavenged." London sent word of the end of hostilities with the sloop-of-war *Favorite* to Admiral Cochrane, who because of the slow progress of the sailing ship did not receive the word until February 11. President Madison referred the treaty to Congress, who accepted it on February 18. As a result of the delay in word reaching North America, the battle of New Orleans was fought on January 8, 1815, two weeks after the war was over.

After the Duke of Wellington turned down the post held by Sir George Prevost, it was given to General Sir George Murray and Prevost was notified of his relief of duties. Wellington wrote to Murray in an effort to clarify the situation in Canada:

Sir George Prevost's conduct in Canada had been in the highest degree admirable and his defense of the Province, against the vastly superior forces of the Americans is one of the brightest pages in the Military annals of Great Britain.—The failure of the expedition against Plattsburg was not to be ascribed to him: it arose from the unprepared state of the fleet before the expedition commenced and the shameful defection of the gun boats which deserted the heroic Downie when on the point of gaining a decisive victory. We have the authority of the greatest military masters of the age, for the assertion that after the destruction of the fleet, any further prosecution of the advance at land could have led to no beneficial result, as the troops could not have obtained supplies when the Americans had the command on the waters. Though Prevost's attack, was not, from the mistake of the guides made at the same time as Downie's that would have had no material effect except by distant encouragement on the issue of the naval combat, as it took place beyond the range of the batteries on shore. That he might have carried the American blockhouses and batteries is indeed certain, but the examples of New Orleans and Chippewa [probably Fort Erie] prove that Americans fight obstinately behind breast works and it could only have been effected by a heavy sacrifice of human life, which with the prospect of a protracted war in Canada was a serious consideration. His decision in regard to the expedience of an immediate retreat therefore after the fleet had been destroyed, was justified in reference to the single objects of that expedition: it is to be regretted only from its having occurred so immediately before the close of the War and thereby afforded the Americans ground for representing as a complete triumph, that by a vigorous application of the military forces at his command, might have been converted into a drawn battle in which the Laurels, barren to both parties, were divided. But in justice to Prevost it must be added that this contingent result could not have been in the certainty foreseen by him, as the duration of the War was uncertain and that the first thought of a General should be the immediate duty with which he is entrusted, rather than the uncertain ultimate results of a course which hazardous daring might perhaps produce.[15]

ACCOLADES

While the British rankled over the defeat, Plattsburgh celebrated, after caring for the casualties and cleaning up the partially destroyed village. The citizens gave a dinner for Macdonough and Macomb at the United States Hotel, within days of the battle. The army band played as they had at the beginning of the battle. After the dinner, the musicians were stretcher bearers and medical attendants. At the dinner, Commodore Macdonough gave a toast, "to Captain Downie our brave enemy." General Macomb conducted a ceremony that honored the dead of both sides on September 14 at the cemetery in the center of the village. Today, the cemetery remains a place of honor, open to visitors, who will find the warriors of both nations intermingled, as they were in battle.

Governor Daniel Tompkins of New York addressed the legislature soon after the battle and reviewed the British battle plan: "one great object . . . was to penetrate . . . Lake Champlain and the Hudson, and, by a simultaneous attack with his maritime force on New York, to form a junction which should sever the communication of the States."[16] The proud state of Vermont purchased for Macdonough one hundred acres of land on Cumberland Bay overlooking the place of victory. New York State gave him a one thousand acres of land, and the state of Delaware, home to the Macdonough family, presented him with a gold-encrusted sword of honor and with silver service. He received the freedom of the New York City and a plot of land in Washington Square. In addition, both he and Macomb had their portraits painted and hung in the city hall as the saviors of the nation. Congress had a gold coin struck for the two heroes, embossed with the words, "with thanks for a decisive and splendid victory." The honors spread as the country learned the importance of the battle to the northern States. Connecticut gave Macdonough a pair of gold-mounted pistols, and the city of Lansingborough, New York, presented him with a silver pitcher and goblets. The presents were accompanied with rhetoric. Secretary of the Navy William Jones said, "Our lakes, hitherto the objects only of natural curiosity, shall fill the pages of future history with the bright annals of our country's fame and the imperishable renown of our naval heroes." The newspapers now referred to the war as the second war of independence.

DISGRACE

We can see from Anne Prevost's diary where the thought of a British court-martial began:

> On 12th October, my Mother and myself and the children returned by the steam boat to Quebec. My Father had previously gone to Kingston [location of Yeo's headquarters]. He had frequent intercourse with Sir J. Yeo—he [Yeo] even stayed in the Government House, thus accepting my Father's hospitality after he had written a public letter calculated to wound his fame for ever—and which he was really afterwards obliged to follow up by the three charges which would have been investigated. No man with a nice sense of honour would have acted in this manner.

In August of 1815 the Royal Navy convened a court-martial proceeding over the loss of the fleet on Lake Champlain, a nearly mandatory attempt to fix blame that occurred after every naval disaster. In true naval tradition, the proceedings were conducted on board HMS *Gladiator,* at rest in Portsmouth harbor, England. The orders of court-martial read:

> To The Right Honorable Charles Manners Sutton, Judge Advocate General of His Majesty's Forces; or his Deputy.

> Orders of Court Martial

> By His Royal Highness, The Prince Regent of the United Kingdom of Great Britain and Ireland "Whereas It hath been most humbly represented

unto us, that the following charges have been preferred against Lt. Gen. Sir George Prevost, Bart, Colonel of His Majesty's 16th, for the Bedfordshire Regiment of Foot.

1st "For having on or about the Eleventh day of September 1814, by holding out the expectation of a co-operation of the Army under his command, induced Captain Downie late of His majesty's Ship Confiance, to attack the American squadron on Lake Champlain, when it was highly imprudent to make such attack without the co-operation from the land forces, and for not having afforded that Co-operation".

2nd "For not having stormed the American Works on Shore, at nearly the same time that the said Naval action commenced, as he had given Captain Downie reason to expect."

3rd "For having disregarded the Signal for Co-operation, which had been previously agreed upon and which was duly given by Captain Downie."

4th "For not having attacked the Enemy on Shore either during the said Naval Action, or after it was ended, whereby His Majesty's Naval Squadron under the command of Captain Downie, might have been saved or recovered."

Which charges we have thought fit should be inquired into by a General Court Martial. Our Will and Pleasure therefore is, in the name and on behalf of His Majesty, that a General Court Martial be forthwith held upon this occasion, which is to consist of General Sir John Francis Cradock, Grand Cross of the Order of the Bath, Colonel of His Majesty's 43rd for the Monmouthshire Regiment of Foot, whom we appoint President thereof, and of a sufficient number of other officers of competent Rank and Quality, who can be conveniently summoned to attend the same, and you are to order the Provost Marshal General of His Majesty's Forces or his Deputy, to give notice to the said President and officers, and all others whom it may concern, when and where the said Court Martial is to be held and to summon such witnesses as may be able to give testimony touching the charges above specified. The said Provost Marshal General and his Deputy being hereby required to obey your orders and give their attendance where it shall be required; and we do hereby authorize and empower the said General Court Martial, to hear and examine into all such matters and Information as shall be brought before them, touching the charges against the said Lt. General Sir George Prevost, Bart. as aforsaid, and to proceed in the trial and in giving sentence, according to the rules of the Military Discipline and for so doing this shall be as well to you, as to the said General Court Martial and all others whom it may concern, a sufficient Warrant. Given at bar Court at Carlton House, this twenty seventh day of September 1815, In the Fifty fifth year of His Majesty's Reign.

By Command of His Royal Highness, The Prince Regent in the name and on behalf of His Majesty. (signed) Sidmouth

Yeo's charges resulted in the following verdict on August 28, 1815, while Sir George was on his way back to England to defend himself:

The court having maturely weighed the evidence is of the opinion that the capture of H.M.S. Confiance and the remainder of the squadron by the American squadron was principally caused by the British squadron having been urged into battle previous to its being in a proper state to meet the enemy, by the promised co-operation of the land forces not being carried into effect, and by the pressing letters of their commander-in-chief, whereby it appears that he had on the 10th of September, 1814, only waited for the naval attack to storm the enemy's works. That the signal of the approach on the following day was made by the scaling of the guns as settled between Captain Downie and Major Coote, and the promised co-operation was communicated to the other officers and crews of the British squadron before the commencement of the action.

The court, however, is of opinion that the attack would have been attended with more effect if a part of the gunboats had not withdrawn themselves from the action and others of the vessels had not been prevented by baffling winds from getting into the stations assigned them. That Captain Pring of the Linnet, and Lieutenant Robertson, who succeeded to the command of the Confiance after the lamented fate of Captain Downie (whose conduct was marked by the greatest valour), and Lieutenant Christopher James Bell, commanding the Murray, and Mr. James Roberson, commanding the Beresford, gunboats, who appeared to take their trial at this court martial, conducted themselves with great zeal, bravery and ability during the action: that Lieutenant William Hicks, commanding the Finch, also conducted himself with becoming bravery; that the other surviving officers and ship's crew, except Lieutenant McGhie of the Chub who has not appeared here to take his trial, also conducted themselves with bravery; and that Captain Pring, Lieutenant Robertson, Lieutenant Hicks, Lieutenant Bell, and Mr. James

Robertson, and the rest of the surviving officers and ship's company, except Lieutenant McGhie, ought to be most honourably acquitted, and they are hereby most honourably acquitted accordingly.

The popular press picked up the charges and discussed them in depth. In Ireland, the *Cork Mercantile Chronicle,* interested in the battle because of the number of Irish soldiers involved, printed:

Let us examine the evidence which has as yet appeared, connected with these charges. In the first place, we find from anonymous letters, some of which were most probably forged in London for the occasion, that the outcry against Sir George Prevost for preventing the storming of Plattsburg was general in Canada and we hear the names of distinguished officers who are stated to have proceeded to measures almost mutinous, in consequence of threat determination, (a statement which we trust will prove altogether unfounded.) The Dispatches of Sir George have not yet arrived, or, if arrived, have not been published; and it appears to us very strange indeed, if the recall of that Officer has been ordered without hearing his account of the transaction.

We have no official British account of the object of the expedition to Plattsburg; but all the accounts concur in stating that there were ulterior objects, the prosecution of which would require co-operation. This being conceded (and it cannot be denied) the simple question arises, would it have been prudent or justifiable for Sir George Prevost to have risked the loss of a single life towards obtaining these ulterior objects, when the possibility of being supported by that necessary naval co-operation was completely destroyed? Oh, but it would be a gallant affair—very gallant, no doubt! but what would it cost? and when our troops should gain possession of the fort, what would it be worth?—would the benefit of the capture be sufficient compensation for losses sustained in ensuring it? We would recommend the hunters of Sir George to reflect on these little interrogatories before they proceed to run the man down.—Let them recollect that Sir George was too distant from his resources to be sporting the lives of his troops in the pursuit of unprofitable glory, besides, we question very much whether he could spare them. The losses at Fort Erie and the battle of Chippawa, must have reduced his force considerably and therefore he was particularly justified in not exposing himself to certain loss, by contending for the possession of what would be worth nothing when obtained—a mere blind nut. We did not hear any of those mighty charges against Colonel Brooke, who, although he stated, that he had no doubt of succeeding in an attack upon Baltimore nevertheless did not make it, because, as he very properly observed, "it was agreed between the Vice-Admiral and myself, that the capture of the town would not have been a sufficient equivalent to the loss which might probably be sustained in storming the heights." Now, we would ask, why may not the same rule of judgement be applied to Sir George as to Colonel Brooke? Every man approved the determination of Colonel Brooke—why then should they disapprove of a similar determination on the part of Sir George? So far for the first charge, which we think we have disposed of in a manner which must appear satisfactory to every unprejudiced mind.

Now, as to the second charge, of not attacking the battery which co-operated with the naval force of the enemy against our flotilla:—nothing but anonymous imputations and insinuations. We are not told of the relative situations of the two batteries, as to place and distance; and we regret the absence of British official evidence, on this point the more, because it struck us to be the only question which could call for investigation. But the American Commander is explicit on the point. In the general orders published at Plattsburg, Sept. 14 1814, by the American General Macombe, we find the following passage. Speaking of the issue of the naval combat, he says, "the British army was also so posted on the surrounding heights, that it could not but behold the interesting struggle for dominion on the Lake."

From this one would be induced to conclude that the British army was so distant that it could do no more than behold the battle. But we would much wrong General Prevost were we not to insert the following paragraph of General Macombe's official report, which completely vindicates the British officer against the charge of inactivity, Or of indisposition to CO-operate with the naval force. General Macombe states, "at the same hour the fleets engaged, the enemy opened his batteries on our forts, throwing hundreds of shells, balls and rockets, and attempted at the same time to cross the Saranac at three different points to assault the works."

It would be offensive to the public judgement, after such abundant testimony, to hesitate in deciding, that the second charge, of neglect of co-operation, is completely refuted.

During the trial many of the officer participants in the battle testified about their experiences. It was curious that Sir George

Prevost was not called to defend himself. The court found no fault on the part of any naval officer and rested the entire matter on the shoulders of General Prevost, who was preparing to leave Canada to defend himself, having been replaced by Murray. When Sir George arrived in England in September, he discovered that he had been found guilty by the Royal naval court and he demanded an army court-martial to clear his name. He was still supported by the Prince Regent, who asked Prevost to raise a new regiment and granted "supporters" on his personal coat of arms, in recognition of his profound service to Great Britain. It was a rare gift for a baronet to have figures established on either side of his shield. Prevost's were in the form of two soldiers from his regiment, in red coats and white crossbelts. But despite the honor, Prevost was in poor health. The years of service in the Caribbean and the strain of the war had taken its toll. He died on January 5, 1816, at age 49, of dropsy, a building up of fluid in the body which causes heart and kidney failure. The army court-martial was to be established within days. Prevost's loyal wife, Lady Catherine, spent the remainder of her life petitioning government officials and royal friends to open the army court-martial and vindicate her husband. She died six years after her husband.

TIME MARCHES ON

Commodore Macdonough went on to an extensive career. While captain of the *Constitution,* Old Ironsides, stationed in the Mediterranean in 1827, he heard of his wife's death. On the voyage home he died of heart failure. General Alexander Macomb went on to become the commanding general of the U.S. Army in 1828. He instituted many reforms. Opposed to the whiskey ration, since young soldiers often learned to drink in the army, he substituted rice and vegetables, or later sugar or coffee, for it. He established pensions for regular and militia soldiers and widows. He was instrumental in fair treatment for the Indians being removed from their lands, lobbying Congress for Native Americans, whom he believed had the rights to the land they occupied. He died in harness in June 1841 at age of 59. His monument is in the Congressional Cemetery in Washington, inscribed, "It were but a small tribute to his memory to say that, in youth and manhood, he served his country in the profession in which he died, during a period of more than forty years, without a stain or blemish on his escutcheon."[17]

In modern times the battle slid into obscurity. Because the Battle of Baltimore, which gave the United States its national anthem, was fought on nearly the same day, Plattsburgh and Champlain slipped from memory. Scholars from time to time have paid tribute. Theodore Roosevelt remarked that "the battle had a very great effect on the negotiations for peace and that Captain Perry's name is more widely known than that of any other commander. Every schoolboy reads about him, if of no other sea captain, yet he certainly stands in a lower grade than Macdonough. This lake, which had hithertofore played but an inconspicuous part was now become the scene of the greatest naval battle of the War." Even Winston Churchill commented, "In September, under Sir George Prevost, they moved on Plattsburgh, and prepared to dispute the command of Lake Champlain. They were faced by a mere fifteen hundred American regulars, supported by a few thousand militia. All depended on the engagement of the British and American flotillas. As at Lake Erie, the Americans built better ships for fresh water fighting, and they gained the victory. This crippled the British advance and was the most decisive engagement of the war."[18] No other author indicates that the construction of the ships had anything to do with the capability of the two fleets.

Churchill missed the point that two of the British vessels had been captured from the Americans in an earlier battle. John McMaster states of Plattsburgh that it was "the greatest naval battle of the war, and provided this country with the greatest sea captain our country produced down to the Rebellion."[19] The famed American naval historian Alfred T. Mahan wrote, "This lake battle was tiny, but one of the most decisive in American history."[20]

Colonel John Elting sums up the entire affair in the closing paragraph of his book, *Amateurs, To Arms!:* "In cold fact the United States survived only because handfuls of American soldiers and sailors, ill-supported and finally almost abandoned by their central government, ignored and often betrayed by their fellow countrymen, somehow made headway against all odds until England at last wearied."[21]

Appendix A

American, British, and Canadian Army Units

American Army Units

There were no intact regiments. They all had accompanied General Izard to Niagara.

77 men from a variety of regiments
100 from the 15th regiment
200 from the 13th regiment
1,500 from the 6th, 29th, 30th, 31st, 33d, and 34th regiments
50 artillery men
700 New York militia
2,500 Vermont militia

More than 500 of the 1,927 regulars were sick in hospital. The vast majority of the 700 New York Militia had gone before the Vermont militia arrived.

British and Canadian Army Units

19th Light Dragoons   Yellow facings, gold lace
1st Battalion of Royal Marines   Blue facings piped in white
1st Regiment   The Royal Scots, blue facings, gold lace

3rd Infantry Regiment	The Buffs, East Kent, buff facings, silver lace
5th Infantry Regiment	Northumberland, green facings, gold lace
6th Infantry Regiment	The Warwickshire, yellow facings, silver lace
8th Kings Regiment	A royal regiment, blue facings, gold lace
9th Infantry Regiment	East Norfolk, yellow facings, silver lace
13th Infantry Regiment	1st Somersetshire, buff facings, silver lace
27th Infantry Regiment	The Inniskillings, buff facings, gold lace
37th Infantry Regiment	North Hampshire, yellow facings, silver lace
39th Infantry Regiment	Dorsetshire, pea green facings, gold lace
49th Infantry Regiment	Princess Charlotte of Wales, green facings, gold lace
57th Infantry Regiment	West Middlesex, yellow facings, gold lace
58th Infantry Regiment	Rutlandshire, black facings, gold lace
76th Infantry Regiment	No affiliation, red facings, silver lace
81st Infantry Regiment	No affiliation, buff facings, silver lace
88th Infantry Regiment	Connaught Rangers, yellow facings, silver lace
100th Infantry Regiment	Prince of Wales Volunteers, green facings, yellow lace
Royal Artillery	Six companies plus one company of rockets

These units were sent in support of the secret plan and added to the four thousand British troops involved in the defense of Canada. Some regiments sent more than one battalion.

MAJOR GENERAL THOMAS BRISBANE'S brigade consisted of the 13th, 49th, and 2/8th infantry regiments. In addition, there were regiments of Canadian fencibles, voltigeurs, and chasseurs, and De Meuron's Swiss, enough to make up an entire brigade.

MAJOR GENERAL FREDERICK ROBINSON'S brigade consisted of the combined light infantry companies and the 39th, 76th, 88th, and 3/27th (the 39th was taken for the crews of the Royal Navy).

MAJOR GENERAL MANLEY POWERS'S brigade consisted of at least the 3d, 5th, and 58th, and the 1st/3d and 5th battalions of the 27th.

MAJOR GENERAL JAMES KEMPT'S BRIGADE, which was in Montreal, was used for the diversion to the west and consisted of the 9th, 37th, 57th, and 81st regiments.

Source note: There are several conflicting lists of regimental assignments, but the most complete comes from Robert S. Quimby's excellent book, *The U.S. Army in the War of 1812: An Operational and Command Study* (East Lansing: Michigan State University Press, 1984), 598.

BRITISH PARTICIPANTS

ANDERSON, ALEXANDER, Captain, Royal Marines, killed during the naval battle

BATHURST, EARL, Secretary of State for the colonial affairs

BAYNES, Adjutant to Sir George Prevost

BRISBANE, THOMAS, Major General, commander of a brigade at Plattsburgh

BROCK, ISAAC, Major General commanding at Detroit and killed in action at Queenstown

BRYDEN, Sailing Master of the *Confiance*

BURGOYNE, JOHN, Major General, American Revolution, lost the battle of Saratoga

COCHRANE, SIR ALEXANDER, Vice Admiral, commander of the diversionary force on the American coast

COCKBURN, GEORGE, Admiral, commander of the fleet that captured Washington, D.C.

CONGREVE, WILLIAM, gun designer and director of ordnance in Great Britain

COOTE, RICHARD, Captain, in the service of Great Britain raided American ports for money

CRAIG, JAMES, Governor General of Canada, prior to the War of 1812

DE ROTTENBURG, FRANCIS, Major General, deputy commanding general at Plattsburgh

DE SALABERRY, CHARLES, Colonel, hero of the Canadian army

DOWNIE, GEORGE, Captain, Royal Navy, commodore of the flotilla, killed at Plattsburgh

FISHER, PETER, Captain, Royal Navy, built *Confiance,* relieved by Downie

GORDON, Captain, Royal Navy, commanded the task force that attacked Alexandria, Virginia

HICKS, WILLIAM, Lieutenant, captain of the *Finch*

LEA, R., Midshipman, *Confiance*

MCGHIE, JAMES, Lieutenant, captain of the *Chub*

MURRAY, JOHN, Lieutenant Colonel, led a raid on Lake Champlain in 1813

NOADIE, CAPTAIN, King's 8th Infantry

POWERS, MANLEY, Major General, commander of a brigade at Plattsburgh

PREVOST, ANNE, daughter of Sir George

PREVOST, AUGUSTIN, father of Sir George, served during the American Revolution

PREVOST, SIR GEORGE, Governor General of Canada

PRINCE REGENT, son of George III, who acts in place of his ill father

PRING, DANIEL, Captain, Royal Navy, Provincial Marine during the entire war

SHERBROOKE, JOHN, Governor General of New Brunswick

SIMONS, WILLIAM, shipwright of the *Confiance*, killed at Plattsburgh

ROBERTSON, Lieutenant, Royal Navy, surviving captain of the *Confiance*

ROBINSON, FREDERICK, Major General, quartermaster general at Plattsburgh

ROBINSON, WILLIAM HENRY, Major General, brigade commander at Plattsburgh

ROSS, ROBERT, Major General, commander of the army force that captured Washington, D.C.

TECUMSEH, Indian chief in the Old Northwest, killed at the Battle of Thames

WELLINGTON, ARTHUR WELLESEY, Duke, commanding general in Spain, ambassador to France, and a representative for Great Britain at the Congress of Vienna

WELLINGTON, JAMES, Lieutenant Colonel, commander of the 3d Infantry Regiment "Buffs," killed at Plattsburgh

YEO, SIR JAMES LUCAS, Admiral, commander of all British naval forces in Canada

AMERICAN PARTICIPANTS

AIKIN, MARTIN, Captain, New York militia, commander of Aikin's volunteers

APPLING, DANIEL, Lieutenant Colonel, commander at Dead Creek bridge

ARMSTRONG, JOHN, Secretary of War, replaced William Eustis after the burning of Washington

BROWN, NOAH, U.S. Navy shipbuilder from the Brooklyn navy yard

BRUM, Sailing Master, *Ticonderoga*

CASSIN, STEPHEN, Lieutenant, U.S. Navy, commander of the *Ticonderoga*

CHITTENDEN, MARTIN, Governor, Vermont

CLARK, ISAAC, Colonel, Vermont militia, conducted successful raid into Canada

CONOVER, Midshipman, in charge of a gunboat, supported Cassin

DARUSIE, R. E., Lieutenant, Corps of Engineers, drew the map of the battle

DEARBORN, HENRY, Major General, secretary of war under Jefferson, then commander of American army until 1813. He was the senior general but commanded the Army of the North.

DUNCAN, SILAS, Midshipman, from *Saratoga,* rescued gunboats, decorated by Congress

EUSTIS, WILLIAM, secretary of war under Madison.

FLAGG, AZARIAH, Lieutenant, New York militia, leader in Aikin's Volunteers

FOWLER, Lieutenant, commanded a blockhouse at Plattsburgh

HAMPTON, WADE, Major General, subordinate to Wilkinson in 1813

HARRISON, WILLIAM HENRY, Major General, western campaign, later president of the United States

HULL, WILLIAM, Commanding General of the Army, Northwest, appointed June 1812

IZARD, GEORGE, Major General, commanding the Army of the North, the spring of 1814

JEFFERSON, THOMAS, President of the United States, 1801–09

JONES, WILLIAM, Secretary of the Navy

LEONARD, Captain, commanded the artillery at Beekmantown and the bridge

LOOMIS, JARVIS, Sailing Master, *Growler,* captured at Ille aux Noix in 1813

MACDONOUGH, THOMAS, Lieutenant, U.S. Navy, commodore of the Lake Champlain flotilla

MACOMB, ALEXANDER, JR., Brigadier General, commander at Plattsburgh

MADISON, JAMES, President of the United States, 1809–17

MANN, JOHN, maintained the hospital on Crab island during the battle

MCGLASSIN, GEORGE, Captain, commanded the raid on the British rocket battery

MONROE, JAMES, Secretary of State, appointed acting secretary of war after the burning of Washington, D.C.

MOOERS, BENJAMIN, Major General, New York militia

PAULDING, HIRAM, Midshipman, *Ticonderoga,* fired guns with a pistol

PHELPS, BENJAH, twelve-year-old boy who witnessed the battle

PIKE, ZEBULON, Brigadier General, killed in action at York, Upper Canada

PLATT, CHARLES, Midshipman, *Saratoga,* took command of the beaten *Chub*

STAFFORD, CAPTAIN, New York militia, dragoon at Dead Creek bridge

SAILLY, PETER, Customs Director, spymaster.

SCOTT, WINFIELD, Brigadier General, fought at Queenstown, Fort George

SMITH, JOHN, Lieutenant, commanded a blockhouse manned by the sick at Plattsburgh

SMITH, MALANCTON, Lieutenant Colonel, commanded Fort Moreau

SMYTH, ALEXANDER, Brigadier General, campaigned after Queenston in the Niagara

SPROUL, ROBERT, Captain, commanded a company of the 13th Infantry

STANDISH, MATTHEW, Lieutenant, New York militia, dragoon

STORES, HUCKENS, Lieutenant Colonel, commanded Fort Brown

STRONG, SAMUEL, Major General, Vermont militia (Green Mountain Boys)

TAYLOR, ZACHARY, Captain, under Harrison in the western campaign, later president of the United States

TERRY, SAM, Private, New York militia, shot Lieutenant Colonel Wellington

TOTTEN, JOSEPH G., Major, Corps of Engineers, designed the defenses at Plattsburgh

VAN RENSSELAER, SOLOMON, Lieutenant Colonel, New York militia, killed at Queenstown

VAN RENSSELAER, STEPHEN, Major General, New York militia, fought at Queenston, 1812

VAUGHAN, Captain, Vermont militia, Pike's Cantonment

VINSON, THOMAS, Major, commanded the remnants of the 33d and 34th regiments

WAIT, ROSWELL, Lieutenant, New York militia, dragoon

WILKINSON, JAMES, Major General, succeeded Dearborn as commanding general in north

WINDER, WILLIAM, Brigadier General, commanded the defensive force at Bladensburg

WOOL, JOHN E., Captain at Queenston, Major at Plattsburgh

YOUNG, GUILFORD DUDLEY, Major, commander of the Troy, New York, militia

APPENDIX B

Naval Weaponry

BRITISH AND AMERICAN SHIPS

Name	Country	Commander	Guns	Crew
Confiance	Great Britain	Downie	37	270
Linnet	Great Britain	Pring	16	99
Chub	Great Britain	McGhie	11	41
Finch	Great Britain	Hicks	11	32
Saratoga	United States	Macdonough	26	250
Eagle	United States	Henley	20	142
Ticonderoga	United States	Cassin	17	115
Preble	United States	Budd	7	43

BREAKDOWN OF THE GUNS BY SHIP (ROYAL NAVY)

	Cannons	Carronades
Confiance	27 long (24 lb)	4 (32 lb)
Linnet	16 long (12 lb)	6 (24 lb)
Chub	1 long (6 lb)	10 (18 lb)
Finch	4 long (6 lb)	7 (18 lb)

The Royal Navy had eleven gunboats: *Yeo, Blucher, Drummond, Murray, Wellington, Bereford, Popham, Prevost, Simcoe, Beckwith,* and *Brock.* More than half of the crews were French Canadian, and under the command of Captain Roumzie.

If *Finch* still had only her guns from before her capture in 1812, then there may have been one columbiad on board.

The total crew for all Royal Navy vessels was believed to be just under one thousand.

BREAKDOWN OF THE GUNS BY SHIP (U.S. NAVY)

	Cannons	Carronades
Saratoga	8 long (24 lb)	6 (42 lb)
		12 (32 lb)
Eagle	8 long (18 lb)	12 (32 lb)
Ticonderoga	4 long (18 lb)	5 (32 lb)
	8 long (12 lb)	
Preble	7 long (9 lb)	

American gunboats: *Borer, Centipede, Wilmer, Nettle, Allen, Viper, Burrows, Ludlow, Alwyn,* and *Ballard.*

The twenty-four-pound long cannons on *Saratoga* were not the same gun that *Confiance* carried. The British flagship was equipped with the latest Congreve technology and her twenty-fours had longer range and were more accurate.

I have seen many gun counts and those in the tables above seems to be the most accurate. I believe the American ship count is taken from a document at the Shelburn Museum, written in Macdonough's hand before the battle. This simple list has often led people to comment that the fleets seemed nearly equal. But there was a decided advantage to the Royal Navy because of the superior range and throwing weight.

The total crew for all the American vessels was believed to be over 800.

Note: The Royal Navy, as a rule, did not count the carronades in the gun totals, while the Americans counted everything. *Chub* and *Finch,* former American vessels, were believed to be gunned with their original carronades, although some disagree. The gunboats on both sides were armed with one cannon, twenty-, eighteen-, and twelve-pounders. Four of the British gunboats had thirty-two-pound carronades. Although some had a center gun, it was not often used.

APPENDIX C

Postbattle Assessments

To: Thomas Macdonough, Esq. commanding
     United States' squadron on Lake Champlain

Sir,

I have the honor to enclose you a list of the killed and wounded on board the different vessels of the squadron under your command in the action of the 11th inst.

It is impossible to ascertain correctly the loss of the enemy. From the best information received from the British officers, from my own observations, and from various lists found on board the Confiance, I calculate the number of men on board at 270, of 180, at least, were killed and wounded; and on board the other captured vessels at least 80 more, making in the whole, killed or wounded, 260. This doubtless short of the real number, as many were thrown overboard from the Confiance during the engagement.

The muster books must have been thrown overboard, or otherwise disposed of, as they are not to be found.

I am, sir, respectfully,
Your obedient servant,

GEORGE BEALE, Jr. purser.

The *Saratoga* killed in action

    Peter Gamble,   lieutenant
    Thomas Butler,   quarter gunner

James Norberry, boatswain's mate
Abraham Davis, quarter master
William Wyer, sail maker
William Brickell, seaman
Peter Johnson, "
John Coleman, "
Benjamin Burrill, ordinary seaman
Andrew Parmlee, "
Peter Post, seaman
David Bennett, "
Ebenezer Johnson, "
Joseph Couch, landsman
Thomas Stephens, seaman
Randall M'Donald, ordinary seaman
John White, "
Samuel Smith, seaman
Thomas Malony, ordinary seaman
Andrew Nelson, seaman
John Sellack, "
Peter Hanson, "
Jacob Laraway, "
Edward Moore, "
Jerome Williams, ordinary seaman
James Carlisle, marine
John Smart, seaman
Earl Hannemon, "

The *Saratoga* wounded in action

James M. Baldwin, acting midshipman
Joseph Barron, pilot
Robert Gary, quarter gunner
George Cassin, quarter master

John Hollingworth, seaman
Thomas Robinson, "
Purnall Smith, "
John Ottiwell, "
John Thompson, ordinary seaman
William Tabee, "
William Williams, "
John Roberson, seaman
John Towns, landsman
John Shays, seaman
John S. Hammond, "
James Barlow, "
James Nagle, ordinary seaman
John Lanman, seaman
Peter Colberg, "
William Newton, ordinary seaman
Neil J. Heidmont, seaman
James Steward, "
John Adams, landsman
Charles Ratche, seaman
Benjamin Jackson, marine
Jesse Vanhorn, "
Joseph Ketter, "
Samuel Pearson, "

The schooner *Ticonderoga* killed in action

John Stansbury, lieutenant
John Fisher, boatswain's mate
John Atkinson, "
Henry Johnson, seaman
Deodrick Think, marine
John Sharp, "

The schooner *Ticonderoga* wounded in action

Patrick Cassin,	seaman
Ezekiel Gound,	"
Samuel Sawyer,	"
William Le Count,	"
Henry Collins,	"
John Condon,	marine

The sloop *Preble* killed in action

Rogers Carter,	acting sailing master
Joseph Bowe,	boatswain's mate

Gun Boats (galleys) crewmen killed in action

Arthur W. Smith,	On board *Borer*
Thomas Gill,	"
James Day,	"

Gun Boats (galleys) crewmen wounded in action

Ebenezer Cobb,	On board *Borer*
James Taylor,	On board *Centipede*
Peter Frank,	On board *Wilmer*

Below is a partial list of the crew of the brig Eagle. *It does not in-clude the names of the prisoners from the American army stock-ade who were enlisted at the last minute to help man the vessel. Among musicians, the list only gives the names of those who were killed, and not of the five men and one musician's wife who sur-vived. Otherwise, the list may be of the original crew that boarded her upon launch that summer of 1814. The complement* *during the battle was 142. Of the 57 listed from this roster, 15 were killed and 20 were wounded, 4 were sick in the hospital on Crab Island, and 4 deserted. Those listed as "marines" were actually army infantry afloat. Note that "+" stands for killed and "*" stands for wounded.*

Robert Henley	Master Command (Captain)
Joseph Smith *	First Lieutenant
William Spencer *	Second Lieutenant
Jarvis Loomis	Master
Daniel Records	Sailing Master
William Machesney	Midshipman
William Chamberlain	Midshipman
Henry Tardy	Midshipman
Francis Breeze *	Master's Mate
Peter Vandermere +	Master's Mate
Abraham Waters *	Pilot
William C. Allen *	Quartermaster
John Wilson	Boatswain
Charles B. Johnson	Carpenter
Edward Smith	Gunner
James Duick *	Quarter Gunner
Isaac Stoddard	Surgeon
James Willis +	Seaman
John Ribero +	Seaman
Jacob Lindman +	Seaman
Andrew McEwan *	Seaman
Zebediah Conklin *	Seaman
Joseph Valentine *	Seaman
John Hartley *	Seaman
John Micklan *	Seaman
Robert Buckley *	Seaman
John Craig *	Seaman

John McKenney *	Seaman
Perkins Moore +	Ordinary Seaman
James Winship +	Ordinary Seaman
Thomas Anwright +	Ordinary Seaman
Nace Wilson +	Ordinary Seaman
Parnel Boice +	Ordinary Seaman
Thomas Lewis +	Boy
Aaron Fitzgerald *	Boy
Garrison Gibbs	Sick in hospital prior to battle
John Davis	Sick in hospital prior to battle
Thomas Maloney	Sick in hospital prior to battle
Joseph Richardson	Sick in hospital prior to battle
Stephen Bostick	Rank unlisted
Christen Frederick	Rank unlisted
Cornelius Moore	Rank unlisted
Joseph Foquet	Rank unlisted
James Springer	Rank unlisted
John Lewis	Deserted August 20th at Vergennes
John Brown	Deserted August 21st at Vergennes
Horace Lane	Deserted August 25th at Vergennes
Joseph Morrison *	Lieutenant, marine [U.S. Army]
Mathew Scriver *	Marine
George Mainwaring *	Marine
John Wallace +	Marine
Joseph Heaton +	Marine
Henry Jones *	Marine
John McCarty *	Marine
James M. Hale +	Musician
John Wood +	Musician
William Wier +	Sailmaker

Navy enlistment was for two years

Below is Beale's recapitulation, which has some errors.

	Killed	Wounded
Saratoga,	28	29
Eagle,	13	20
Ticonderoga,	6	6
Preble,	2	
Gun Boats,	3	3
Total	52	58

The Royal Navy acknowledges 57 killed and 72 wounded, with 17 officers and 340 seamen captured. There was a much larger number of crewmen on board the fleet. These figures more than likely include only the Royal Navy men and not the battalion of Dorset infantry, which numbered near to five hundred. Poor record keeping, considering the ships were manned on both sides by soldiers who had only been aboard for a week, is understandable. It is known that many were lost to the lake who may never have been recorded as having been on board.

The following are extracts from a letter written by Commodore Thomas Macdonough to Commodore John Rodgers, president of the Board of the Navy Commissioners. In today's terminology, the letter is a fitness, or efficiency, report, to be used for promotions and assignments for those discussed. It was not uncommon at that time for reports to be very critical, often harsh, with the intent to reform bad habits.

Washington May 6th 1815

Sir,

In obedience to the order of the Commissioners I herewith transmit an impartial and as far as I am capable of Judging a correct report of the character, and qualifications of each of the

Commissioned & Warrant officers who were attached to my command on Lake Champlain commencing with Captain Henly of whom I have had but little opportunity to form an opinion, though I look upon him to be very deficient in seamanship and in the equipment of a Vessel of War he is a stranger. His disposition I take to be Malicious and base. He behaved like a brave Man on the 11th Sept. last, though his Vessel was badly Managed. [Henly arrived on Lake Champlain on August 12, one month before the battle, to command the *Eagle.* He wanted to name the ship the *"Surprise"* and wrote on this matter directly to the secretary of the navy, going over Macdonough's head. He was promoted to captain in March 1825.]

Captain Cassin, I consider a Man of firmness when put to the test, as good a seaman as Most Men of his age and experience, whose Judgment is good, and who behaved very well on the 11th Sept. 1814. [Cassin was captain of the *Ticonderoga.*]

Captain Sidney Smith, I consider no Seaman, though an amiable Man he is deficient in Seamanship and the knowledge of fitting out a Vessel. Heretofore has been indifferent about the Service or did not seem to feel or take an individual interest in it. Since his promotion he May be More attached to the Service though his rank Must be above his Merits. [The year before, Smith had lost the two vessels that the British converted to the *Chub* and *Finch* and used against Macdonough in the battle of Plattsburgh. Smith was released in a prisoner exchange in July 1814. It is unknown what his duties were during the battle—perhaps none.]

Lt. Francis I. Mitchell. Must be well known to the board as the Most profane Man in the Service. He is no Seaman neither do I consider him a Man of Courage. Speaking from What I was eye Witness to on Lake Champlain, I think he does the service

More disgrace than honor. [Mitchell commanded the gunboat *Viper* during the battle.]

Lt. Charles A Budd, Is an intemperate Man Whose habits of intemperance are I believe so firmly rooted as to be nearly immovable. His best quality is his seamanship, he is careless or regardless of the service, all it appeared to me that he wished was to remain at home draw his pay—and live an idle life—he did not behave well on the 11th September. [After the battle, Macdonough publicly defended Budd's action in leaving the line, saying that had he done otherwise, his ship, *Preble,* surely would have been boarded and taken.]

Lt. EAF Vallette. Is an excellent young Man, a good seaman, sober, steady—studious & brave. [Vallette was the officer in charge of the quarter gun division on *Saratoga* during the battle.]

Lt. Silas Duncan. Is a brave cool and deliberate young Man something of a Seaman whose habits are good, he was badly wounded on the 11th Septr. He will I believe make a valuable officer though he should have practice in his profession. [As third Lieutenant on the *Saratoga,* Duncan was sent to recall the gunboats, when he was wounded. He was later decorated by Congress.]

Lt. Wm. Augustus Spencer. I am sorry that it is out of my power compatible with candor & impartiality to give a good character of this young Man, he did not from all accounts behave well on the 11th Septr. and I regret that I believe there is too Much cause for those accounts to be true, he is a well looking young Man but, his external is the best, he is not much of a Seamen yet he May make an officer of value to the Service. [Spencer served as the second lieutenant on the *Ticonderoga.*]

Doctor William Caton. Is I believe a Man very deficient in the necessary knowledge of his profession. I am sure he is in Moral charter of the Man, he was complained of much by the officers & particularly by the Men in the Hospital. He drank hard on the Lake, for which he should have been arrested but for the apparent impossibility of getting another Surgeon, his conduct had been bad, I do not think he will ever Make a good Surgeon for the Navy, or a good Member of Society.

Surgeons Mate Gustavus R. Brown. I cannot say much of this young Man, he is or was fond of drink. His knowledge of his profession I believe is good and he Might Make a Surgeon of some Value though he should be a good one or none for I believe that Several Men who Might have recovered from their Wounds, with skilled attention died through the want of it in Dr. Caton, as well as some of the Surgeons of the Army.

George Beale Purser. I believe this to be an excellent young man who has done as Much if not More Justice to the Men whose purser he was, than any other purser in the Navy—his principles and Judgment are good, I consider him an excellent purser. [Beale had been in Macdonough's command since August 3, 1813.]

William M. Robins Sailing Master. Has once been a man who might have been of Value to the Service he is now old & infirmed subject to intoxication occasionally for he does not Make it a constant practice to get so/ A Seamen, but, not to be trusted with Much, as he is unsteady, he would make a good Master for a Navy Yard as he is neat in arrangement & careful of public property. He behaved well on the 11th of September in the galleys. [Robins commanded the gunboat *Allen* in the battle.]

Daniel S. Stellwagen Sailing Master. A Man who in my opinion cannot think he has Much claim to public favour or patronage, I believe him to be a good Seaman, but feels more calling to be supported by the Service than to give his individual aid to the service, he did not behave well on the 11th September in the Galleys. [Stellwagen commanded the gunboat *Wilmer* during the battle.]

Philip Brum Sailing Master. A man who I would have been much pleased to see promoted for his good conduct on the 11th Septr. as master of *Saratoga*. He is a Seamen a Man of steady and Manly habits. Has commanded several times to Canton. I think a Valuable officer.

I have the honor to be
Sir, your ob Servt.

(signed) T. Macdonough

Members of Macdonough's own crew on board the Saratoga *fared much better in his assessments than members of his command who were not under his personal supervision. This is not an uncommon occurrence, even in today's military. It is human nature for a commander to reward those closest to him.*

APPENDIX D

After-Action Reports

THE AFTER-ACTION REPORT OF ALEXANDER MACOMB

The governor-general of the Canadas, Sir George Prevost, having collected all the disposable force in Lower Canada, with a view of conquering the country as far as Crown Point, and Ticonderoga, entered the territories of the United States on the 1st of the month, and occupied the village of Champlain; there he avowed his intentions, and issued orders and proclamations, tending to dissuade the people from their allegiance, and inviting them to furnish his army with provisions. He immediately began to impress the wagons and teams in the vicinity, and loaded them with his heavy baggage and stores. From this I was persuaded he intended to attack this place. I had but just returned from the lines, where I had commanded a fine brigade, which was broken up to form the division under Major-general Izard, and ordered to the westward. Being senior officer, he left me in command; and, except the four companies of the 6th regiment, I had not an organized battalion among those remaining. The garrison was composed of convalescents and recruits of the new regiments, all in the greatest confusion, as well as the ordnance and stores, and the works in no state of defense. To create emulation and zeal among the officers and men in completing the works, I divided them into detachments, and placed them near the several forts; declaring in orders that each detachment was the garrison of its own work, and bound to defend it to the last extremity. The enemy advanced cautiously and by short marches, and our soldiers worked day and night, so that by the time he made his appearance before the place we were prepared to receive him. General Izard named the principal work Fort-Moreau and, to remind the troops of the actions for their brave countrymen, I called the redoubt on the right Fort-Brown, and that on the left Fort-Scott. Besides these three works, we had two block-houses strongly fortified. Finding, on examining the returns for the garrison, that our force did not exceed 1500 effective men for duty, and well informed that the enemy had as many thousands, I called on general Mooers, of the New York militia, and arranged with him plans for bringing forth the militia en masse. The inhabitants of the village fled with their families and effects, except a few worthy citizens and some boys who formed themselves into a party, received rifles, and were exceedingly useful. By the 4th of the month, general Mooers collected about 700 militia, and advanced seven miles on the Beekmantown road, to watch the motions of the enemy, and to skirmish with him as he advanced; also to obstruct the roads with fallen trees, and to break up the bridges. On the lake-road, at Dead creek bridge, I posted 200 men, under captain Sproul, of the 13th regiment, with orders to abattis the woods, to place obstruction in the road, and to fortify himself; to this party I added two field-pieces. In advance of that position was lieutenant-colonel Appling, with 110 riflemen, watching the movements of the enemy, and procuring intelligence. It was ascertained that before day-light on the 6th, the enemy would advance in two columns, on the two roads before mentioned, dividing at Sampson's a little below Chazy village. The column on the Beekman-town road proceeded most rapidly; the militia skirmished with his advanced parties, and except a few brave men, fell back most precipitately in the greatest disorder, notwithstanding the British troops did not deign to fire on them, except by their flankers and advanced patrols. The night previous, I ordered major Wool to advance with a detachment of 250 men to support the militia, and set them an example of firmness; also captain Leonard, of the light-artillery, was directed to proceed with two pieces to be on the ground before day; yet he did not make his appearance until eight o'clock, when the enemy had approached within two miles of the village. With his conduct, therefore, I am not well pleased. Major Wool, with his party, disputed the road with great obstinacy, but the militia could not be prevailed on to stand, notwithstanding the exertions of their general and staff-officers; although the fields were divided by strong stone walls, and they were told that the enemy could not possibly cut them off. The state dragoons of New York wear red coats; and they being on the heights to watch the enemy, gave constant alarm to the militia, who mistook them for the enemy, and feared his getting in their rear.

Finding the enemy's columns had penetrated within a few miles of Plattsburg, I dispatched my aid de camp, lieutenant Root, to bring off the detachment at Dead creek, and to inform lieutenant-colonel Appling that I wished him to fall on the enemy's right flank. The colonel fortunately arrived just in time to save his retreat, and to fall in with the head of a column debauching from the woods. Here he poured in a destructive fire from his riflemen at rest, and continued to annoy the enemy until he formed a junction with major Wool. The field-pieces did considerable execution among the enemy's columns. So undaunted, however, was the enemy, that he never deployed in his whole march, always pressing on in column. Finding that every road was full of troops, crowding on us on all sides, I ordered the field-pieces to retire across the bridge, and form a battery for its protection and to cover the retreat of the infantry, which was accordingly done, and the parties of Appling and Wool, as well as that of Sproul, retired, alternately keeping up a brisk fire until they got under cover of the works.

The enemy's light troops occupied the houses near the bridge, and kept up a constant firing from the windows and balconies, and annoyed us much. I ordered them to be driven out with hot shot, which soon put the houses in flames, and obliged those sharpshooters to retire. The whole day, until it was too late to see, the enemy's light troops endeavored to drive our guards from the bridge, but they suffered dearly for their perseverance. An attempt was also made to cross the upper bridge, where the militia handsomely drove them back. The column which marched by the lakeroad was much impeded by the obstructions, and the removal of the bridge at Dead creek; and, as it passed the creek and beach, the galleys kept up a lively and galling fire. Our troops being now all on the south side of the Saranac, I directed the planks to be taken off the bridges and piled up in the form of breast-works, to cover our parties intention for disputing the passage, which afterwards enabled us to hold the bridges against very superior numbers. From the 7th to the [11th], the enemy was employed in getting on his battering-train, and erecting his batteries and approaches, and constantly skirmishing at the bridges and fords. By this time the militia of New York and the volunteers of Vermont were pouring in from all quarters. I advised general Mooers to keep his force along the Saranac to prevent the enemy's crossing the river, and to send a strong body in his rear to harass him day and night, and keep him in continual alarm. The militia behaved with great spirit after the first day, and the volunteers of Vermont were exceedingly serviceable. Our regular troops, notwithstanding the constant skirmishing, and repeated endeavors of the enemy to cross the river, kept at their work day and night, strengthening the defenses, and evinced a determination to hold out to the last extremity. It was reported that the enemy only waited the arrival of his flotilla to make a general attack. About eight in the morning of the 11th, as was expected, the flotilla appeared in sight around Cumberland

Head, and at nine bore down and engaged at anchor in the bay off the town. At the same instant the batteries were opened on us, and continued throwing bomb-shells, shrapnells, balls, and Congreve rockets, until sun-set, when the bombardment ceased, every battery of the enemy being silenced by the superiority of our fire. The naval engagement lasted but two hours, in full view of both armies. Three efforts were made by the enemy to pass the river at the commencement of the cannonade and bombardment, with a view of assaulting the works, and they had prepared for that purpose an immense number of scaling ladders. One attempt to cross was made at the village bridge, another at the upper bridge, and a third at a ford about three miles from the works. At the two first he was repulsed by the regulars—at the ford by the brave volunteers and militia, where he suffered severely in killed, wounded, and prisoners; a considerable body crossed the stream, but were either killed, taken, or driven back. The woods at this place were very favorable to the operations of the militia. A whole company of the 76th regiment was here destroyed, the three lieutenants and 27 men prisoners, the captain and the rest killed. I cannot forego the pleasure of here stating the gallant conduct of captain M'Glassin, of the 15th regiment, who was ordered to ford the river, and attack a party consisting of 150, and defeated a covering party of the same number, killing one officer and six men in the charge, and wounding many. At dusk the enemy with drew his artillery from the batteries, and raised the siege; and at nine, under cover of the night sent off, in a great hurry, all the baggage he could find transport for, and also his artillery. At two the next morning the whole Army precipitately retreated, leaving the sick and wounded to our generosity; and the governor left a note with a surgeon, requesting the humane attention of the commanding-general.

Vast quantities of provision were left behind and destroyed; also an immense quantity of bomb-shells, cannon-balls, grape-shot, ammunition, flints, &c, entrenching tools of all sorts, also tents and marquees. A great deal has been found concealed in ponds and creeks, and buried in the ground, and a vast quantity carried off by the inhabitants. Such was the precipitance of his retreat, that he arrived at Chazy, a distance of eight miles, before we discovered he had gone. The light troops, volunteers, and militia, pursued immediately on learning of his flight, and some of the mounted men made prisoners five dragoons of the 19th regiment, and several others of the rear-guard. A continual fall of rain and a violent storm prevented further pursuit. Upwards of 300 deserters have come in, and many are hourly arriving. We have buried the British officers of the army and navy with the honors of war, and shown every attention and kindness to those who have fallen into our hands. The conduct of the officers, non-commissioned officers, and soldiers of my command, during the trying occasion, cannot be represented in too high terms.

Alex. Macomb.

THE AFTER-ACTION REPORT OF THOMAS MACDONOUGH

U.S. Ship Saratoga,
Plattsburgh Bay, Sept. 13th, 1814

Sir; I have the honor to give you the particulars of the action which took place on the 11th inst. on this lake.

For several days the enemy were on their way to Plattsburg by land and water, and it being well understood that an attack would be made at the same time by their land and naval forces, I determined to await at anchor the approach of the latter.

At 8AM. The lookout boat announced the approach of the enemy. At 9 he anchored in a line ahead at about 300 yards distance from my line, his ship opposed to the Saratoga, his brig to the Eagle, Capt. Robe. Henley, his galleys, thirteen in number, to the schooner, sloop and a division of our galleys, one of his sloops assisting their ship and brig, the other assisting their galleys. Our remaining galleys with the Saratoga and Eagle. In this situation the whole force on both sides became engaged, the Saratoga suffering much from the heavy fire of the Confiance. I could perceive at the same time, however, that our fire was very destructive to her. The Ticonderoga, Lt. Commt. Cassin, gallantly sustained her full share of the action. At 1/2 10 the Eagle, not being able to bring her guns to bear, cut her cable and anchored in a more eligible position between my ship and the Ticonderoga, where she very much annoyed the enemy but unfortunately leaving me exposed to a galling fire from the enemy's brig. Our guns on the starboard side being nearly all dismounted or not manageable, a stern anchor was let go, the bower cable cut and the ship winded with a fresh broadside on the enemy's ship, which soon after surrendered. Our broadside was then sprung to bear on the brig, which surrendered in about fifteen minutes after.

The sloop that was opposed to the Eagle had struck some time before and drifted down the line, the sloop which was with their galleys having been struck also. Three of their galleys are said to be sunk; the others pulled off. Our galleys were about obeying with alacrity the signal to follow them when all the vessels were reported to me to be in a sinking state. It then became necessary to annul the signal to the galleys and order their men to the pumps. I could only look at the enemy's galleys going off in a shattered condition, for there was not a mast in either squadron that could stand to make sail on; the lower rigging, being nearly all shot away, hung down as though it had been just placed over the mast heads.

The *Saratoga* had fifty-five round shot in her hull; the Confiance one hundred and five. The enemy's shot passed principally just over our heads, as there were not 20 whole hammocks in the nettings at the close of the action which lasted, without intermission, two hours and twenty minutes.

The absence and sickness of Lt. Raymond Perry left me without the services of that excellent officer. Much ought fairly to be attributed to him for his great care and attention in disciplining the ship's crew as her first lieutenant. His place was filled by a gallant young officer, Lt. Peter Gamble, who, I regret to inform you, was killed early in the action. Acting Lt. Vallette worked the 1st and 2nd divisions of guns with able effect. Sailing Master Brum's attention to the springs and in the execution of the order to wind the ship and occasionally at the guns meets with my entire approbation; also Capt. Youngs, commanding the acting marines, who took his men to the guns. Mr. Beale, purser, was of great service at the guns and in carrying my orders throughout the ship, with Midshipman Montgomery. Master's Mate Joshua Justin had command of the 3rd division. His conduct during the action was that of a brave and correct officer. Midshipmen Monteath, Graham, Williamson, Platt, Thwing, and acting Midshipman Baldwin, all behaved well and gave evidence of their making valuable officers.

The Saratoga was twice set on fire by hot shot from the enemy's ship.

I close, sir, this communication with feelings of gratitude for the able support I received from every officer and man attached to the squadron which I have the honor to command.

I have the honor to be with great respect, sir, yr. mot ob st.

T. Macdonough.

THE AFTER-ACTION REPORT OF DANIEL PRING

Letter to Admiral Sir James Lucas Yeo, commander of the Royal Navy in Canada. Note that it is sent from on board the American flagship.

U. States Ship Saratoga, Plattsburg Bay
Lake Champlain, Sept 12, 1814

Sir; The painful task of making you acquainted with the circumstances attending the capture of his Majesty's squadron, yesterday, by that of the American, under Commodore Macdonough, it grieves me to state, becomes my duty to perform, from the ever-to-be-lamented loss of that worthy and gallant officer, Capt. Downie, who unfortunately fell early in the action.

In consequence of the earnest solicitation of his Excellency Sir George Prevost for the co-operation of the naval force on this lake to attack that of the enemy, who were placed for the support of their works at Plattsburg, which he proposed should be stormed by the troops at the same moment the naval action should commence in the bay, every possible exertion was used to accelerate the armament of the new ship that the military movements might not be postponed at such an advanced season of the year longer than was absolutely necessary. On the 3d inst. I was directed to proceed in command of the flotilla of gunboats to protect the left flank of our army advancing toward Plattsburg; and on the following day, after taking possession and paroling the militia of Isle La Motte, I caused a battery of 3 long 18 pounder guns to be constructed for the support of our position abreast of Little Chazy, where the supplies for the army were ordered to be landed.

The fleet came up on the 3d inst. but for want of stores for the equipment of the guns, cold not move forward until the 11th. At daylight we weighed, and at 7 were in full view of the enemy's fleet, consisting of a ship, brig, schooner, and 1 sloop, moored in line abreast of their encampment, with a division of 5 gunboats on each flank. At 40 minutes past 7, after the officers commanding vessels and the flotilla had received their final instructions as to the plan of attack, we made sail in order of battle. Capt. Downie had determined on laying his ship aftward-hawse of the enemy's directing Lieut. McGhie, of the Chub, to support me in the Linnet in engaging the brig to the right, and Lt. Hick, of the Finch, with the flotilla of gunboats, to attack the schooner and sloop on the left of the enemy's line.

At 8 the enemy's gunboats and smaller vessels commenced a heavy and galling fire on our line. At 10 minutes after 8 the Confiance, having 2 anchors shot away from her larboard bow, and the wind baffling, was obliged to anchor (though not in the situation proposed) within two cable length of her adversary. The Linnet and Chub soon afterwards took their allotted stations, something short of that distance, when the crews on both side cheered and commenced a spirited and close action. A short time, however, deprived me of the valuable services of Lt. McGhie, who from having his cables, bow-sprit and main boom shot away, drifted within the enemy's line and was obliged to surrender.

From the light airs and smoothness of the water, the fire on each side proved very destructive from the commencement of the engagement, and, with the exception of the brig, that of the enemy appeared united against the Confiance. After two hours severe conflict with our opponent she *[Eagle]* cut her cable, run down and took shelter between the ship and schooner, which enabled us to direct our fire against the division of the enemy's gunboats and ship *[Saratoga]*, which had so long annoyed us during our close engagement with the brig without any return on our part. At this time the fire of the enemy's ship slackened considerably, having several of her guns dismounted, when she cut her cable and winded her larboard broadside to bear on the Confiance, who, in vain, endeavored to effect the same operation. At 33 minutes after 10 I was much distressed to observe that the Confiance struck her colors. The whole attention of the enemy's force then became directed towards the Linnet. The shattered and disabled state of the masts, sails, rigging and yards precluded the most distant hope of being able to effect an escape by cutting the cable. The result of doing so must in few minutes have been her drifting along side the enemy's vessels, close under our lee; but in the hope the flotilla of gunboats, who had abandoned the object assigned them, would afford a reasonable prospect of being towed clear, I determined to resist the then destructive cannonading of the whole of the enemy's fleet, and at the same time dispatched Lt. H. Drew to ascertain the state of the Confiance. At 45 minutes after 10 I was apprised of the irreparable loss she has sustained by the death of her brave commander (whose merits it would be presumptuous in me to extol) as well as the great slaughter which had taken place on board, and observing from the maneuvers of the flotilla that I could enjoy no further expectations of relief, the situation of my gallant comrades, who had so nobly fought and even now fast falling by my side, demanded the surrender of his Majesty's brig entrusted to my command to prevent a useless waste of valuable lives, and, at the request of the surviving officers and men, I gave the painful orders for the colours to be struck.

Lieut. Hicks, of the Finch, had the mortification to strike on a reef of rocks to the eastward of Crab Island about the middle of the engagement, which prevented his rendering that assistance to the squadron that might, from an officer of such ability, have been expected.

The misfortune which this day befell us by capture will, sir, I trust, apologize for the lengthy detail which, in justice to the sufferers, I have deemed necessary to give of the particulars which led to it; and when it is taken into consideration that the Confiance was 16 days before the stock, with an unorganized crew composed of several drafts of men who had recently arrived from different ships at Quebec, many of whom only joined the day before and were totally unknown either to the officers or to each other, with the want of gunlocks as well as other necessary appointments not to be procured in the country, I trust you will feel satisfied of the decided advantage the enemy possessed, exclusive of their great superiority in point of force, a comparative statement of which I have the honor to annex. It now becomes the most pleasing part of my duty to notice to you the determined skill and bravery of the officers and men in this unequal contest; but it grieves me to state that the loss sustained in maintaining it has been so great; that of the enemy, I understand, amounts to something more than the same number.

The fine style in which Capt. Downie conducted the squadron into action, amidst a tremendous fire, without returning a shot until secured, reflects the greatest credit to his memory for his judgement and coolness as also on Lieuts. McGhie and Hicks for so strictly attending to his example and instructions. Their own accounts of the capture of their respective vessels, as well as that of Lt. Robertson, who succeeded to the command of the Confiance, will, I feel assured, do ample justice to the merits of the officers and men serving under their immediate command; but I cannot omit noticing the individual conduct of Lieuts. Robertson, Creswick and Hornby and Mr. Bryden, master, for their particular exertion in endeavoring to bring the Confiance's larboard side to bear on the enemy after most of their guns were dismounted on the other.

It is impossible for me to express to you my admiration of the officers and crew serving under my personal orders. Their coolness and steadiness, the effect of which was proved by their irresistible fire directed towards the brig opposed to us, claims my warmest acknowledgments, but more particularly for preserving the same so long after the whole strength of the enemy had been directed against the Linnet alone. My first lieutenant, Mr. William Drew, whose merits I have before had the honor to report to you, behaved on this occasion in the most exemplary manner.

By the death of Mr. Paul, acting second lieutenant, the service has been deprived of a most valuable and brave officer; he fell early in the action. Great credit is due to Mr. Giles, purser, for volunteering his services on deck; to Mr. Mitchell, surgeon, for the skill he evinced in performing some amputations required at the moment, as well as his great attention to the wounded during the action, at the close of which the water was nearly a foot above the lower deck from the number of shot which struck her between wind and water. I have to regret the loss of the boatswain, Mr. Jackson, who was killed a few minutes before the action terminated. The assistance I received from Mr. Mickel, the gunner, and also from Mr. Clark, master's mate, Messrs. Toorke and Sinclair, midshipmen, the latter of who was wounded in the head, and Mr. Guy, my clerk, will, I hope, recommend them, as well as the whole of my gallant little crew to your notice. I have much satisfaction in making you acquainted with the humane treatment the wounded have received from Commodore Macdonough. They were immediately removed to his own hospital on Crab Island and were furnished with every requisite. His generous and polite attention also, to myself, officers and men, will ever hereafter be gratefully remembered.

I have, &c.

Dan. Pring.

Note: Pring was the captain of the Royal Navy's Linnet *and second in command.*

Appendix E

Extracts of Original Source Material and Letters

United States' brig Eagle,
Plattsburgh, Sept. 12, 1814.

To The Honorable William Jones,
  Secretary of the Navy

Sir,

I am happy to inform you that all my officers and men acted bravely, and did their duty in the battle of yesterday, with the enemy.

I shall have the pleasure of making a more particular representation of the respective merits of my gallant officers, to the honorable secretary of the navy.

I have the honor to be,
Respectfully, sir,

Your most obedient servant,

ROBERT HENLEY

P. S. We had thirty-nine round shot in our hull, (mostly 24 pounders) four in our lower masts, and we were well peppered with grape. I enclose my boatswain's report.

United States' ship Saratoga.
September 15, 1814, off Plattsburgh

To Captain Daniel Pring, Royal Navy,

Sir.

As Providence has given into my command the squadron on Lake Champlain, of which you were, (after the fall of captain Downie,) the commanding officer, I beg you will, after the able conflict you sustained, and evidence of determined valor you evinced on board his Britannic majesty's brig Linnet, until the necessity of her surrender, accept of your enclosed parole, not to serve against the United States, or their dependencies, until regularly exchanged.

I am, &e. &e.

T. MACDONOUGH

This parole enabled Captain Pring to return to England, where he was court-martialed by the Royal Navy. Pring was exonerated and the navy blamed army Lieutenant General Sir George Prevost for the loss. Sir George was not present for the court and sought a court-martial from the Army to clear his name. The court never convened because Sir George died the day before of heart failure.

General Hospital, Isle Aux Noix

21 September 1814

Dear Brother; While we lay at Brandy pots, hearing that Captain Downie had a command on Lake Ontario, I volunteered my services for that place, and I embarked on board a brig, together with 48 seamen and 14 marines, with orders to proceed and join the fleet with all possible dispatch. We went to Montreal in the brig, and from that place I took open boats for the remainder of our passage, which was nine days. The passage from Montreal upwards was awfully grand. The immense cataracts or rapids of water, which we had to haul the open boats through, at once strike terror in the mind of every person who had never before witnessed it, but we arrived safe, when I made myself known to Captain Downie, who was very glad to see me and took me into his own ship, the Montreal. I remained here about seven days, when Captain Downie received an order to go to Lake Champlain and there took command of the fleet, on which he and myself proceeded to the place, where he hoisted his broad pendent, as commander of the lake, on board the Confiance, which was not complete when we got here. Captain Downie gave me command of his Majesty's cutter Icicle, which I held until we had completed the ship, when I joined her, and we immediately sailed in quest of the Yankee fleet, which on Sunday, the 11th of September, we described lying off Plattsburg, with springs on their cables and all in line of battle, ready to receive us. At nine, A.M. (just after breakfast) we beat to quarters; at half past 9 made signal to our fleet to form the line of battle; at 40 minutes after 9 run down alongside the Yankee commodore's ship and came to anchor, when the action commenced by a vigorous cannonade of all the Yankee fleet on our ship, which we immediately returned. A little before 10 o'clock the action was general, and kept up with the greatest spirit until 25 minutes after noon, when our spring and rudder being shot away, all our masts, yards and sails so shattered that one looked like so many bunches of matches, and the other like a bundle of old rags. The captain was killed about ten minutes after the action commenced, and not above five men but what were killed or wounded, and her hull like a riddle. As she was foundering very fast, we were necessitated, though with the greatest reluctance, to strike to the enemy. About 15 minutes before we struck, I received a wound from a grape shot, which, after striking my foot, passed through the palm of my left hand. My fingers are very much shattered. The enemy immediately took possession of us and we were sent on shore to the hospital, where we lay two days, when we were sent down here on our parole. The havoc on both sides is dreadful. I don't think there are more than five of our men out of 300 but what are killed or wounded. Never was a shower of hail so thick as the shot whistling about our ears. Were you to see my jacket, waistcoat, trousers and hat, you would be astonished how I escaped as I did, for they are literally torn all to rags with shot and splinters. The upper part of my hat was also shot away. There is one of our marines who was in the Trafalgar action with Lord Nelson, who says it was a mere fleabite in comparison with this. At the time we attacked the shipping, our army made an attack on the town, and were in the act of scaling the walls when Sir George Prevost sounded the retreat.

Note: This letter was written by Midshipman Robert Lea to his brother in England.

Navy Department, October 3, 1814.

To The Honorable Charles Tate,
    Chairman of the naval committee of the senate.

Sir,

In compliance with your request, I have now the honor, to enclose copies of all the documents received from captain Macdonough, in relation to the brilliant and extraordinary victory achieved by the United States' squadron under his command, over that of the enemy in Plattsburgh Bay, on Lake Champlain.

This action, like that of its prototype on Lake Erie, cannot be portrayed in language corresponding with the universal and just admiration inspired by the exalted progress, consummate skill, and persevering intrepidity, which will ever distinguish this splendid and memorable event.

This like those brilliant naval victories which preceded it, has its peculiar features, which mark it with a distinct character. It was fought at anchor. The firm, compact, and well formed line; the preparations for all the evaluations of which the situation was susceptible, and the adroitness and decisive effect with which they were performed in the heat of battle, mark no less the judgment which planned, than the valor and skill displayed in the execution.

All these are heightened by the contemplation of a vigorous and greatly superior foe, moving down upon this line, in his own time, selecting his position, and choosing his distance; animated by the proximity of a powerful army in co-operation, and stimulated by the settled confidence of victory.

To view it in the abstract, it is not surpassed by any naval victory on record; to appreciate its results, it is perhaps one of the most important events in the history of our country.

That it will be justly estimated, and the victors duly honored by the councils of the nation, the justice and liberality hither displayed on similar occasions, is a sufficient pledge.

I have the honor to be,
Very respectfully, sir,
Your obedient servant,

W. JONES
(Secretary of the Navy)

War of 1812
Letter from Lieutenant James Willey, American Army
Camp at Plattsburgh, (New York), 11 October 1814
to
Mrs. Honor Willey

We have so few officers . . . reported fit for duty that my task is
rather hard, having to mount guard two or three times a week
with neither sleep to my eyes nor slumber to my eye lids. . . .
Captain Dinsmore behaved manfully in the late battle. . . . Having myself counted nineteen bullet holes through an innkeeper's
sign under which he with fifty men was stationed, I concluded he
must have had hot work. . . . We are building our barracks. . . .
The old ones [were] burned before the battle. . . . [W]e are at
present so fortunate as to drive the enemy [back].

*This letter appeared in an auction catalog of Fine Manuscript
and Printed Americana as lot number 160.*

APPENDIX F

Discussion of the Existence of a Shot Furnace on board *Confiance*

Why is there a difference of opinion between the British and American participants over the existence of a shot furnace on board the Royal Navy flagship? It was a matter of interest during the court-martial conducted by the Royal Navy in the summer of 1815. Charges had been brought by Sir James Yeo, commander of all Royal Navy ships in Canada, against Sir George Prevost. Yeo had replaced the commander of the British fleet twice in four months. At Plattsburgh, Downie had been killed in action and the fleet totally defeated and captured. Yeo knew that Royal Naval would demand an accounting for this humiliation. So he tried to place the blame on the army or, more precisely, the commanding general who would not be able to appear at the court to defend himself. Yeo knew that this solution would play well with the powers at the admiralty. Prevost had been vilified in the Canadian and London press for the previous two and one half years, making him an easy target. Yeo also did not appear at the court and therefore was represented by his four written charges against Prevost and the officers he had appointed to command, and who had lost the battle. Yeo could expect that in the nine months before the trial, among the dozen officers who were to testify, which included the army generals subordinate to Prevost, a consonance would occur that would establish a body of testimony to support the charges. After all, the charges mentioned the actions only of Prevost, not those of any other participant. Key to the

239

testimony was the fact that the American defense was superior to the Royal Navy attack from the start. This of course was nonsense, as a simple accounting would show. But if the testimony could prove otherwise, then defeat would not seem so ignominious.

The testimony from the British naval officers states that the Royal Navy flotilla was attacked not only by the U.S. Navy but by the army gun battery at Fort Scott, which should have been silenced by the British army. As proof that the American artillery was firing on the Royal Navy, the officers stated that the USS *Saratoga* was set on fire by hot shot that could only have come from the same land battery that set the houses on fire in Plattsburgh. The British naval officers learned of the house fires from the British army generals who testified before the court. The *Saratoga* could not have been set on fire by hot shot from the *Confiance,* since there was no shot furnace on board. It was policy in the Royal Navy not to use hot shot because of the danger of fire at sea. The French used shot furnaces and hot shot, which were known to have lit the very ships attempting to fire the shot. That the *Saratoga* was set on fire established that the British fleet was under fire not only from the guns of the American navy but also from the shore artillery, thereby increasing the hazard and accounting for the defeat.

The court would not hear the testimony of Prevost, nor that of the American naval officers who captured the British fleet, which was still in the hands of the Americans. They were half a world away. However, Commodore Thomas Macdonough, in his official after-action report, states, "The *Saratoga* was twice set on fire by hot shot from the enemy ship." *Confiance* is always reported as the "ship" while the other British vessels are called "brig," "sloop," "gunboat," etc. If the fires had been caused by shore fire, Macdonough would have known, since the hot cannonballs would have come from the opposite direction, behind him. If he had been receiving supporting fire from Macomb's land artillery, he would have mentioned it in this report or in his other writings in the years to come. Also, Macomb does not mention that he supported Macdonough's flotilla with cannon fire. Macomb was totally committed to the enemy in front of him, who had been pouring cannon and rocket fire on him from six batteries for four days. In addition, he was occupied with a veteran land army four times the size of his own. It is doubtful that he could have spared any guns or ammunition for the lake battle. In addition, there was no American gun that could range the British ships, since they were two miles from the beach, as stated on the map which accompanied Macomb's after-action report.

Robert S. Quimby, in *The U.S. Army in the War of 1812* (613, n. 71), says, "It is curious how strongly the British officers denied that they had any means of heating shot. The fact that the *Saratoga* was twice set on fire by hot shot during the action led them to assert that the shot must have come from American shore battery. However, every American officer who visited *Confiance* remarked on the furnace, and several heated shot were reported as found on board when she was occupied."

Adrian Caruana, author of the definitive book on the history of smooth-bore cannon, *The History of English Sea Ordnance 1523–1875*, makes only one reference to the lake battle at Plattsburgh and expresses his incredulity that the *Confiance* was firing "hot shot," which was not done anywhere else by the Royal Navy. However, he said to me during our research that being on a relatively calm body of water might account for the uncharacteristic use of hot shot.

APPENDIX G

The Congreve Rockets

The information below is an extract from the field manual published in 1804 by the Royal Artillery. The manual, on the operation of the rocket system, is reprinted and available at the Rotunda Museum at the Old Military Academy, Woolwich.

Capt. Wm Congreve—wounded in the Americas—was selected by the Master General of Ordnance to found the Royal Military Repository in the Arsenal in 1778. His son, also William, became a scientist and inventor within the Board of Ordnance and is the better known of the two as he invented the Congreve Rocket System. He was at one time the Superintendent of the Royal Laboratory in the Royal Arsenal, which is where ammunition was developed and where his expertise was invaluable. He later became the Superintendent of the Royal Military Repository, responsible for the development of the collections in the Rotunda museum at Woolwich which is still open to visitors today.

Congreve's rocket system arose from the experience the British had in India, where the East India Company's forces frequently met rockets in the hands of the Indian princes. These were not part of a well-developed system, but they were nonetheless unpleasant weapons to face, and since we had nothing like it, Congreve set about studying the principles. In his typically enthusiastic way, he went on to produce not merely a workable rocket, but a complete system for their use, as evidenced in the publication produced in 1814.

The rockets were tried out in the Napoleonic Wars, mainly in the bombardments of the French coast at Boulogne and the Danish capital, Copenhagen.

NOTES

CHAPTER 1

1. At that time, wives of very notable figures, as a courtesy, were commonly referred to as "Lady" but their husbands were not called "Lord."

2. New York and Vermont Historical Society bulletins.

3. Public Records Office of Canada, RG 8, C-506, reel B 2176.

4. National Archives, Washington D.C. For the many documents excerpted in this book, original spelling and capitalization is retained.

5. England treated all small nations with the same contempt and thought little of those who could not stand up to the Royal Navy, which was 90 percent of the world.

6. The 62d later became the famous 60th Light Infantry.

7. Henry J. Morgan, *Sketches of Celebrated Canadians and Persons Connected with Canada* (London: Hunter, Rose, 1934), 222.

8. Donald R. Hickey, *The War of 1812: A Forgotten Conflict* (Urbana: University of Illinois Press, 1990), 33.

9. British Canada was divided into two parts: Lower Canada, extending from Montreal east to the Atlantic, and Upper Canada, west of Montreal into the wilderness and the Great Lakes.

10. John Elting, *Amateurs, to Arms!: The Military History of the War of 1812* (New York: Da Capo, 1995), 13.

11. The "*Oneida*" was at Sackets Harbor on Lake Ontario.

12. *War of 1812,* New York State History, vol. 26 (Clinton and Franklin County, 1932).

13. Horse Guards is the headquarters of the British army, located near the Palace of Westminster, London.

14. *North Country Notes* no. 19 (November 1964). The letter was sent to General Joseph Bloomfield, commander of the northern army at Burlington, Vermont.

15. Karen Campbell, "Antiquities Collection, War of 1812," University of Vermont Library, 11, p. 121.

16. Harvey Strum, "Smuggling in the War of 1812," *History Today* 29 (August 1979): 332–37.

17. Found in the Public Records Office, Kew Gardens, London.

18. Correspondence of Thomas Macdonough, Macdonough-Boden Papers, Shelburne Museum, Burlington, Vermont, MS 41.25.

19. Printed in William S. Dudley, *The Naval War 1812: A Documentary History,* Vol. 1 (Washington, D.C.: Naval History Center, Department of the Navy, 1985), 241.

20. Phillip J. Haythornthwaite, *Wellington's Military Machine* (Turnbridge Wells, England: Spellmount, 1951), 155.

21. Captain Adrian B. Caruana (Royal Artillery, retired), personal interview at the Old Royal Military Academy, Woolwich, England.

22. Macdonough-Boden Papers, MS 21.3.

23. John R. Elting, *Amateurs, To Arms!* 155.

24. Morgan, *Sketches of Celebrated Canadians,* 222.

25. Dennis M. Lewis, *British Naval Activity on Lake Champlain During the War of 1812* (Plattsburgh, N.Y.: Clinton County Historical Association, 1994), 19.

CHAPTER 2

1. John K. Mahon, *The War of 1812* (Gainesville: University Press of Florida, 1972), 317.

2. The secret order was found among the private family papers of Sir Christopher Prevost, 6th Baronet, at his home in Albufeira, Portugal. The order remained secret into the next century. The famous American naval writer, Admiral Alfred T. Mahan, knew of the order and the gist of the content but had never seen it in 1905, when he wrote about the battle of Plattsburgh. It was discovered at the British Public Records Office in 1922 but lost again soon after. This copy of the order, Sir George's, was unearthed with the help of Sir Christopher. It does not appear in the record of Daniel Pring's court-martial held by the Royal Navy in 1815.

3. Taken from an article in the *London Gazette* on famous Canadians, found in the private papers of the Prevost family.

4. Among the books found in Sir George's library in Portugal were histories of Napoleon's then very recent campaigns against the Austrians and Russians.

5. Henry J. Morgan, *Sketches of Celebrated Canadians and Persons Connected with Canada* (London: Hunter, Rose, 1934), 222. The reference to Chippawa is in doubt since I could not find any other reference that supported his presence.

6. See the appendix for the exact type of guns and other details of the fleets.

7. It is also said that the regiment was taken into British service after the capture of Ceylon in 1795.

8. H. E. W. Laws, *Battle Records of the Royal Artillery 1716–1889* (Woolwich, England: Royal Artillery Institute, 1921). Courtesy of the Royal Artillery Academy Library.

9. Francis Duncan, *History of the Royal Regiment of Artillery* (London: Murray, 1874), 188–89.

10. William Congreve, son of Captain William Congreve, was a scientist and inventor within the Ordnance Board and invented the Congreve rocket system. He was at one time the superintendent of the Royal Laboratory in the Royal Arsenal, where ammunition was developed.

11. The Ordnance Board originated in the fifteenth century and was the government department responsible for all warlike stores. It was headed by the master general of the ordnance—a post of great privilege because, as it developed, the incumbent came to have a seat on the cabinet on a par with the ministers of the army and navy.

12. William Congreve, *Details of the Rocket System* (London: Woolwich Arsenal, 1814). Available courtesy of the Royal Artillery Institute Library, Woolwich, England.

13. The number of troops sent into the United States comes from many sources, none of which agree with each other. They range from a high of 16,000 to as low as 9,000. It is most probable that it was at least 12,000 if not more. Many believe 15,000.

CHAPTER 3

1. Jane E. Rupp, "Peter Sailly of Plattsburgh," manuscript in the Clinton County Historical Society, quoted by permission of the author.

2. John R. Elting, *Amateurs, to Arms! The Military History of the War of 1812* (New York: Da Capo, 1995), 180.

3. Taken from Charles Fairbank, "The Old Soldier's History" (1861), Vermont Antiquities Collection, University Library, University of Vermont, Burlington.

4. Figures on the sick, lame, and lazy vary widely from contemporary reports. It is safe to say that, under the conditions, the numbers grew steadily and were very high.

5. Alfred T. Mahan, *Seapower in Its Relation to the War of 1812* (Boston: Little, Brown, 1905), 319.

6. Terence Wise, *Artillery Equipment of the Napoleonic Wars* (London: Osprey, 1979), 3.

7. Today the infantry is known as the "Queen of Battle" at the infantry school at Fort Benning, Georgia, which is a recently adopted name. The U.S. Artillery calls itself the "King of Battle."

8. Today that is Spellman Road, near the high school.

9. Papers held privately by Thomas Macdonough Russell.

10. William S. Dudley, ed. *The Naval War of 1812: A Documentary History*, Vol. 1, (Washington, D.C.: Naval History Center, Department of the Navy, 1985), 371.

11. *North Country Notes* no. 10 (September 1964).

12. Elting, *Amateurs, to Arms!*, 220.

13. Historical Records Located at the Headquarters of Fort Lesley J. McNair, Washington D.C. (visitor pamphlet). In all 64 were killed and 185 were missing during the entire action.

14. See appendix A, "American Army."

15. Not to be confused with the ocean-going *President,* a frigate. The lake vessel had been damaged in an earlier mishap and was not fit for combat.

CHAPTER 4

1. Russell P. Bellico, *Sails and Steam in the Mountains* (Fleischmanns, N.Y.: Purple Mountain, 1992), 218.

2. The continental dollar, even after thirty years, did not enjoy the desirability of gold and was somewhat suspect.

3. No roads existed due west from Plattsburgh, so the army had to go south to Schenectady, 140 miles, before it could turn west and then north for a march of nearly five hundred miles.

4. Personal diary of Miss Anne Prevost, 1814, unpublished, privately held at Albufeira, Portugal, by Sir Christopher Prevost, Bt.

5. Henry J. Morgan, *Sketches of Celebrated Canadians and Persons Connected with Canada* (London: Hunter, Rose, 1934), 222

6. Testimony from the court-martial proceedings of the Royal Navy, aboard H.M.S. *Gladiator*, Portsmouth Harbor, August 1815, Public Records Office, Kew Gardens, London.

7. W. H. Robinson to Mr. Clarkson, September 10, 1814, Public Archives of Canada. 24 I 21 MG, American War of 1812.

8. *North Country Notes* (November 1965).

9. This is a widely told folk story associated with the battle.

10. John R. Elting, *Amateurs, to Arms! The Military History of the War of 1812* (New York: Da Capo Press, 1995).

11. "Order of battle" is a listing of the units, attachments, and affiliations of a military force.

12. "Abbatis" is a military term meaning to fell trees on either side of a road so that they fall, often in a herring-bone pattern, facing the oncoming enemy column, thereby creating an obstacle to movement. If there is time, the ends pointing at the enemy can be sharpened. The obstacle is very difficult and time-consuming to breach, even with modern engineering tools.

13. Macomb ordered the artillery sent, but only two guns went.

14. *North Country Notes* no. 103 (May 1974). Extract taken from the Bailey Collection, Burnt Hills, N.Y.

15. Richard Dawson's writings and Benson Lossing, in *The Pictorial Field Book of the War of 1812* (New York, Harper Brothers, 1868) give the militia more credit for interrupting the British movement.

16. Antiquities Record, War of 1812, Vermont Historical Collection. University of Vermont Library, Burlington, Vermont.

17. Report from Major General Macomb to the Secretary of War, 15 September 1814, Armstrong Correspondence, War of 1812, U.S. Army Military History Institute, Carlisle Barracks, Pennsylvania.

18. For example, "J. B. L. Skinner joins the regular army in later years and rises to the rank of Major General during the Civil War fifty years later."

19. Letter from Major General John E. Wool to B. J. Lossing, in the author's collection. Wool (1784–1869) was the inspector general of the army and served in the Mexican War and Civil War, before his retirement in 1862.

20. Letter from Sproul to Roberts, Battle of Plattsburgh file, Clinton County Historical Association, Plattsburgh, New York.

21. Brevet is a promotion in rank without commensurate pay. Lathum survived and lived into his eighties.

22. C. R. B. Knight, "Historical Records of the Buffs (east Kent regiment), 3rd Foot, 1814–1914," East Kent Regimental Museum, Canterbury, England.

23. The graves of all the combatants are in the Riverside Cemetery in Plattsburgh.

24. Silas Duncan's heroic actions were recognized in 1826 by the Congress of the United States, when they passed a resolution of thanks for his gallantry. There were no medals issued at that time and Congress had to act on each event individually.

25. "Fastness" is a stronghold made up of a combination of widely spread but connecting, mutually supporting fortifications.

26. Benjah Phelps, "Memories of Benjah Phelps," *Outlook* (June 1901).

27. Letter from George Freligh to his brother, Dr. Michael Freligh, Battle of Plattsburgh collection, State University of New York.

28. Court-Martial proceedings of the Royal Navy, August 1815, on board HMS *Gladiator,* Portsmouth, England, Royal Naval Collection, Public Record Office, Kew Gardens, London. Whenever there was a military disaster for Britain, a court would be called to inquire into the circumstances and fix blame. If a commander, officer, or sergeant were deemed derelict or culpable, he would at least be removed from a position of trust to protect the troops under his command.

29. James Henry Craig, *Memoirs of the Administration of the Colonial Government of Lower-Canada* (privately published, 1818), found among the papers of Sir Christopher Prevost, Albufeira, Portugal.

30. John K. Mahon, *War of 1812* (Gainesville: University Press of Florida, 1972). Here, Mahon is comparing cannons to carronades.

31. "To scale the guns" meant to fire without a cannonball in place. The guns are here used as a signaling device. It was a common practice even on land and Napoleon would fire them in a certain rhythm to provide a variety of commands, as with drumbeats.

32. "Map of the Battle of Plattsburgh prepared by Major DeRussy U.S.A.," in Report from Major General Macomb.

33. Francis Duncan, *History of the Royal Regiment of Artillery, Major Francis Duncan* (London: Murray, 1874), 188–89. Copy found at the Old Royal Military Academy Library. Woolwich, England.

34. Allen S. Everest, *The War of 1812 in the Champlain Valley* (Syracuse, N.Y.: Syracuse University Press, 1981).

35. William Walcutt, "Anecdotes of the Battle of Plattsburg," Antiquities Collection, University Library, Vermont University, Burlington.

36. War of 1812 in the Champlain Valley, Antiquities Collection, University Library, University of Vermont, Burlington.

37. Transcript of a January 1996 conversation held in the archives of the Clinton County Historical Association, with Jane Rupp, curator.

CHAPTER 5

1. The captain's gig on the *Confiance* was a rowboat powered by six men that was generally reserved for the use of the captain and therefore in very good repair. It was reserved to convey the captain to other ships or to shore and used by other officers with permission of the captain. In land terms, it was his chauffeur-driven command car.

2. Carol Oman, *Nelson,* 2d ed. (London: Greenhill, 1996), 619.

3. Geoffrey Bennett, *Nelson the Commander* (New York: Scribner's, 1972), 54.

4. Philip J. Haythorn-thwaite, *Wellington's Military Machine,* reprint ed. (Ipswich, England: Cowell, 1989), 154.

5. Oscar Bradenburg, *The Battle of Plattsburgh Bay: The British Navy's View* (Plattsburgh, N.Y.: Clinton County Historical Association, 1978), 71–80.

6. Testimony of Captain Daniel Pring from court-martial proceedings in 1815 appears very convenient, if not contrived, to support the charge made by Sir James Yeo that Prevost, not the Royal Navy, was at fault in the battle. According to Pring, Downie said to his crew, "There are the enemy's ships; at the same moment we attack the ships, our Army are to storm the enemy's works at the moment we engage, and mind, don't let us be behind."

7. Interview with Captain Adrian Caruana, Royal Artillery, noted gun expert and regimental historian, conducted at the Old Royal Military Academy, Woolwich, England, January 1994.

8. Theodore Roosevelt, *The Naval War of 1812* (New York: Putnam, 1882), 349. The prayer comes from the U.S. Navy's *Book of Prayer.*

9. Patrick Griffith, *French Artillery: Nations in Arms, 1800–1815* (New Malden, England: Almark, 1991), 11.

10. Carl von Clausewitz, *On War,* ed. and trans. Michael Howard and Peter Paret (Princeton, N.J.: Princeton University Press, 1976).

11. At Chatham Dock Yard in England, I watched Captain Adrian Caruana fire an unrestrained Congreve cannon that was set on a concrete sidewalk. The man next to me said it was one of Caruana's "party tricks." He used a bag of wet sand in the proper proportion to simulate a cannonball and placed behind it a full charge of gunpowder. Not only did the white smoke fill the football pitch (soccer playing field), obscuring everything to the front for a hundred yards, but the cannon rolled thirty-six feet to the rear. It took a dozen men to push and pull it back into position. See Adrian Caruana, *The Pocket Artillerist*

(Rotherfield, England: Jean Boudroit, 1987), 123. I have videotape of the demonstration at the soccer pitch.

12. Julius Hubbell's account, Clinton County Historical Association records. Hubbell viewed the battle from the road on Cumberland Head.

13. The gun that killed Captain Downie is mounted in front of Macdonough hall at the U.S. Naval Academy, Annapolis, Maryland. The muzzle is clearly marked where the American shot struck.

14. Interview with Adrian Caruana, Royal Artillery Rotunda Museum, Woolwich, England, 1994. Caruana had researched why the *Confiance* hull was shot up with numerous holes, while the *Saratoga* received little damage to the hull but lost all her rigging and masts.

15. Personal letter from Lieutenant James McGhie to Captain Daniel Pring, written while in American custody the day after the battle, Court-Martial Record, Public Records Office, Kew Gardens, London.

16. Bradenburg, *The Battle of Plattsburgh Bay.*

17. Paulding's method was demonstrated for the author by Brigadier K. A. Timbers, historical secretary of the Royal Artillery Historical Trust, Old Military Academy Library, at the Rotunda, using one of the Duke of Wellington's pistols: "With his pistol loaded with powder and no ball, Paulding would fire the pistol at the primer, which protruded slightly from the touch hole, on the rear of the gun. He attempted to direct the flash of the pistol barrel so as to set off the primer and therefore fire the gun. It must have taken many attempts to get the gun to go off. Very tricky, I can't imagine that taking place for two hours in the heat of battle."

18. Charles A. Budd to Commodore T. Macdonough, September 13, 1814, Thomas MacDonough Papers, U.S. Naval Academy Library, Annapolis, Maryland.

19. Trafalgar, the decisive naval battle of the Napoleonic Wars, occurred in 1805 off the eastern coast of Spain near Gibraltar, where a hundred ships of the line from England and France fought. Nelson was victorious and killed in the battle. It may seem an exaggeration to compare the two and call the action on Lake Champlain more rigorous, but war is a very personal thing and impressions are often made by where one views the action.

20. C. H. J. Snider, *In the Wake of the Eighteen Twelvers* (London: Cornmarket Press, 1969), 42–43.

21. John M. Stahl, *The Battle of Plattsburgh, War of 1812: A Study in and of the War of 1812* (Chicago: Van Trump, 1918), 118.

22. The colors of the *Confiance* hang today in the corridor of the main hall of the U.S. Naval Academy, Annapolis, Maryland, across the quadrangle from

Macdonough Hall. The red flags of the other English ships are on the balcony in the speaker's hall.

23. *What Historians Say about the Battle of Plattsburgh,* pamphlet provided by the city of Plattsburgh on the 100th anniversary of the battle (1914). This is taken from the section attributed to Theodore Roosevelt. Many of the guns on both fleets were fired by means of a detachable flintlock mechanism known as a "lock spring."

24. Carl von Clausewitz's *Vom Kriege* (On War) was published in 1832 by his wife, at his request upon his death. Since then it has become a significant guide for explaining the most complex of human activity, the conduct of war, in understandable terms.

25. "Memoirs of the Administration of the Colonial Government of Lower-Canada," from the collection of Sir Christopher Prevost, Albufeira, Portugal.

CHAPTER 6

1. Macdonough-Boden Papers, Shelburne Museum, Burlington, Vermont, MS 20.8.

2. Benjah Phelps, "Memories of Benjah Phelps," *Outlook* (June 1901).

3. The best guess for the Royal Navy is that over 100 were killed in action and 160 seriously wounded of the 442 (a very dubious number) reported to have been required to man their fleet of principal ships. For the U.S. Navy, close to 85 were killed in action, with 150 hospitalized out of a requirement for crews that numbered 550. It is not known if the crew requirements were met or not. Nearly everyone on the eight principal combatant was injured to some degree.

4. The Purple Heart was instituted during the Revolution by George Washington. Then, it was a cloth badge in the shape of a heart. Resurrected shortly before World War II, it was then a gold medallion with ribbon and the profile of General Washington emblazoned on the medallion.

5. A letter by William Dent, October 10, 1814, British Army Museum, London. Printed in Leonard Woodford, *Medical Student's Career in the Early 19th Century* (1814).

6. The letter and the desk on which Macdonough wrote it are in the Navy Museum in Washington, D.C.

7. Lieutenant Macdonough was granted leave and he and his wife went to Connecticut for several months.

8. "Retrospective and Miscellaneous," *Naval Chronicle* 32 (September–October), 335–36. Held at the Royal Navy Museum, Greenwich, England. The piece ends with, "Want of room obliges us to pass over many interesting points connected with the American naval war." The loser in any war records it most briefly.

9. Guernsey, "New York City in the War of 1812," New York Public Library.

10. The Prevost papers, Sir Christopher Prevost, Albufeira, Portugal.

11. Castlereagh Correspondence X, 186–188, printed in A. Allson, *Lives of Lord Castlereagh and Sir Charles Stewart* (London: 1831), 512.

12. John Elting, *Amateurs, to Arms! The Military History of the War of 1812.* (New York: De Capo, 1995), 274.

13. Walter Lord, *The Dawn's Early Light* (New York: Norton, 1972), 310.

14. Allen S. Everest, *The War of 1812 in the Champlain Valley* (Syracuse, N.Y.: Syracuse University Press, 1981), 241.

15. Wellington to Sir George Murray, Prevost papers, Sir Christopher Prevost, Albufeira, Portugal. The letter includes a note: "I approve highly indeed, I go further, I admire all that has been done by the Military in America so far as I understand it. Generally whether Sir George Prevost was right or wrong in his decision at Lake Champlain is more than I can tell: though of this I am certain, he must equally have returned to Kingston after the Fleet was beaten and I am inclined to think he was right. I have told the Ministers repeatedly that a naval superiority on the Lakes is a 'sine qua non' of success in war on the frontiers of Canada, even if our object should be totally defensive."

16. Quoted in James MacGregor Burns, *The Vineyard of Liberty* (New York: Knopf, 1981), 213.

17. Allan S. Everest, *The Military Career of Alexander Macomb* (Plattsburgh, N.Y.: Clinton County Historical Association, 1989).

18. Winston S. Churchill, *History of the English Speaking People, Vol. 3: The Age of Revolution* 3d ed. (New York: Dorset, 1990), 363.

19. John McMaster, *A History of the People of the United States from the Revolution to the Civil War, Vol. 4* (Philadelphia: University of Pennsylvania Press, 1960), 361.

20. John K. Mahon, *The War of 1812* (Gainesville: University Press of Florida, 1972), 335.

21. Elting, *Amateurs, to Arms!,* 328.

INDEX

About the Author

Colonel David G. Fitz-Enz served as a regular army officer for thirty years. In the Vietnam War, he was a combat photographer and paratrooper in the 173d Airborne Infantry Brigade and, on his second tour, a signal officer in the 10th Cavalry, 4th Infantry Division. Among his decorations are the Soldier's Medal for heroism, the Bronze Star for Valor with four oak leaf clusters, the Air Medal, and the Legion of Merit with three oak leaf clusters. He is the author of *Why a Soldier?* a memoir published in 2000, and a graduate of Marquette University, the Command and General Staff College, and the Army War College. Presently, he is the vice president for production of Cannonade Filmworks, which produced the television film *The Final Invasion.* He is married to Carol, his researcher. They have three grown sons and reside near Lake Placid, New York, with their two West Highland terriers.

OTHER COOPER SQUARE PRESS TITLES OF INTEREST

THE WAR OF 1812
Henry Adams
New Introduction by Col. John R. Elting
377 pp., 27 b/w maps & sketches
0-8154-1013-1
$16.95

THE LIFE AND TIMES OF AKHNATON
Pharaoh of Egypt
Arthur Weigall
320 pp., 33 b/w illustrations
0-8154-1092-1
$17.95

AUGUSTUS
The Golden Age of Rome
G. P. Baker
376 pp., 17 b/w illustrations, 8 maps
0-8154-1089-1
$18.95

CONSTANTINE THE GREAT
and the Christian Revolution
G. P. Baker
384 pp., 3 b/w illustrations, 7 maps
0-8154-1158-8
$18.95

HANNIBAL
G. P. Baker
366 pp., 3 b/w illustrations, 5 maps
0-8154-1005-0
$16.95

SULLA THE FORTUNATE
Roman General and Dictator
G.P. Baker
328 pp., 5 b/w illustrations, 8 maps & diagrams
$18.95
0-8154-1147-2

THE LIFE AND TIMES OF MUHAMMAD
Sir John Glubb
416 pp., 12 maps
0-8154-1176-6
$18.95

HAROLD AND WILLIAM
The Battle for England, 1064–1066 A.D.
Benton Rain Patterson
256 pp., 30 b/w illustrations
0-8154-1165-0 cl.
$25.95

GENGHIS KHAN
R. P. Lister
256 pp., 1 b/w illustration
0-8154-1052-2
16.95

THE DREAM AND THE TOMB
A History of the Crusades
Robert Payne
456 pp., 37 b/w illustrations, 11 maps
0-8154-1086-7
$19.95

AGINCOURT
Christopher Hibbert
176 pp., 33 b/w illustrations, 3 b/w maps
0-8154-1053-0
$16.95

HISTORY OF THE CONQUEST OF MEXICO &
HISTORY OF THE CONQUEST OF PERU
William H. Prescott
1330 pp., 2 maps
0-8154-1004-2
$29.95

WOLFE AT QUEBEC
The Man Who Won the French and Indian War
Christopher Hibbert
208 pp., 1 b/w illustration, 4 b/w maps
0-8154-1016-6
$15.95

IMPERIAL SUNSET
The Fall of Napoleon, 1813–14
R. F. Delderfield
328 pp., 16 b/w photos
0-8154-1119-7
$18.95

ON CAMPAIGN WITH THE ARMY OF THE POTOMAC
The Civil War Journal of Theodore Ayrault Dodge
Edited by Stephen W. Sears
304 pp., 11 b/w illustrations
0-8154-1030-1 cl.
$28.95

THE CIVIL WAR REMINISCENCES OF GENERAL BASIL W. DUKE,
C.S.A.
New Introduction by James Ramage
536 pp., 1 b/w illustration
0-8154-1174-X
$19.95

MEMOIR OF MY LIFE AND TIMES
John Charles Fremont
696 pp., 89 b/w illustrations
0-8154-1164-2
$24.95

THREE WHO MADE A REVOLUTION
A Biographical History of Lenin, Trotsky, and Stalin
Bertram D. Wolfe
680 pp., 54 b/w photos
0-8154-1177-4
$23.95

THE SELECTED LETTERS OF THEODORE ROOSEVELT
Edited by H. W. Brands
464 pp., 20 b/w photos and illustrations
0-8154-1126-X cl.
$29.95

GENERAL OF THE ARMY
George C. Marshall, Soldier and Statesman
Ed Cray
876 pp., 24 b/w photos
0-8154-1042-5
$29.95

THE GI's WAR
American Soldiers in Europe During World War II
Edwin P. Hoyt
with a new preface
664 pp., 29 b/w photos, 6 maps
0-8154-1031-X
$19.95

CORREGIDOR
The American Alamo of World War II
Eric Morris
560 pp., 23 b/w photos, 4 maps
0-8154-1085-9
$19.95

KASSERINE PASS
Rommel's Bloody, Climactic Battle for Tunisia
Martin Blumenson
358 pp., 18 b/w photos, 5 maps
0-8154-1099-9
$19.95

ANZIO
The Battle That Failed
Martin Blumenson
224 pp., 4 b/w maps
0-8154-1129-4
$17.95

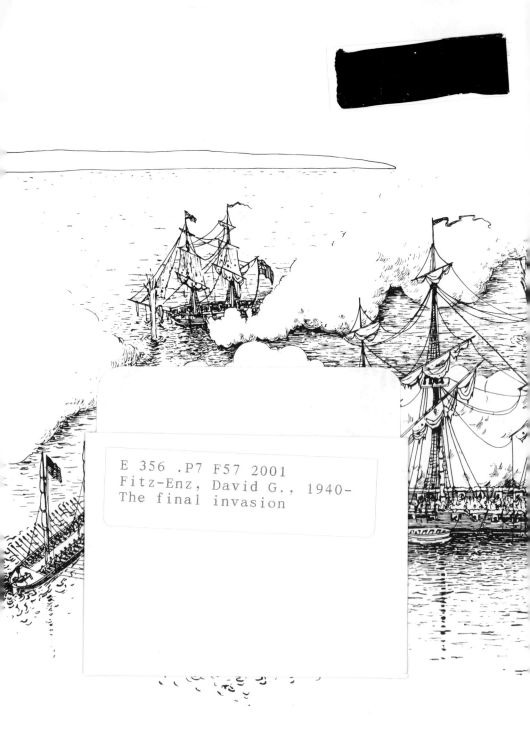